FIFTH EDITION

THE SOCIOLOGY STUDENT WRITER'S MANUAL

William A. Johnson, Jr.
University of Central Oklahoma

Richard P. Rettig
Eastern Oregon University

Gregory M. Scott
University of Central Oklahoma

Stephen M. Garrison
University of Central Oklahoma

PEARSON
Prentice
Hall

UPPER SADDLE RIVER, NEW JERSEY 07458

Library of Congress Cataloging-in-Publication Data

The sociology student writer's manual/William A. Johnson, Jr. . . . [et al.].—5th ed.
   p. cm.
  Includes bibliographical references and index.
  ISBN 0-13-192851-1
  1. Sociology—Authorship—Handbooks, manuals, etc. 2. Sociology—Research—Handbooks, manuals, etc. 3. Report writing—Handbooks, manuals, etc. I. Johnson, William A.
  HM585.S638 2006
  808'.066301—dc22

2005011348

Editorial Director: Leah Jewell
Publisher: Nancy Roberts
Executive Editor: Christopher DeJohn
Editorial Assistant: Kristin Haegele
Senior Marketing Manager: Marissa Feliberty
Marketing Assistant: Anthony DeCosta
Assistant Manufacturing Manager: Mary Ann Gloriande
Cover Art Director: Jayne Conte
Cover Design: Bruce Kenselaar
Interior Design: John P. Mazzola
Composition/Full-Service Project Management: Kari Callaghan Mazzola and John P. Mazzola
Printer/Binder: Courier Companies, Inc.
Cover Printer: Courier Companies, Inc.

This book was set in 10/12 Cheltenham.

Pearson Education LTD.
Pearson Education Singapore, Pte. Ltd
Pearson Education, Canada, Ltd
Pearson Education–Japan
Pearson Education Australia PTY, Limited

Pearson Education North Asia Ltd
Pearson Educación de Mexico, S.A. de C.V.
Pearson Education Malaysia, Pte. Ltd
Pearson Education, Upper Saddle River, NJ

10 9 8 7 6 5 4 3 2 1
ISBN 0-13-192851-1

*To my faithful friends
Max and Mango.
Thanks for the memories.*
—Billy J.

CONTENTS

TO THE STUDENT

Successful students, like successful social scientists, are competent writers. As sociology students, we observe social institutions and behavior. We write to record what we observe, to explain what we record, and to defend what we explain. As citizens, we write to take part in making decisions that direct our nation, our community, and our private lives. From the Declaration of Independence to the Emancipation Proclamation, from the United Nations Charter to President Kennedy's inaugural address, writing has brought us the freedom we enjoy today.

This newly revised fifth edition of *The Sociology Student Writer's Manual* is designed to help you do two things: (1) learn how to research and write in sociology; and (2) improve your writing ability. These objectives are addressed in the four major sections of this book. The Introduction explains what sociology is all about. Intended for both first-time and experienced sociology students, it offers a basic historical orientation and a challenging account of current theoretical perspectives in the field.

Part I, A Handbook of Style for Sociology, addresses fundamental concerns of all writers, exploring the reasons we write, describing the writing process itself, and examining those elements of grammar, style, and punctuation that most often cause confusion among writers. It also explains the importance of formatting the research paper properly—the title page, table of contents, and so on—along with citing and referencing sources using the American Sociological Association's Style Guide. The fifth edition of *The Sociology Student Writer's Manual* contains several writing style updates from the American Sociological Association. A vital concern throughout Part I, and the rest of the book as well, is the three-way interrelationship among writer, topic, and audience. Our discussion of this relationship aims at building your self-confidence as you clarify your goals. Writing is not a magical process beyond the control of most people; it is a series of interconnected skills that any writer can improve with practice, and the end result of this practice is power. Part I of this manual treats the act of writing not as an empty exercise undertaken only to produce a grade, but as a powerful learning tool as well as the primary medium by which sociologists accomplish their goals.

Part II, Conducting Research in Sociology, focuses on the research process. The first chapter in this part, Chapter 5, describes the research process in detail, explaining how you can maintain self-confidence by establishing control over your project and assume the crucial responsibility of every writer to use source material ethically. Chapter 6 lists and describes traditional sources of information for sociology researchers, including libraries, government agencies, and private research organizations that may provide you with information not available in your library. Chapter 7 includes information available on the Internet and World Wide Web specific to sociology. It demonstrates how to find and obtain resources in this burgeoning new territory. It also deals with distance learning as it relates to the Internet. The fifth edition of *The Sociology Student Writer's Manual* has revised and updated the chapter on using the Internet and distance learning, including reference to Prentice Hall's *Research Navigator*™ (on-line navigation system) for sociological research. The final chapter in Part II, Chapter 8, explains the role of the scientific method in doing social research.

Part III, How to Write Different Types of Sociology Papers, includes examples of writing assignments, two of which are new to the fifth edition. This section includes a variety of writing exercises—issue reaction paper, social issue analysis paper, book review, article critique, literature review, annotated bibliography, quantitative research design, survey-based design, and qualitative case study— that are commonly assigned in sociology classes. Each chapter begins by exploring the purposes and characteristics of the paper covered. Next, the steps for writing a successful paper are spelled out and typical formats are provided. Each chapter encourages you to use your imagination and resourcefulness in confronting the paper's requirements. Your professor may give you a specific writing assignment from one of these chapters. If your assignment is not specific, you may want to select an assignment and discuss your selection with your instructor before proceeding.

This manual is designed to help you organize your thoughts and directions in order to write more clearly and accurately. To assist you in becoming a better writer within the discipline, a glossary of terms associated with sociology is included. If you learn to write well, you will be more valuable in whatever line of work you pursue. As you continue to use this manual throughout your college and professional career, we hope your writing skills evolve and aid you in attaining your professional goals and objectives.

TO THE INSTRUCTOR

How many times have you assigned papers in your sociology classes and found yourself teaching the class how to write the paper—not only content but also form and grammar? This newly revised fifth edition of *The Sociology Student Writer's Manual* may accompany the primary text you assign in any sociology class or may stand on its own. It allows you to assign one of the papers explained in Part III with the understanding that virtually everything the student needs to know—from grammar to sources of information to source citation—is within this book.

The new fifth edition of *The Sociology Student Writer's Manual* has revised and updated the chapter on using the Internet and distance learning, including reference to Prentice Hall's *Research Navigator*™ (on-line navigation system) for sociological research. Several chapters have new or revised examples of specific writing assignments, including issue reaction papers and social issue analysis papers. There are also minor revisions throughout the book, with several specific updates for citing and referencing sources using American Sociological Association guidelines.

The fifth edition of *The Sociology Student Writer's Manual* makes assigning papers easier than ever. For example, you might direct your students in courses on introductory sociology or social problems to write an issue reaction paper according to the directions in Chapter 9. Instruct them to follow the guidelines in Part I for formatting, grammar, and source citations, and in Part II for organization of the research process and use of available resources. Most questions a student could ask about the paper are answered in this book, but the book also allows you to supplement your assignment with special instructions. Examples are included.

Assigning students to write an issue reaction paper, following the directions in Chapter 9, is an excellent exercise for beginning or advanced students, because reaction papers are exercises in logic and problem-solving. Our directions help students do the following:

1. Select a suitable reaction statement
2. Clearly define the issue addressed in the statement
3. Clearly state a position on the issue
4. Defend the position
5. Conclude concisely

By using the guidelines in this manual to complete an issue reaction paper—or any of the other assignments that are included—your students learn to define and focus clearly on issues or problems that are germane to their world. They will become more competent problem-solvers and develop skills that are important in every profession.

As you know, writing skills are essential to professional success in sociology—or in any other profession. By combining the latest sociology research and writing techniques with a broad spectrum of writing activities—based on a total of over ninety years of experience in teaching courses in sociology, criminal justice, political science, and English—we have written this book to assist you in leading students toward success.

As a final note, we would like to thank the following reviewers for their helpful suggestions: Linda Grant of the University of Georgia and Charles Tompkins of Whatcom Community College.

INTRODUCTION:
WELCOME TO THE STUDY OF SOCIOLOGY

If you are about to write your first paper in sociology, this introduction is for you. It will enhance your confidence and ability to present ideas and issues at every level of the discipline, from introductory sociology to sociological theory and advanced sociological research. Reading this section will help you understand what sociology is all about and what sociologists are trying to achieve when they write. It provides a brief overview of the discipline, which will help you understand basic sociological concepts, methods, and theories and apply them in your writing. The knowledge it offers can save you time, energy, and confusion.

Sociology is taught under different conditions at different colleges and universities by instructors who have varying amounts and types of resources at their disposal. If you have already studied sociology in some detail, you may choose to skip this introduction and read Chapters 1 through 8 before selecting the chapters in Part III that provide directions for the specific type of paper you have been assigned. However, you may find that reading this introduction will help to refresh your memory and establish your writing efforts more firmly within the broader framework of the discipline. Wherever you are in your progress toward mastering the methods and contributing to the rich tradition of sociology, we encourage you to read this section.

WHAT IS SOCIOLOGY?

Sociology, the study of human interaction, attempts to remove the mystery from human behavior. Although we, like the Hebrew prophet Isaiah, often become weary of finding the answers we seek, we continue nonetheless, for the price of ignorance has far too often proven—not only for the Jews—too costly. Because

1

it deals with the effects of social systems on people's behavior, there is virtually no topic that sociology does not touch. Therefore, it is sometimes difficult to see where sociology is distinct from other disciplines. Perhaps the best way to begin is with an example from everyday life taken from Hess, Markson, and Stein (1988):

> Sometime this week you will probably eat at a luncheonette or restaurant. As you pay your bill, you will probably leave a tip. Why do that? Do you have a deep psychological urge to give money to people who provide a service? Is it biological? Do you have a "tipping gene" that programs your actions? Or has some divine power commanded you to do so? The answer to all three questions is, of course, "no." Then why, in our society, is this behavior almost automatic? Students pondering this question typically give such responses as, "It's expected," "I was taught to," "If you don't, they'll spill soup on you the next time you eat there," or "It's the way they make a living because their wages are so low." Regarding the amount of the tip, some students will point to group pressure and to "wanting to be taken as a big shot" by restaurant personnel, other customers, or their dates. And some will point out that if the size of the tip is directly related to the quality of service, it serves to motivate high levels of performance.
>
> Notice that all of these answers involve some form of interaction: They assume that your behavior is linked to that of other people, and that you are acting within expectations and mutual influence. Under some circumstances—when trying to impress someone, or eating in a crowd—we will probably leave larger tips than when dining alone. Tipping also varies according to the eating place—the more expensive the meal, the proportionately higher the tip. Also, in general, men tend to tip more generously than do women. And if you have traveled across this country or abroad, you will probably have noticed regional and national variations in tipping expectations.
>
> Once you realize that these differences have little to do with how hungry you are or how you were toilet trained, you can begin to grasp the essence of the sociological perspective: Human beings live in groups; these groups are characterized by rules that govern behavior; the rules are learned; and we take other people into account when we choose how to behave. In other words, our thoughts and actions are largely shaped by forces outside ourselves—by the social context and how we interpret it.
>
> But notice also that we can choose not to tip, and that the amount we leave depends on a number of considerations—what we think is customary, a fear of retaliation or of looking like a cheapskate, what we consider a fair reward for service, or a means of adding to the income of low-paid workers. Thus, although there is an outside patterning or structure to which we are reacting, human beings are not robots or puppets; we can choose not to react or we can give varying meanings to our actions. Nevertheless, the raw material on which our choices are based also comes from what we have learned as members of the society. (Pp. 2–3)

From this example, we can see that sociology is the systematic study of the social behavior of individuals. It is the examination of the workings of social groups, organizations, cultures, and societies.

DIFFERENT KINDS OF SOCIOLOGY

There is no one sociology. Instead, there are several different sociological approaches to the study of human behavior in society. Unlike disciplines more limited in scope, such as economics or political science, sociology can deal with all aspects of society and human behavior, a fact that adds to the excitement of the field. The discipline's diversity virtually ensures that every student will find something of particular interest to study—from urban sociology to the sociology of art.

A sociologist who is asked, "What kind of sociologist are you?" will likely respond by listing his or her specialties; for example, some aspect of human behavior such as deviance, or some characteristic of social life such as politics. Although most sociologists have a theoretical preference, many utilize several approaches, depending on what's being studied.

SOME FUNDAMENTAL IDEAS OF SOCIOLOGY

Social Change

Most sociologists agree that it is the actions and behaviors of humans that create social settings and social laws, and that these actions, behaviors, and settings change over time. For example, consider the widespread use of slavery in developing countries and the widespread abolition of slavery in developed countries. Changes in women's right to vote, in the legal and illegal use of drugs, in the legal custody of minor children, and in the family system itself are just a few of the myriad examples of social change.

Every day people affirm or modify their social settings and thus maintain or change them. Each time a major change occurs, some people resist. Sociology is concerned with the way individuals and groups support or change their social surroundings.

The Sociological Imagination

Some sociologists believe that society can be understood only by looking at both the subjective/personal and the objective/historical side of any given period. The sociological imagination demands that thinking people (1) view their world by locating themselves in their time period; and (2) become conscious of how the broader social structure directly affects their lives (Mills 1959).

People often view their personal lives in narrow frames that tend to exclude the effects of structural transformations like population migration to the Sun Belt or evolution of local industries from textile manufacturing to high-technology products. They may feel stifled by an inability to handle society's rapid pace of change. The sociological imagination allows people to envision what happens among them in society. It helps them to distinguish their personal problems from broader social issues and thereby to understand the effect of cultural values and norms on their own lives. In other words, personal problems can be better understood by "seeing" them within the social structure in which they occur.

Three basic questions frame the classic study of people in particular societies:

1. What is the structure of the society in general?
2. Where does the society stand in human history?
3. What types of men and women prevail in this society and period of time?

Social issues—such as unemployment, divorce, and terrorism—are directly related to personal problems. Linking people to their social surroundings and the historical period in which they live tells us about their individual and social potentials. This linking activity requires sociological imagination, and this book will help you identify and sharpen your own social imagination.

Creating the Person

Socialization refers to the process by which people learn to conform to their society's norms, values, and roles. All social settings influence or constrain our behavior. Primary socialization refers to the process by which the newborn baby is molded into a social being. Secondary socialization occurs later in childhood and adolescence, as the person is influenced by adults and peers outside the family. Our personal attitudes, beliefs, and behaviors about everything—morality, politics, religion, work, entertainment, and so on—are formed and changed by social settings.

Different stages of our lives instigate the change process, as do educational opportunities, a new job, new surroundings, and new historical times. Moving from one stage to another is often accompanied by a rite of passage, especially if the change is considered very important in that society. Graduation from high school marks a significant shift for some individuals in American society: The graduation ceremony, or ritual, is the traditional rite of passage that illuminates the transition from adolescence to adulthood.

In advanced technological societies like the United States, the movement from one stage of cultural evolution to another is often more subtle than in societies where the current stage is relatively primitive, such as the Aborigines of the Australian outback. Their "walkabout" rite of passage requires that each postpubescent male adolescent be left alone in an unfamiliar place far from the village with only a spear. If he is able to make his way back to the village—a trip, often filled with life-threatening events, that sometimes takes up to two weeks—he is welcomed home with a ceremony that christens his arrival to adult status within the Aborigine society.

Looking further into understanding the socialization process, we find many unsolved issues that may be of interest to you as a student. One example centers around the relative strength of biological and/or social influences on human development—a critical issue in many areas of sociology, including criminology and social psychology. This discussion is known as the *nature versus nurture* debate. It questions the impact of heredity on the sense of self, versus the effect of social environments on socialization over time and within social circumstances. As sociologists study human behavior, they often discover that facts run contrary to popular beliefs. For example, within the context of the nature versus nurture debate, popular belief often holds that criminals are "born" with a predisposition to break laws. However, most social scientists agree that criminals are "socially constructed," or affected by numerous external influences, not "born that way."

Cultural Relativism

The concept that cultures are "blueprints for living," drawn from particular environmental and situational conditions, is called *cultural relativism*. In a now classic study demonstrating cultural eccentricities and underscoring the idea of cultural relativism, Miner (1956) describes the way of life of the Nacirema, a North American group whose chief lives on the banks of the Camotop River. The tribe is obsessed with rituals centered on deforming the human body: changing its color, its smell, and its shape. Under the guidance of "holy-mouth-men," whom they seek out once or twice a year, the Nacirema engage in a daily ritual of inserting bundles of hogs' hair and magical powders into the mouth and "then moving the bundle in a highly formalized series of gestures" (p. 505). Nacirema ceremonies can be quite painful, as when the men scrape their faces with sharp instruments and the women bake their heads in small ovens.

Described in this way, such customs appear very strange. Perhaps you'd be tempted to call them "primitive." Surely a person from the modern industrial world would not behave in this fashion. Yet Miner was simply looking at American (*Nacirema* spelled backwards) society from a different perspective. Can you see it?

Look at some of our other behaviors. Consider tattooing, a process that is far from painless and is supposed to make the bearer's body both more attractive and somehow more powerful for having endured the pain. Another painful process, hair transplanting, is a fairly involved procedure designed to counter baldness.

No behavior should be considered out of the context of the culture in which it originates, because what is natural to us will not necessarily be so to members of other societies (Hess et al. 1988).

Awareness and understanding of other cultures are important today because we all live in an international and global community. Cross-cultural studies involving reports and descriptions of societies other than our own allow students to become aware of and knowledgeable about how other societies function, which in turn diminishes ethnocentrism—the idea that one's own culture or group is best.

A BRIEF HISTORY OF SOCIOLOGY

Emergence of the Discipline

As a discipline, sociology emerged in Europe as a direct result of the political, economic, demographic, social, and scientific changes precipitated by the Industrial Revolution in the late eighteenth and early nineteenth centuries. The Industrial Revolution, along with the French and other political revolutions, and a desire to apply the scientific method to the study of society, provided the vision to view society as a whole and the resources to accomplish that task. According to Charon (1996),

> Not only was sociology born in a time of science, but also in a time when industrialization and urbanization were transforming the very basis of society. [This led some sociologists to view] industrialization as they saw science: a means by which the problems that plagued humanity would be banished. . . . Other sociologists, such as Karl Marx, reacted to the extremes of inequality and poverty that the Industrial Revolution telescoped, while still others, such as Durkheim and Weber, saw basic changes in the old ways of society occurring—changes such as the declining importance of traditional religion and the growing bureaucratic organization of society. (P. 12)

Standing on the Shoulders of Giants

Many modern sociologists believe the aforementioned French and German scholars, with a few exceptions, laid the foundation for the basic issues and concepts that define sociology today. They spoke directly to the effects of social change and stability that were inherent in the revolutions on both continents. Robert K. Merton (1910–2003) notes that sociology has progressed to its current position as a scientific discipline by (borrowing Sir Isaac Newton's phrase) "standing on the shoulders of giants." The following is a brief summary of the contributions of several of these "giants."

Frenchman Auguste Comte (1798–1857) is often called the founder of sociology because he gave the emergent discipline its name—from the Latin *socius,* meaning "companion with others," and the Greek *logos,* meaning "the study of reason." A child of the Age of Enlightenment, Comte subscribed to its ideals of progress, political and economic freedom, individualism, the scientific method, and a profound belief in the ability of human beings to solve social problems. Highly influenced by the French Revolution and the tremendous changes it brought to European societies, Comte sought to help restore order and tranquility to French society. He believed that sociology should be recognized as the science of society, beneath which all other sciences should be placed. He had tremendous faith in science as a means to solve such social problems as war, revolution, crime, and poverty, and rejected theological and philosophical approaches (although traces of them remained in his work).

Many of the ideas and concepts that are still germane to sociology sprang from scholars' attempts to explain the social milieu of their time. They defined economic aspects of social life, such as class, status, and power, and described the growing gap between urban and rural life, and rational and traditional thinking.

German philosopher Karl Marx (1818–1883) drew attention to the class conflict that arises between those who own the means of production and those who do not—the "haves" versus the "have-nots." He focused on the conflict that generated the change process. For Marx the superstructure of society— a cultural foundation composed of politics, religion, law, education, government, and family—constitutes a level of social life that is shaped primarily by economics.

Although it would not be entirely appropriate to label Marx a sociologist, his social analysis and political philosophy laid the foundation for conflict theory, which, along with functionalism and symbolic interactionism (which we will discuss later), is one of the three major models or perspectives of sociological explanation today. Marxist analysis of social change proved to be a watershed of ideas for thinkers like Weber and Durkheim.

German sociologist Max Weber (1864–1920) disagreed with Marx that the superstructure was always a product of economic institutions and that economic conflict was always the precursor of social change. His classic work *The Protestant Ethic and the Spirit of Capitalism* (1930) supports the hypothesis that capitalism as an economic system was dependent on and flourished within the normative structure of Protestant religion, and that the Protestant ethic became the precursor of capitalism because it supported the belief that God approves of working hard, enjoying the material benefits of labor, and subsequently being generous to others.

Weber also believed that the emerging rationality of the modern age would ultimately transform social institutions into bureaucracies, wherein occupational specialization and the rational ordering of people would become a way of life. From a technical point of view, the bureaucratic type of administrative organization is the most rational, efficient, precise, and disciplined means of exerting control over human beings. No one recognized and feared the possible consequences of this trend more than Weber (1969):

> [I]t is still more horrible to think that the world could one day be filled with nothing but those little cogs, little men clinging to little jobs and striving towards bigger ones—a state of affairs which is to be seen once more, as in the Egyptian records, playing an ever-increasing part in the spirit of our present

administrative system, and specially of its offspring, the students. This passion for bureaucracy . . . is enough to drive one to despair. It is as if . . . we were deliberately to become men who need "order" and nothing but order, who become nervous and cowardly if for one moment this order wavers, and helpless if they are torn away from their total incorporation in it. That the world should know no men but these: it is in such an evolution that we are already caught up, and the great question is therefore, not how we can promote and hasten it, but what can we oppose to this machinery in order to keep a portion of mankind free from this parceling-out of the soul, from this supreme mastery of the bureaucratic way of life. (P. 455)

Much of what Weber predicted has come to pass. Bureaucratic organizations have become dominant in most institutions of the modern world, including the military, religions, universities, government, and the economy.

French sociologist Emile Durkheim (1858–1917) examined the economic changes of the nineteenth century in a somewhat different light. His classic work *La Suicide* ([1897] 1951) linked personal actions to much larger social forces—mainly the degree of social integration experienced by the individual. His work demonstrated for the first time that a personal act such as suicide could be properly understood only in terms of social facts such as religious beliefs and marital status.

Durkheim generated many insights related to social order and social relations. He believed that social solidarity is maintained by similar ideals internalized by people's personalities, and that complex social relations are governed by negotiations between individuals.

German sociologist Ferdinand Toennies (1855–1936) emphasized the widening gap between the Gemeinschaft (traditional, communal relationships that exist in small, rural societies and are based on personal emotions and long-standing customs) and Gesellschaft (large, urban societies characterized by a modern type of associational relationship that is based on impersonal, rational, secondary group relations). He believed that as science uncovers the laws of nature, some of the wonder and mystery of existence is destroyed, and social organization moves from the Gemeinschaft to the Gesellschaft. He called this process the "disenchantment of the world."

Herbert Spencer (1820–1903), an English social historian, was one of the first to suggest that social scientists should suspend their own opinions and wishes when studying the facts of society. Spencer applied the predominant economic and biological models already available to the emergent discipline of sociology. Using the theory of evolution originated by English naturalist Charles Darwin (1809–1882) to help explain social change, Spencer's social evolution model provided critical justification for the growth of capitalism. He was influential for decades because his explanations supported rather than challenged the economy and social structure in which they were based.

Austrian physician Sigmund Freud (1854–1939), the founder of psychoanalysis, is considered the creator of the medical model of mental illness. His works *Totem and Taboo* ([1913] 1952) and *Civilization and Its Discontents* (1930), among others, significantly influenced the creators of modern sociological theory. He stressed the interplay between internal (conscious and unconscious) personality forces and external social factors. Freud's contribution to sociology is important particularly because he stressed the ongoing conflict between the individual and society. For Freud, the socialization process consists of the progressive development of a social conscience (superego) through the increasing submission of individual impulses (sublimation) to societal wishes and requirements.

THE RISE OF AMERICAN SOCIOLOGY

By the turn of the nineteenth century, the Industrial Revolution had begun in the United States. Industrial expansion brought waves of immigrants from Europe, and the United States experienced a tremendous population increase. The period from 1880 to 1920 produced not only a rapid increase in population but also a dramatic change in the composition of the population. As droughts and crop failures plagued the nation's heartland, the United States became primarily urban for the first time, and urban life assumed new dimensions of social and technological challenge.

Responding to these developments, American sociologists first examined social changes, urbanization, racism, and crime. They also explored the gap between personal action and social structure, borrowed liberally from European influences, and generated new ideas of their own.

Charles Horton Cooley (1864–1929) and George Herbert Mead (1863–1931) were two major influences in the development of this new social psychology from a sociological perspective. In his classic work *Human Nature and the Social Order* (1902), Cooley rejected the belief that human nature is determined predominantly by genetic heritage and biological maturation. He argued that human development is instead a product of interaction with other humans in social group situations.

Mead, in his book *Mind, Self, and Society* (1934), published posthumously by his students, argued that both mind and self are social products that represent the outcomes of interactions with others in social situations rather than biological inheritance. He emphasized that the use of significant symbols—namely, language—is fundamental to human development. For Mead, socialization is never a finished product. His three-stage process—play, game, and identification with the generalized other (rules of society)—ultimately provides the frame of reference from which the child views himself or herself. Mead argued that the self is never a finished product but rather is subject to significant modification throughout one's lifetime.

From the 1920s through the early 1970s, sociology enjoyed considerable growth as an academic discipline at major universities and colleges in the United

States. Many sociology departments were formed, faculties hired, and theory and research programs developed. Although the field remains a highly abstract intellectual enterprise, it has also supplied the theoretical and methodological structure for more applied disciplines such as social work and criminal justice. This alignment with these more applied disciplines has great potential both in the discipline of sociology and in the amelioration of significant problems in the world.

MAJOR SOCIOLOGICAL PERSPECTIVES

According to Farley (2000:71–72), a perspective is usually composed of three elements: (1) an approach to a topic that helps to determine the kinds of questions that are asked about the topic; (2) a theory or set of theories describing what are believed to be the realities of the topic; and (3) stated or unstated values concerning potentially controversial issues related to the topic.

We close this section by reexamining and expounding on the three major sociological perspectives introduced earlier: functionalism, conflict theory, and symbolic interactionism. Each perspective has unique assumptions and consequently different explanations or theories about social structure and human behavior. The first two perspectives, functionalism and conflict theory, compete with one another within what is known as the *order versus conflict* debate—a disagreement concerning whether society's institutions are the outgrowth of natural human impulses to order or conflict.

Functionalism

Functionalism—often labeled *structural-functionalism, equilibrium theory, consensus theory,* or *systems theory*—is a product of Durkheim's attempt to show that Marx was mistaken in many of the assumptions and explanations that he associated with class conflict. Functionalism has been further developed, refined, and elaborated by such modern American theorists as Talcott Parsons (1902–1975) and Merton.

Functionalism emphasizes the order perspective, which assumes that every pattern of activity or structure in a given society makes some contribution—positive (functional) or negative (dysfunctional)—to the overall maintenance of that society. Functionalists view social structure as a regular pattern of social interaction and persistent social relationships, such as the patterned social relationship between races and ethnic groups, or the patterns of family organization. Functions represent a positive purpose or consequence, one necessary for the continued existence of the society. Manifest functions are intended and well recognized, while latent functions are less obvious and often unintended. Major criticisms of this perspective center around its difficulty in explaining social change, and its tendency to affirm established power and the status quo.

Conflict Theory

The Marxist model of power and class struggle is the bastion for the conflict theory in the order versus conflict debate. A central assumption of Marxist theory is that "the distribution of wealth . . . determines other aspects of society, such as the political system and the culture, including social norms, values and beliefs" (Farley 2000:74). These norms, values, and beliefs were labeled "ideology" by Marx, who believed that conflict is inevitable because of the scarcity of economic resources in society. Differences in access to these scarce economic resources allow one group or class (the haves) to dominate the other (the have-nots). The dominant social class is always the one that controls the means of economic production. Divergent values and interests create struggle that ensures the disenfranchisement and impoverishment of the weak. Since the ideological superstructure supports the dominant class (the middle class in a capitalistic system), the subordinate laboring class eventually experiences alienation—especially from work—and the potential for revolution increases. Conflict theory has been refined and elaborated by such modern American theorists as C. Wright Mills (1916–1962) and Ralf Dahrendorf (born 1929).

Symbolic Interactionism

Symbolic interactionism is mainly a product of American sociology, and stems mostly from the ideas of Cooley, Mead, W. I. Thomas (1863–1947), and Florian Znaniecki (1882–1957). It focuses on the role of symbols—especially those embodied in language—that communicate meanings among people, and on a common "definition of the situation." According to this social-psychological perspective, people in a given society share an understanding of most commonly used symbols. Humans have a unique ability to use words. As they grow, word learning moves from the concrete to the abstract. We are influenced initially by the significant others in our lives, such as relatives and friends, who help us develop a sense of self. As we grow and mature, we adopt a perspective within the generalized other—society's values and normative structure. By understanding the meanings people attach to things through the use of words and other symbols, it is possible to understand much of human behavior.

A FINAL NOTE

The key proposition of all sociological thought is that human behavior—wherever you find it—is mediated, shaped, channeled, and influenced by social relationships and social systems. According to all sociological perspectives, answers to the human condition are not found in the genes or the phases of the moon but in the structure of social life, among the variations of social institutions and organizations such as the family, education, religion, ethnicity, social status, and nationality.

Sociology develops its understanding of all propositions through writing. Ideas do not crystallize until they are set forth on paper or in electronic form. This manual was written to help and encourage you to make your own unique contribution to society's understanding of how we live together, and to join the marvelous pursuit of the branch of knowledge known as sociology.

A Handbook of Style for Sociology

WRITING AS COMMUNICATION

1.1 WRITING TO LEARN

Writing is a way of ordering your experience. Think about it: No matter what you are writing—a paper for your introductory sociology class, a short story, a limerick, or a grocery list—you are putting pieces of your world together in new ways and making yourself freshly conscious of these pieces. This is one of the reasons writing is so hard. From the infinite welter of data that your mind continually processes and locks in your memory, you are selecting only certain items significant to the task at hand, relating them to other items, and phrasing them in a new coherence. You are mapping a part of your universe that has hitherto been unknown territory. You are gaining a little more control over the processes by which you interact with the world around you.

This is why the act of writing, no matter where it leads, is never insignificant. It is always communication, a way of making a fresh connection with your world. Writing, therefore, is also one of the best ways to learn. This statement, at first, may sound odd. If you are an unpracticed writer, you may share a common notion that the only purpose writing can have is to express what you already know or think. Any learning that you as a writer might do has already been accomplished by the time your pen meets the paper. In this view, your task is to inform or even surprise the reader. But if you are a practiced writer, you know that, at any moment as you write, you are capable of surprising yourself. And it is surprise that you look for: the shock of seeing what happens in your own mind when you drop an old, established opinion into a batch of new facts or bump into a cherished belief from a different angle. Writing synthesizes new understanding for the writer. E. M. Forster's famous question "How do I know what I think until I see what I say?" is one that all of us could ask. We make meaning as we write, jolting ourselves by little, surprising discoveries into a larger and more interesting universe.

1.1.1   The Irony of Writing

Good writing often helps the reader become aware of the ironies and paradoxes of human existence. One such paradox is that good writing expresses that which is unique about the writer and, at the same time, that which is common, not to the writer alone, but to every human being. Many of our most famous political statements share this double attribute of mirroring the singular and the ordinary. For example, read the following excerpts from President Franklin Roosevelt's first inaugural address, spoken on March 4, 1933, in the middle of the Great Depression. Then answer this question: Is what Roosevelt said famous because its expression is extraordinary, or because it appeals to something that is basic to every human being?

> This is pre-eminently the time to speak the truth, the whole truth, frankly and boldly. Nor need we shrink from honestly facing conditions in our country today. This great nation will endure as it has endured, will revive and will prosper.
>
> So first of all let me assert my firm belief that the only thing we have to fear is fear itself—nameless, unreasoning, unjustified terror that paralyzes needed efforts to convert retreat into advance.
>
> In every dark hour of our national life a leadership of frankness and vigor has met with that understanding and support of the people themselves that is essential to victory. I am convinced that you will again give that support to leadership in these critical days.
>
> In such a spirit on my part and on yours we face our common difficulties. They concern, thank God, only material things. Values have shrunken to fantastic levels; taxes have risen; our ability to pay has fallen; government of all kinds is faced by serious curtailment of income; the means of exchange are frozen in the currents of trade; the withered leaves of industrial enterprise lie on every side; farmers find no markets for their produce; the savings of many years in thousands of families are gone.
>
> More important, a host of unemployed citizens face the grim problem of existence, and an equally great number toil with little return. Only a foolish optimist can deny the dark realities of the moment.
>
> Yet our distress comes from no failure of substance. We are stricken by no plague of locusts. Compared with the perils that our forefathers conquered because they believed and were not afraid, we have still much to be thankful for. Nature still offers her bounty and human efforts have multiplied it. Plenty is at our doorstep, but a generous use of it languishes in the very sight of the supply. . . .
>
> The measure of the restoration lies in the extent to which we apply social values more noble than mere monetary profit.
>
> Happiness lies not in the mere possession of money; it lies in the joy of achievement, in the thrill of creative effort.
>
> The joy and moral stimulation of work no longer must be forgotten in the mad chase of evanescent profits. These dark days will be worth all they cost us if they teach us that our true destiny is not to be ministered unto but to minister to ourselves and to our fellow-men. (quoted in Commager 1963:240)

The benefits of writing in learning and in controlling what we learn are why sociology instructors will require a great deal of writing in their classes. Learning the complex and diverse world of sociology takes more than a passive ingestion of facts. You have to understand and come to grips with social issues and with your own attitudes toward them. When you write in an introductory sociology or minorities in American society class, you are entering into the world of the sociologist in the same way he or she does—testing theory against fact, fact against belief, belief against reality.

Writing is the entryway into social and political life. Virtually everything that happens in education, politics, and so on, happens on paper first. Documents are wrestled into shape before their contents can affect institutions and/or the public. Great speeches are written before they are spoken. Meaningful social programs must be spelled out before they are implemented. The written word has helped free slaves, end wars, create new opportunities in the workplace, and shape the values of nations. Often, gaining recognition for our ourselves and our ideas depends less on what we say than on how we say it. Accurate and persuasive writing is absolutely vital to the sociologist.

1.1.2   Learning by Writing

Here is a way to test the notion that writing is a powerful learning tool: Rewrite the notes you have taken from a recent class lecture. It does not matter which class—it can be history, chemistry, or advertising. Choose a difficult class, if possible, one in which you are feeling somewhat unsure of the material and in which you have taken copious notes. As you rewrite, provide the transitional elements (connecting phrases, such as *in order to, because of, and, but, however*) that you were unable to supply in class because of time constraints. Furnish your own examples or illustrations of the ideas expressed in the lecture.

This experiment forces you to make your own thought processes coherent. See if the time it takes you to rewrite the notes is not more than compensated for by a gain in your understanding of the lecture material.

1.1.3   Challenging Yourself

There is no way around it—writing is a struggle. Do you think you are the only one to feel this way? Take heart! Writing is hard for everyone, great writers included. Bringing order into the world is never easy. Isaac Bashevis Singer, winner of the 1978 Nobel Prize in literature, once wrote: "I believe in miracles in every area of life except writing. Experience has shown me that there are no miracles in writing. The only thing that produces good writing is hard work" (quoted in Lunsford and Connors 1992:2). Hard work was evident in the words of John F. Kennedy's inaugural address. Each word is crafted to embed an image in the reader's mind. As you read the following excerpts from Kennedy's speech, what images come to mind? Historians tend to consider a president "great" when his words live longer than his deeds in the minds of the people. Do you think this will be true of Kennedy?

> We observe today not a victory of party but a celebration of freedom—symbolizing an end as well as a beginning—signifying renewal as well as change. For I

have sworn before you and Almighty God the same solemn oath our forebearers prescribed nearly a century and three-quarters ago.

The world is very different now. For man holds in his mortal hands the power to abolish all forms of human poverty and all forms of human life. And yet the same revolutionary beliefs for which our forebearers fought are still at issue around the globe—the belief that the rights of man come not from the generosity of the state but from the hand of God.

We dare not forget today that we are the heirs of that first revolution. Let the word go forth from this time and place, to friend and foe alike, that the torch has been passed to a new generation of Americans—born in this century, tempered by war, disciplined by a hard and bitter peace, proud of our ancient heritage—and unwilling to witness or permit the slow undoing of those human rights to which this nation has always been committed, and to which we are committed today at home and around the world. . . .

In the long history of the world, only a few generations have been granted the role of defending freedom in its hours of maximum danger. I do not shrink from this responsibility—I welcome it. I do not believe that any of us would exchange places with any other people or any other generation. The energy, the faith, the devotion that we bring to this endeavor will light our country and all who serve it—and the glow from that fire can truly light the world.

And so, my fellow Americans: ask not what your country can do for you—ask what you can do for your country.

My fellow citizens of the world: ask not what America will do for you, but what together we can do for the freedom of man. (quoted in Commager 1963:688–689)

One reason for the difficulty of writing is that it is not actually a single activity but a process consisting of several activities that can overlap each other, with two or more sometimes operating simultaneously as you labor to organize and phrase your thoughts (this will be discussed in greater detail later in this chapter). The writing process tends to be sloppy for everyone—an often frustrating search for the best way to articulate meaning.

Frustrating though that search may sometimes be, however, it need not be futile. Remember that the writing process makes use of skills that we all have. In other words, the ability to write is not some magical competence bestowed on the rare, fortunate individual. Although few of us may achieve the proficiency of Isaac Singer, we are all capable of phrasing thoughts clearly and in a well-organized fashion. But learning how to do so takes practice: The one sure way to improve your writing is to write.

Remember also that one of the toughest but most important jobs in writing is to maintain enthusiasm for your writing project. Commitment may sometimes be hard to come by given the difficulties inherent in the writing process—difficulties that can be made worse when the project assigned is unappealing at first glance. For example, how can you be enthusiastic about having to write a paper analyzing welfare reform, when you know little about the American welfare system and see no real use in doing the project?

One of the worst mistakes that unpracticed writers sometimes make is failing to assume responsibility for keeping themselves interested in their writing. No matter how hard it may seem at first to drum up interest in your topic, you have to do it—that is, if you want to write a paper you can be proud of, one that contributes useful material and a fresh point of view to the topic. One thing is guaranteed: If you are bored with your writing, your reader will be, too.

So what can you do to keep your interest and energy level high? Challenge yourself. Think of the paper not as an assignment for a grade, but as a piece of writing that has a point to make. Getting this point across persuasively is the real reason that you are writing, not the simple fact that a teacher has assigned a project.

If someone were to ask you why you are writing your paper, what would you answer? If your immediate, unthinking response is, "Because I've been given a writing assignment," or "Because I want a good grade," your paper may be in trouble. If, on the other hand, your first impulse is to explain the challenge of your main point—"I'm writing to show how welfare reform will benefit both welfare recipients and the American taxpayer"—then you are thinking usefully about your topic.

1.1.4   Maintaining Self-Confidence

Having a sense of confidence in your ability to write well about your topic is essential for good writing. This does not mean that you will always know what the end result of a particular writing activity will be. In fact, you have to cultivate your ability to tolerate a high degree of uncertainty while weighing evidence, testing hypotheses, and experimenting with organizational strategies and wording. Be ready for temporary confusion and for seeming dead-ends, and remember that every writer faces them. It is from your struggle to combine fact with fact, to buttress conjecture with evidence, that order arises.

Do not be intimidated by the amount and quality of work already done in your field of inquiry. The array of opinion and evidence that confronts you in the published literature can be confusing. But remember that no important topic is ever exhausted. There are always gaps—questions that have not yet been satisfactorily explored either in the published research on a subject or in the prevailing popular opinion. It is in these gaps that you establish your own authority, your own sense of control.

Remember that the various stages of the writing process reinforce one another. Establishing a solid motivation strengthens your sense of confidence about the project, which in turn influences how successfully you organize and write. If you start out well, using good work habits, and give yourself ample time for the various activities to gel, you should produce a paper that will reflect your best work, one that your audience will find both readable and useful.

1.2   THE WRITING PROCESS

As you engage in the writing process, you are doing many different things at once. While planning, you are no doubt defining the audience for your paper at the same time that you are thinking about the paper's purpose. As you draft the paper, you may organize your next sentence while revising the one you have just written. Different parts of the writing process overlap, and much of the difficulty of writing is that so many things happen at once. Through practice—in other words, through writing—it is possible to learn how to control those parts of the process that can be controlled and to encourage those mysterious, less controllable activities.

No two people go about writing in exactly the same way. It is important for you to recognize routines—modes of thought as well as individual exercises—that help you negotiate the process successfully. And it is also important to give yourself as much time as possible to complete the process. Procrastination is one of the writer's greatest enemies. It saps confidence, undermines energy, and destroys concentration. Working regularly and keeping as close as possible to a well-thought-out schedule often make the difference between a successful paper and an embarrassment.

Although the various parts of the writing process are interwoven, there is, naturally, a general order to the work you have to do. You have to start somewhere! What follows is a description of the various stages of the writing process—planning, using intervention strategies, outlining, drafting, revising, editing, and proofreading—along with suggestions as to how to get the most out of each.

1.2.1   Planning

Planning includes all activities that lead up to the writing of the first draft. These activities differ from person to person. For instance, some writers prefer to compile a formal outline before writing that draft. Others perform brief writing exercises to jump-start their imaginations. Some draw diagrams; others doodle. Later on we'll look at a few starting strategies, and you can determine which may be of help to you.

Right now, however, let us discuss some early choices that all writers must make during the planning stage. These choices concern topic, thesis, purpose, and audience—four elements that help make up the writing context, the terms under which we all write. Every time you write—even if you are writing a diary entry or a note to the delivery person—these four elements are present. You may not give conscious consideration to all of them in each piece of writing that you do, but it is extremely important to think carefully about them when writing a sociology paper. Some or all of these defining elements may be dictated by your assignment, yet you will always have a degree of control over them.

Selecting your topic.   No matter how restrictive an assignment may seem to be, there is no reason to feel trapped by it. Within any assigned subject you can find a range of topics to explore. What you are looking for is a topic that engages your own interest. Let your curiosity be your guide. For example, if you have been assigned the subject of welfare reform, then try to find some issues concerning welfare reform that interest you. (How does receiving something for nothing affect an individual's self-esteem? What would be the repercussions of limiting the amount of time anyone could receive welfare benefits?) Any good topic comes with a set of questions; you may well find that your interest picks up if you simply begin asking questions. One strong recommendation: Ask your questions on paper. Like most other mental activities, the process of exploring your way through a topic is transformed when you write down your thoughts as they come instead of letting them fly through your mind unrecorded. Remember the old adage from Louis Agassiz: "A pen is often the best of eyes" (quoted in Pearce 1958:106).

Although it is vital to be interested in your topic, you do not have to know much about it at the outset of your investigation. In fact, having too heartfelt a commitment to a topic can be an impediment to writing about it; emotions can get in the way of objectivity. Often it is better to choose a topic that has piqued your interest yet remained something of a mystery to you—a topic discussed in one of your classes, perhaps, or mentioned on television or in a conversation with friends.

Narrowing your topic.   The task of narrowing your topic offers you a tremendous opportunity to establish a measure of control over the writing project. It is up to you to hone your topic to just the right shape and size to suit both your own interests and the requirements of the assignment. Do a good job of it, and you will go a long way toward guaranteeing yourself sufficient motivation and confidence for the tasks ahead of you. Do it wrong, and somewhere along the way you may find yourself directionless and out of energy.

Generally, the first topics that come to your mind will be too large to handle in your research paper. For example, the topic of a national health policy has generated a tremendous number of news articles and reports recently published by experts in the field. Despite all the attention turned toward this topic, however, there is still plenty of room for you to investigate it on a level that has real meaning to you and that does not merely recapitulate the published research. What about an analysis of how one of the proposed U.S. health policies might affect insurance costs in a locally owned company?

The problem with most topics is not that they are too narrow or too completely explored; it is that they are too rich. There are so many useful ways to address a topic that choosing the best focus is often difficult. Take your time narrowing the topic. Think through the possibilities that occur to you, and—as always—jot down your thoughts.

The following is a list of topics assigned to undergraduate students in a course on social theory. Their task was to choose a topic and write an essay of 2,500 words. Next to each topic is an example of how a student narrowed it to make it a manageable paper topic.

General Topic	**Paper Topic**
Plato	Plato's philosophy of the role of women in politics
Freedom	A comparison of Rousseau's concept of freedom with Locke's

Community	Arguments for the necessity of community used by Amitai Etzioni
Max Weber	Weber's definition of bureaucracy

Without taking time to research them, see what kinds of viable narrowed topics you can make from the following general topics:

crime in America	political corruption
international terrorism	military spending
education	affirmative action hiring policies
freedom of speech	freedom of religion
gun control	abortion rights

Example

general topic:	the family
narrowed topics:	cultural demands that keep family members isolated the effect of substance abuse on family stability the impact of the single-parent family on work in America

Finding your thesis.   As you plan, be on the lookout for an idea that would serve as your thesis. A thesis is not a fact that can be immediately proven by recourse to recorded information, but a hypothesis worth discussing, an argument with more than one possible conclusion. Your thesis sentence will reveal to your reader not only the argument you have chosen, but also your orientation toward it—the conclusion that your paper will attempt to prove.

In looking for a thesis, you do many jobs at once:

1. You limit the amount and kind of material that you must cover, making it manageable.
2. You increase your own interest in the narrowing field of study.
3. You work to establish your paper's purpose—the reason that you are writing about your topic. (If the only reason you can see for writing is to earn a good grade, then you probably won't!)
4. You establish your notion of who your audience is and what sort of approach might best catch their interest.

In short, you gain control over your writing context. For this reason, it is a good idea to establish a thesis early on—a working thesis—that will very probably change as your thinking deepens but that will allow you to establish a measure of order in the planning stage.

Writing your thesis sentence.   The introduction of your paper will contain a sentence that expresses in a nutshell the task that you intend to accomplish. This thesis sentence communicates your main idea—the one you are going to support or defend or illustrate. The thesis sets up an expectation in the reader's mind that you must satisfy. But it is more than just the statement that informs your reader of your goal; in the planning stage, the thesis is a valuable tool to help you narrow your focus and confirm in your own mind your paper's purpose.

Developing your thesis.   A class on crime and society was assigned a twenty-page paper studying a problem currently being faced by the municipal authorities in their own city. The choice of the problem was left up to the students. One student, Richard Gonzales, decided to investigate the problem posed to the city by the large number of abandoned buildings in a downtown neighborhood that he drove through on his way to the university. Richard's first working thesis was: "Abandoned houses result in negative social effects to the city."

The problem with this thesis, as Richard found out, was that it was not an idea that could be argued, but a fact corroborated easily by the sources he began to consult. As he read reports from various sources, such as the Urban Land Institute and the City Planning Commission, and talked with representatives from the Community Planning Department, Richard began to get interested in the dilemma faced by his city in responding to the problem of abandoned buildings.

Richard's second working thesis was: "Removal of abandoned buildings is a major problem facing the city." This thesis narrowed the topic somewhat and gave Richard an opportunity to use material gleaned from his research, but there was still no real comment attached to it. It still states a bare fact, easily proved. At this point, Richard became interested in the still narrower topic of how building removal should best be handled. He found that the major issue was funding and that different civic groups favored different methods of funding the demolition. As Richard explored the arguments for and against funding plans, he began to feel that one of them might be best for the city.

Richard's third working thesis was: "Assessing a 'demolition fee' to each sale of a property offers a viable solution to the city's building removal problem." Note how this thesis narrowed the focus of his paper still further than the other two yet presents an arguable hypothesis. This thesis told Richard what he had to do in his paper, just as it tells his reader what to expect.

At some time during your preliminary thinking on a topic, you should consult the library to see how much published work has already been done. This search is beneficial in at least two ways:

1. It acquaints you with a body of writing that will become very important in the research phase.
2. It gives you a sense of how your topic is generally addressed by the community of scholars you are joining. Is the topic as important as you think it is? Has there already been so much research on the topic as to make your inquiry, in its present formulation, irrelevant? These questions can be answered by reviewing the literature.

As you go about determining your topic, remember that one goal of sociology writing in college is to enhance your own understanding of the social and/or social-psychological process, to build an accurate model of the way societies work. Let this goal help you: Aim your research into those subject areas that you know are important to your understanding of the discipline.

Defining your purpose.   There are many ways to classify the purposes of writing, but in general most writing is undertaken either to inform or to persuade an audience. The goal of informative or expository writing is, simply, to impart information about a particular subject, whereas the aim of persuasive writing is to convince your reader of your point of view on an issue. The distinction between expository and persuasive writing is not hard and fast. Most sociology writing has elements of both exposition and persuasion. However, most effective writing has a clearly chosen focus of either exposition or persuasion. When you begin writing, consciously select a primary aim of exposition or persuasion, and then set out to achieve that goal.

Suppose you have been required to write a paper explaining how parents' attitudes affect their children's choice of college. If you are writing an expository paper, your task could be to describe in a coherent and impartial way the attitudes of the parents and the choices of their children.

If, however, your paper attempts to convince your reader that parental attitudes often result in children making poor choices, you are now writing to persuade, and your strategy is radically different. You will now need to explain the negative effects of parental attitudes. Persuasive writing seeks to influence the opinions of its audience toward its subject. Writing assignments in sociology may break down the distinction between expository and persuasive writing in a number of ways. You may be called on to analyze sociopolitical situations, evaluate government programs, speculate on directions in social policy, identify or define problems within a range of fields, or suggest solutions and predict results. It is very important to spend planning time sharpening your sense of purpose.

Know what you want to say. By the time you begin working on your final draft, you must have a very sound notion of the point you wish to argue or the position you wish to support. If, during the writing of the final draft, someone were to ask you to state your thesis, you should be able to give a satisfactory answer with a minimum of delay and no prompting. On the other hand, if you have to hedge your answer because you cannot easily form a notion of your thesis in your own mind, you may not yet have arrived at a final draft.

For example, two writers have been asked what point they wish to make in their papers. One of these writers has a better grip on her writing task.

Writer 1: My paper is about tax reform for the middle class.

Writer 2: My paper argues that tax reform for the middle class would be unfair to the upper and lower classes, who would then have to share more responsibility for the cost of government.

The second writer has a clear view of her task; the first knows what her topic is—tax reform for the middle class—but may not yet know what it is about tax reform that she wishes to support. It may be that you will have to write a draft or two or engage in various prewriting activities to arrive at a secure understanding of your task.

Watch out for bias! There is no such thing as pure objectivity. You are not a machine. No matter how hard you may try to produce an objective paper, every choice you make as you write is influenced to some extent by your personal beliefs and opinions. What you tell your readers is influenced—sometimes without your knowing—by a multitude of factors: your environment, upbringing, and education; your attitude toward your audience; your political affiliation; your race and gender; your career goals; and your ambitions for the paper you are writing. The influence of these factors can be very subtle, and it is something you must work to identify in your own writing as well as in the writing of others in order not to mislead or be misled. Remember that one of the reasons you write is for self-discovery. The writing you will do in sociology classes—as well as the writing you will do for the rest of your life—will give you a chance to discover and confront honestly your own views on your subjects. Responsible writers keep an eye on their own biases and are honest with their readers about them.

Defining your audience.   It may sometimes be difficult to remember that the point of your writing is not simply to jump through the technical hoops imposed by the assignment. The point is communication—the transmission of your knowledge and your conclusions—to the reader in a way that suits you. Your task is to pass to your reader the spark of your own enthusiasm for the topic. Readers who were indifferent to your topic should look at it in a new way after reading your paper. This is the great challenge of writing: to enter into your reader's mind and leave behind new knowledge and new questions.

It is tempting to think that most writing problems would be solved if the writer could view his or her writing as if it had been produced by another person. The ego barrier between writer and audience is the single greatest impediment to accurate communication. To reduce the discrepancy between your understanding and that of your audience, it is necessary to consider the audience's needs. By the time you begin drafting, most—if not all—of your ideas have begun to attain coherent shape in your mind, so that virtually any words in which you try to phrase those ideas will reflect your thought accurately—to you. Your reader, however, does not already have in mind the conclusions that you have so painstakingly achieved. If you leave out of your writing the material that is necessary to complete your reader's understanding of your argument, he or she may not be able to supply that information himself.

The potential for misunderstanding is a given for any audience—whether it is made up of general readers, experts in the field, or your professor, who is reading, in part, to see how well you have mastered the constraints that govern the relationship between writer and reader. Make your presentation as complete as possible, writing always as if to an audience whose previous knowledge of your topic is limited to information easily available to the general public.

John F. Kennedy's Pastry Mistake

President Kennedy was one of America's greatest speechmakers. He had a gift for understanding and speaking directly to the audience he was addressing. At one point during the Cold War, the Soviet Union banned shipments of supplies across East Germany to West Berlin, the part of the city governed by the Western, noncommunist countries. It was a tense moment in East–West relations.

Going to Berlin on June 26, 1963, Kennedy spoke to the besieged people as if he were one of them. The people responded warmly, cheering his speech continuously. At the climactic moment, Kennedy boldly proclaimed, in words that became famous, "Ich bein ein Berliner." He was attempting to say, in German, "I am a citizen of Berlin," meaning, "I am one of you; I share your concerns in this moment of crisis." What he said instead was German for "I am a pastry." His mistake was in inserting the article *ein—ein Berliner* is a kind of pastry in Germany.

Communicating to your audience can sometimes be more difficult than it first appears.

1.2.2   Using Invention Strategies

In this chapter, we have discussed methods of selecting and narrowing the topic of a paper. As your focus on a specific topic sharpens, you naturally begin to think about the kinds of information that will go into the paper. In the case of papers not requiring formal research, that material comes largely from your own recollections. Indeed, one of the reasons why instructors assign unresearched papers is to convince you of the incredible richness of your memory, the vastness and variety of the "database" that you have accumulated and that, moment by moment, you continue to build.

So vast is your horde of information that it is sometimes difficult to find within it the material that would best suit your paper. In other words, finding out what you already know about a topic is not always easy. Invention—a term borrowed from classical rhetoric—refers to the task of discovering, or recovering from memory, information about your topic. As we write, all of us go through some sort of invention procedure that helps us explore our topic. Some writers seem to have little problem coming up with material; others need more help. Over the centuries writers have devised different exercises that can help locate useful material housed in memory. We shall look at a few of these briefly.

Freewriting.   Freewriting is an activity that forces you to get something down on paper. There is no waiting around for inspiration. Instead, you set yourself a time limit—three minutes or five minutes—and write for that length of time without stopping, not even to lift the pen from the paper or your hands from the typewriter or computer keyboard. Focus on the topic, and don't let the difficulty of finding relevant material stop you from writing. If necessary, you may begin by writing, over and over, some seemingly useless phrase, like, "I cannot think of anything to write about," or perhaps the name of your topic. Eventually, something else will occur to you. (It is surprising how long a three-minute freewriting can seem to take!) At the end of the freewriting, look over what you have produced for anything of use. Granted, much of the writing will be unusable, but there may be an insight or two that you did not know you possessed. In addition to its ability to recover usable material for your paper, freewriting yields a few other benefits. First, it takes little time to do, which means you may repeat the exercise as often as you like within a relatively short span of time. Second, it breaks down

---

An Example of Freewriting

The professor in Shelby Johnson's second-year Family as a Social Institution class assigned a paper focusing on some aspect of American family life. Shelby, who felt her understanding of the family as an institution was modest, tried to get her mind started on the job of finding a topic that interested her with a three-minute freewriting exercise. Thinking about the family and child development, Shelby wrote steadily for three minutes without lifting her pen from the paper. Here is the result of her freewriting:

> Okay, now, what do I know about the family? I was raised in one. I have a father, mother, and sister. Both parents were present all my life. Both worked. Professionals. Sometimes I wished Mom was at home. That might be interesting: working parents, the effects on kids. Two-paycheck families. I like it. Where to start? I could interview my parents. I need to find some recent statistics on two-paycheck families.

---

some of the resistance that stands between you and the act of writing. There is no initial struggle to find something to say; you just write.

Brainstorming.   Brainstorming is simply the process of making a list of ideas about a topic. It can be done quickly and, initially, without any need to order items into a coherent pattern. The point is to write down everything that occurs to you as quickly and as briefly as possible, as individual words or short phrases. Once you have a good-sized list of items, you can then group the items according to relationships that you see among them. Brainstorming allows you both to uncover ideas stored in your memory and to make useful associations among those ideas.

A professor in a political sociology class asked her students to write a 700-word paper, in the form of a letter to be translated and published in a Warsaw newspaper, giving the Polish readers useful advice about living in a democracy. Carrie Nation, a student in the class, started thinking about the assignment by brainstorming. First, she simply wrote down anything that occurred to her:

Life in a Democracy

voting rights	welfare	freedom of the press
protest movements	everybody equal	minorities
racial prejudice	American Dream	injustice
the individual	no job security	lobbyists and PACs
justice takes time	psychological factors	aristocracy of wealth
size of bureaucracy	market economy	

Thinking through her list, Carrie decided to rearrange her list into two: one devoted to positive aspects of life in a democracy, the other to negative aspects. At this point she decided to discard some items that were redundant or did not seem to have much potential. As you can see, Carrie had some questions about where some of her items would fit.

Positive	Negative
voting rights	aristocracy of wealth
freedom of the press	justice takes time
everybody equal	racial prejudice
American Dream	welfare
psychological factors	lobbyists and PACs
protest movements	size of bureaucracy

At this point, Carrie decided that her strongest inclination was to explore the ways in which money and special interests affect a democratically elected government. Which of the remaining items in her two lists would be of help to Carrie?

Asking questions.   It is always possible to ask most or all of the following questions about any topic: Who? What? When? Where? Why? How? These questions force you to approach it the way a journalist does, setting it within different perspectives that can then be compared to discover insights within the material.

For a class in the sociology of law, a professor asked her class to write a paper describing the impact of Supreme Court clerks on the decision-making process. Here are some questions that a student in the class might logically ask to begin thinking about a thesis.

- Who are the Supreme Court's clerks? (How old? What racial and gender mix are they? What are their politics?)
- What are their qualifications for the job?
- What exactly is their job?
- When during the court term are they most influential?
- Where do they come from? (Is there any discernible geographical pattern in the way they are chosen? Any pattern regarding religion? Do certain law schools contribute a significantly greater number of clerks than any others?)
- How are they chosen? (Are they appointed? elected?)
- When in their careers do they serve?
- Why are they chosen as they are?
- Who have been some influential court clerks? (Have any gone on to sit on the bench themselves?)

Can you think of other questions that would make for useful inquiry?

Being flexible.   As you engage in invention strategies, you are also doing other work. You are still narrowing your topic, for example, as well as making decisions that will affect your choice of tone or audience. You move forward on all fronts, with each decision you make affecting the others. This means you must be flexible enough in your understanding of the paper's development to allow for adjustments or alterations in your understanding of your goal. Never be so determined to prove a particular theory that you fail to notice when your own understanding of it changes. Stay objective.

1.2.3   Organizing Your Writing by Outlining

A paper that contains all the facts but provides them in an ineffective order will confuse rather than inform or persuade. Although there are various methods of grouping ideas, none is potentially more effective than outlining. Unfortunately, no organizing process is more often misunderstood.

Outlining for yourself.   There are really two jobs that outlining can do. First, it can serve as a means of forcing you, the writer, to gain a better understanding of your ideas by arranging them according to their interrelationships. As the following model indicates, there is one primary rule of outlining: Ideas of equal weight are placed on the same level within the outline. This rule requires you to determine the relative importance of your ideas. You must decide whether one idea is of the same type or order as another and which subtopic each idea best fits into. If you arrange your ideas with care in a coherent outline in the planning stage, your own grasp of your topic will be greatly enhanced. You will have linked your ideas together logically and given a skeleton to the body of the paper. This sort of subordinating and coordinating activity is difficult, however, and as a result, inexperienced writers sometimes fail to pay the necessary attention to the outline. They begin writing their first draft without an effective outline, hoping for the best. That hope usually disappears, especially in complex papers involving research. Garcia, a student in a second-year class in government management, researched the impact of a worker-retraining program in his state and came up with the following facts and theories. Number them in logical order.

___ A growing number of workers in the state do not possess the basic skills and education demanded by employers.

___ The number of dislocated workers in the state increased from 21,000 in 1982 to 32,000 in 1992.

___ A public policy to retrain uneducated workers would allow them to move into new and expanding sectors of the Oklahoma economy.

___ Investment in high technology would allow the state's employers to remain competitive in the production of goods and services in both domestic and foreign markets.

___ The economy is becoming more global and more competitive.

Outlining for your reader.   The second job of an outline is aimed not at the writer's understanding, but at the reader's. An outline accompanying your paper can serve the reader as its blueprint—a summary of the paper's points and their interrelationships. A busy person can consult your outline to quickly get a sense of your paper's goal and the argument you have used to promote it. This accompanying outline, then, is very important, since its clarity and coherence help to determine how much attention your audience will give to your ideas. As sociology students, you will be given a great deal of help with the arrangement of your material into an outline to accompany your paper. A look at the model presented in other chapters of this manual will show you how strictly these formal outlines are structured. But while you must pay close attention to the requirements of the accompanying outline, do not forget that an outline is a powerful tool in the early planning stages of your paper.

Formal outline pattern.   Following this pattern accurately during the planning stage of your paper helps to guarantee that your ideas are placed logically.

Thesis sentence (prefaces the organized outline)

   I. First main idea
     A. First subordinate idea
       1. Reason, example, or illustration
       2. Reason, example, or illustration
         a. Detail supporting reason 2
         b. Detail supporting reason 2
         c. Detail supporting reason 2
     B. Second subordinate idea
  II. Second main idea

Notice that each level of the paper must have more than one entry: For every A there must be at least a B (and, if required, a C, D, and so on); for every 1 there must be a 2. This arrangement forces you to compare ideas, looking carefully at each one to determine its place among the others. The insistence on assigning relative values to your ideas is what makes your outline an effective organizing tool.

The structure of any particular type of sociology paper is governed by a formal pattern. When rigid external controls are placed on their writing, some writers tend to feel stifled, their creativity impeded by this kind of paint-by-numbers approach to structure. It is vital to the success of your paper that you never allow yourself to be overwhelmed by the pattern rules of a particular type of paper. Remember that such controls are placed on papers not to limit your creativity but to make the paper easy to read and immediately useful to its intended audience. It is as necessary to write clearly and confidently in a social issue paper or a case study as it is in a term paper for English literature, a résumé, a short story, or a job application letter.

1.2.4   Writing Drafts

The rough draft.   After the planning comes the writing of the first draft. Using your thesis and outline as direction markers, you must now weave your amalgam of ideas, researched data, and persuasion strategies into logically ordered sentences and paragraphs. Though adequate prewriting may make the drafting easier than it might have been, it will still not be easy. Writers establish their own methods of encouraging themselves to forge ahead with the draft, but here are some tips to bear in mind:

1. Remember that this is a rough draft, not the final draft. At this stage, it is not necessary that every word you write be the best possible choice. Do not put that sort of pressure on yourself; you must not allow anything to slow you down now. Writing is not like sculpting, in which every chip is permanent—you can always go back to your draft later and add, delete, reword, or rearrange. No matter how much effort you have put into planning, you cannot be sure how much of this first draft you will eventually keep. It may take several drafts to get one that you find satisfactory.

2. Give yourself sufficient time to write. Don't delay the first draft by telling yourself there is still more research to do. You cannot uncover all the material there is to know on a particular subject, so don't fool yourself into trying. Remember that writing is a process of discovery. You may have to begin writing before you can see exactly what sort of final research you need to do. Keep in mind that there are other tasks waiting for you after the first draft is finished, so allow for them as you determine your writing schedule. Giving yourself time is very important for another reason: The more time that passes after you write a draft, the better your ability to view it with greater objectivity. It is very difficult to evaluate your writing accurately soon after you complete it. You need to cool down, to recover from the effort of putting all those words together. The "colder" you get on your writing, the better able you are to read it as if it were written by someone else, which helps you acknowledge the changes needed to strengthen the paper.

3. Stay sharp. It is important to keep in mind the plan you created for yourself as you narrowed your topic, composed a thesis sentence, and outlined the material. But if, as you write, you feel a strong need to change the plan a bit, do not be afraid to do so. Be ready for surprises dealt you by your own growing understanding of your topic. Your goal is to render your best thinking on the subject as accurately as possible.

Authority.   To be convincing, your writing needs to be authoritative; that is, you have to sound as if you have confidence in your ability to convey your ideas in words. Sentences that sound stilted or that suffer from weak phrasing or the use of clichés are not going to win supporters for the aims that you express in your paper. Thus, sounding confident becomes a major concern. Consider the following points as you work to convey to your reader that necessary sense of authority.

Level of formality.   Tone is one of the primary methods by which you signal to the readers who you are and what your attitude is toward them and toward your topic. The major choice you make has to do with the level of language formality that you feel is most appropriate for your audience. The informal tone you would use in a letter to a friend might well be out of place in a paper called "Waste in Military Spending," written for your sociology professor. Remember that tone is only part of the overall decision that you make about how to present your information. To some extent, formality is a function of individual word choices and phrasing. Is it appropriate to use contractions like *isn't* or *they'll?* Would the strategic use of a sentence fragment for effect be out of place? The use of informal language, the personal *I,* and the second-person *you* is traditionally forbidden—for better or worse—in certain kinds of writing. Often, part of the challenge of writing a formal paper is, simply, how to give your prose bite while staying within the conventions.

Jargon.   One way to lose readers quickly is to overwhelm them with jargon—phrases that have a special, usually technical meaning within your discipline, but that are unfamiliar to the average reader. The occasional use of jargon may add an effective touch of atmosphere, but anything more than that will severely dampen a reader's enthusiasm for the paper. Often a reason for jargon is the writer's desire to impress the reader by sounding lofty or knowledgeable. Unfortunately, all jargon usually does is make for confusion. In fact, jargon is often an index of the writer's lack of connection to his audience.

Sociology writing is a haven for jargon. Perhaps writers of professional journals and certain issue papers believe their readers are all completely attuned to their terminology. It may be that these writers occasionally hope to obscure faulty information or potentially unpopular ideas in confusing language. Or the problem could simply be fuzzy thinking on the writer's part. Whatever the reason, sociology papers too often sound like prose made by machines to be read by machines.

Some students may feel that, in order to be accepted as sociologists, their papers should conform to the practices of their published peers. This is a mistake. Remember that it is always better to write a clear sentence than a cluttered or confusing one, and that burying your ideas in jargon defeats the effort that you went through to form them.

Clichés.   In the heat of composition, as you are looking for words to help you form your ideas, it is sometimes easy to plug in a cliché—a phrase that has attained universal recognition by overuse. (Note that clichés differ from jargon in that clichés are part of the general public's everyday language, while jargon is specific to the language of experts in a particular field.) Our vocabularies are brimming with clichés:

It's raining cats and dogs.

That issue is as dead as a doornail.

It's time for the governor to face the music.

Angry voters made a beeline for the ballot box.

The problem with clichés is that they are virtually meaningless. Once color-ful means of expression, they have lost their color through overuse, and they tend to bleed energy and color from the surrounding words. When revising, re-place clichés with words that more accurately convey the specific impression that you wish to create.

Descriptive language.   Language that appeals to the reader's senses will al-ways engage his or her interest more fully than language that is abstract. This is especially important for writing in disciplines that tend to deal in abstracts—such as sociology. The typical sociology paper—with its discussions of abstract principles, demographics, or deterministic outcomes—is often in danger of float-ing off on a cloud of abstractions, drifting farther away in each paragraph from the tangible life of the reader. Whenever appropriate, appeal to your reader's sense of sight, hearing, taste, touch, or smell. Consider the effectiveness of the following second sentence, as opposed to that of the first.

1. The housing project had deteriorated since the last inspection.
2. Since the last inspection, deterioration of the housing project had become ev-ident in stench rising from the plumbing, grime on the walls and floors, and the sound of rats scurrying in the hallways.

Bias-free and gender-neutral writing.   Language can be a very powerful method of either reinforcing or destroying cultural stereotypes. You should try to avoid gender bias and ethnic stereotyping in your writing. By treating the sexes in subtly different ways in your writing, you may unknowingly be commit-ting an act of discrimination. A common example is the use of the pronoun *he* to refer to a person whose gender has not been identified. But there are many other writing situations in which sexist and/or ethnic bias may appear. To avoid gen-der bias, the American Sociological Association (1997) recommends replacing words like *man, men,* or *mankind* with *person, people,* or *humankind.* When both sexes must be referred to in a sentence, use *he or she, her or him,* and *his or hers* instead of *he/she, him/her,* and *his/hers.* Consider the following examples of sex-ist and nonsexist language:

Sexist: A lawyer should always treat his client with respect.

Corrected: A lawyer should always treat his or her client with respect.

Or: Lawyers should always treat their clients with respect.

Sexist: Man is a political animal.

Corrected: People are political animals.

There are other methods of avoiding gender bias in your writing. Some writ-ers, faced with the aforementioned pronoun dilemma, alternate the use of male and female personal pronouns, identifying to the unknown referent as *he* in one section of their text, then as *she* in the next (a strategy often used in this manu-al). You can also change the subject to plural—there is no gender bias in *they.*

Sexist language denies to a large number of your readers the basic right to fair and equal treatment. Be aware of this subtle form of discrimination. Remember that language is more than the mere vehicle of your thoughts; your words shape perceptions for your reader. How well you say something will profoundly affect your reader's response to it.

1.2.5   Revising

After all the work you have gone through writing it, you may feel "married" to the first draft of your paper. However, revising is one of the most important steps in assuring your paper's success. Although unpracticed writers often think of revision as little more than making sure all the i's are dotted and t's are crossed, it is much more than that. Revising is reseeing the paper, looking at it from other perspectives, trying always to align your view with the view that will be held by your audience. Research in the process of composition indicates that we are actually revising all the time, in every phase of the writing process as we reread phrases, rethink the placement of a item in an outline, or test a new topic sentence for a paragraph. Subjecting your entire hard-fought draft to cold, objective scrutiny is one of the most difficult activities to master in the writing process, but it is absolutely necessary. You must make sure that you have said everything that needs to be said clearly and in logical order. One confusing passage, and the reader's attention is deflected from where you want it to be. Suddenly she has to become a detective, trying to figure out why you wrote what you did and what you meant by it. You don't want to throw such obstacles in the path of meaning.

Here are some tips to help you with revision:

1. Give yourself adequate time to revise. As mentioned, you need time to become "cold" on your paper in order to analyze it objectively. After you have written your draft, spend some time away from it. Try to come back to it as if it had been written by someone other than yourself.

2. Read the paper carefully. This is tougher than it sounds. One good strategy is to read it aloud or to have a friend read it aloud while you listen. (Note: Having friends critique your writing may be helpful, but friends do not usually make the best critics. They are rarely trained in revision techniques and are usually so close to you that they are unwilling—often unconsciously so—to risk disappointing you by giving your paper a really thorough examination.)

3. Prepare a list of specific items to check. It is important to revise in an orderly fashion—in stages—looking first at large concerns, such as the overall structure, and then rereading for problems with smaller elements, such as paragraph organization or sentence structure.

4. Check for unity—the clear and logical relation of all parts of the essay to its thesis. Make sure that every paragraph relates well to the whole paper and that it is in the right place.

5. Check for coherence. Make sure there are no gaps among the different parts of the argument and that you have adequate transition everywhere it is needed. Transitional elements are markers indicating places where the paper's focus or attitude changes. Transitional elements can be one-word long—*however, although, unfortunately, luckily*—or as long as a sentence or a paragraph:

"In order to fully appreciate the importance of democracy as a shaping presence in post–Cold War Polish politics, it is necessary to examine briefly the Poles' last historical attempt to implement democratic government." Transitional elements rarely introduce new material. Instead, they are direction pointers, either indicating a shift to new subject matter or signaling how the writer wishes certain material to be interpreted by the reader. Because you—the writer—already know where and why your paper changes direction and how you want particular passages to be received, it can be very difficult for you to determine where transition is needed.

6. Avoid unnecessary repetition.

Avoiding repetition.   There are two types of repetition that can annoy a reader: repetition of content and repetition of wording. Repetition of content leads to redundancy. Ideally, you want to cover a topic once, memorably, and then move on to your next topic. Organizing a paper is a difficult task, however, one that usually occurs through a process of enlightenment as to purposes and strategies. It is possible for an early draft to circle back to a subject you have already covered, and to begin to treat the same material over again. This sort of repetition can happen even if you have made use of prewriting strategies. What is worse, it can be difficult for you as a writer to acknowledge the repetition—to admit to yourself that the material you have worked so hard to shape on page 2 returns on page 5 in much the same shape. As you write and revise, bear this in mind: Any unnecessary repetition of content that you allow into your final draft is a potential annoyance to your reader, who is working to make sense of the argument she or he is reading and does not want to be distracted by a passage that repeats material already encountered. Train yourself, through practice, to read through your draft, looking for material that you have repeated unnecessarily.

Repetition of wording results in boring material. Make sure that you do not overuse any phrases or individual words. This sort of repetition can make your prose sound choppy and uninspired. It is important that your language sound fresh and energetic. Before you turn in your final draft, make sure to read through your paper carefully, looking for such repetition. Here are some examples of repetition of wording:

The subcommittee's report on education reform will surprise a number of people. A number of people will want copies of the report.

The chairman said at a press conference that he is happy with the report. He will circulate it to the local news agencies in the morning. He will also make sure that the city council has copies.

I became upset when I heard how the committee had voted. I called the chairman and expressed my reservations about the committee's decision. I told him I felt that he had let the teachers and students of the state down. I also issued a press statement.

The last passage illustrates a condition known by composition teachers as the "I-syndrome." Can you hear how such duplicated phrasing can make a paper sound disconnected and unimaginative?

Note that not all repetition is bad. You may wish to repeat a phrase for rhetorical effect or special emphasis: "I came. I saw. I conquered." Just make sure that any repetition in your paper is intentional—placed there to produce a specific effect.

1.2.6   Editing

Editing is sometimes confused with the more involved process of revising. But editing happens later, after you have wrestled through your first draft—and maybe your second and third—and arrived at the final draft. Even though your draft now contains all the information you want to impart and the information is arranged to your satisfaction, there are still many factors to check, such as sentence structure, spelling, and punctuation.

It is at this point that an unpracticed writer might let down his guard. After all, most of the work on the paper is finished; the big jobs of discovering material and organizing and drafting it have been completed. But watch out! Editing is as important as any other step in the writing process. Any error that you allow in the final draft will count against you in the reader's mind. It may not seem fair, but a minor error—a misspelling or the confusing placement of a comma—will make a much greater impression on your reader than it perhaps should. Remember that everything about your paper is your responsibility, including getting even the supposedly little jobs right. Careless editing undermines the effectiveness of your paper. It would be a shame if all the hard work you put into prewriting, drafting, and revising were to be damaged because you carelessly allowed a comma splice!

Most of the preceding tips for revising hold for editing as well. It is best to edit in stages, looking for only one or two kinds of errors each time you reread the paper. Focus especially on errors that you remember committing in the past. For instance, if you know you have a tendency to misplace commas, go through your paper looking at each comma carefully. If you have a weakness for writing unintentional sentence fragments, read each sentence aloud to make sure that it is, indeed, a complete sentence. Have you accidentally shifted verb tenses anywhere, moving from past to present tense for no reason? Do all the subjects in your sentences agree in number with their verbs? Now is the time to find out.

Watch out for miscues—problems with a sentence that the writer can easily overlook. Remember that your search for errors is hampered in two ways:

1. As the writer, you hope not to find any errors with your writing. This desire can lead you to miss sighting them when they occur.
2. Because you know your material so well, it is easy, as you read, to unconsciously supply missing material—a word, correct punctuation—as if it were present.

How difficult is it to see that something is missing in the following sentence?

Unfortunately, legislators often have too little regard their constituents.

We can even guess that the missing word is probably *for,* which should be inserted after *regard.* However, it is quite possible that the writer of the sentence will supply the missing *for* automatically as he reads it, as if he has seen it on the page. This is a miscue, and miscues can be hard for the writer to spot because he is so close to his own material.

Editing is the stage in which you finally answer those minor questions that you put off earlier when you were wrestling with wording and organization. Any ambiguities regarding the use of abbreviations, italics, numerals, capital letters, titles (for example, when do you capitalize the title *president?*), hyphens, dashes (usually created on a typewriter or computer by striking the hyphen key twice), apostrophes, and quotation marks have to be cleared up. You must check to see that you have used the required formats for footnotes, endnotes, margins, and page numbers.

Guessing is not allowed. Sometimes unpracticed writers who realize that they don't quite understand a particular rule of grammar, punctuation, or format often do nothing to fill that knowledge gap. Instead they rely on guesswork and their own logic—which is not always up to the task of dealing with so contrary a language as English—to get them through problems that they could solve if only they referred to a writing manual. Remember that it does not matter to the reader why or how an error shows up in your writing; it only matters that you as the writer have dropped your guard. You must not allow a careless error to diminish your hard work.

One tactic for catching mistakes in sentence structure is to read the sentences aloud, starting with the last one in the paper, moving to the next to last, and then the previous sentence, thus going backward through the paper (reading each sentence in the normal, left-to-right manner, of course) until you reach the first sentence of the introduction. This backward progression strips each sentence of its rhetorical context and helps you to focus on its internal structure.

1.2.7   Proofreading

Before you hand in your final version of the paper, it is vital that you check it over one more time to make sure there are no errors of any sort. This job is called *proofreading* or *proofing.* In essence, you are looking for many of the same things you checked for during editing, but now you are doing it on the last draft, which has been typed and is about to be submitted to your audience. Proofreading is as important as editing; you may have missed an error in the previous stages, or an error may have been introduced when the draft was recopied or typed for the last time. Like every other stage of the writing process, proofreading is your responsibility.

At this stage, it is essential that you check for typing mistakes—letters transposed or left out of words, or missing words, phrases, or punctuation. If you have had the paper professionally typed, you still must check it carefully. Do not rely solely on the typist's proofreading abilities. If you typed your paper on a computer or a word processor, it is possible that you unintentionally inserted a command that alters your document drastically—slicing out a word or a line or a sentence at the touch of a key. Make sure such accidental deletions have not occurred.

Above all else, remember that your paper represents you. It is a product of your best thoughts, your most energetic and imaginative response to a writing challenge. If you have maintained your enthusiasm for the project and worked through the different stages of the writing process honestly and carefully, you should produce a paper you can be proud of and one that will serve its readers well.

1.3   LEVELS OF ACADEMIC WRITING

Researchers who study the written work of college students find that several patterns of effort and expertise emerge. Morgan (1981:5–6) refers to these patterns as "levels of academic writing," and believes that they appear in nearly every college class, graduate and undergraduate alike. Although writing quality increases with grade level, many students—no matter what their grade level—have trouble using words effectively.

1.3.1   Level One: The Fact-Gathering Level

Students at this level have little more to offer in their writing than opinions that they have heard others state or that they found in a newspaper or periodical. If asked, "What is Social Security?" a level-one student might answer, "Social Security is welfare for the elderly or disabled," or "Social Security is a liberal program." Students who are stranded at level one or below are unable to advance much further than presenting a fact or two to support their statements. This is the lowest level of scholarship. The level-one student, when assigned a report, will simply go to the library and assemble facts and opinions incoherently and return with a paper. At best, this is a very simple presentation of "What is?" However, mastery of level one is a necessary learning experience.

1.3.2   Level Two: The Informational Level

At this level, students learn to clarify facts and understand them more completely through the process of comparison. When asked the question, "What is Social Security?" the student writing at level two might draw on what she has learned of political science and economics to suggest different ideological perspectives, each with its own facts. A level-two answer shows greater depth of knowledge than a level-one answer; the student has advanced beyond a recitation of facts, taking the initial steps toward analysis.

1.3.3   Level Three: The Analytical Level

At this level, the student becomes familiar with and somewhat proficient in completing various types of sociological analysis. Using the same example, "What is Social Security?" some students might present their facts in numerical terms, using formulas, mathematical curves, statistical tests, or tables to express relationships among variables. Other students might reduce their data to common prose, utilizing different theories to analyze and explain the same phenomena.

1.3.4   Level Four: The Creative Level

This is the highest and most difficult level of academic writing. The student is able to use facts, theories, and analytical ability to reach levels of creativity. At the creative level, the student is essentially alone, trying to discover something new, perhaps an insight that colleagues can't appreciate initially.

To the question, "What is Social Security?" the creative sociologist, utilizing the sociological imagination described in the Introduction, might employ both historical analysis and creative forecasting to discover new information. The creative level is where knowledge is advanced, its frontiers pushed inevitably outward.

It is the purpose of this book to help you advance, from whatever level at which you presently find yourself, to the full professional expression of level four—creative and insightful writing in sociology.

WRITING COMPETENTLY

2.1 GUIDELINES FOR THE COMPETENT WRITER

Good writing places your thoughts in your reader's mind in exactly the way you want them to be there. It tells your reader just what you want him to know without revealing anything you do not wish to say. That may sound odd, but the fact is that writers have to be careful not to let unwanted messages slip into their writing. For example, look at the following passage, taken from a paper analyzing the impact of a worker-retraining program. Hidden within the prose is a message that jeopardizes the paper's success. Can you detect the message?

> Recent articles written on the subject of dislocated workers have had little to say about the particular problems dealt with in this paper. Since few of these articles focus on the problem at the local level.

Chances are, when you reached the end of the second "sentence," you sensed something missing, a gap in logic or coherence, and your eye ran back through both sentences to find the place where things went wrong. The second sentence is actually not a sentence at all. It does have certain features of a sentence—a subject, for example (*few*), and a verb (*focus*), but its first word (*Since*) subordinates the entire clause that follows, taking away its ability to stand on its own as a complete idea. The second "sentence," which is properly called a subordinate clause, merely fills in some information about the first sentence, explaining why recent articles about dislocated workers fail to deal with problems discussed in the present paper.

This sort of error is commonly called a sentence fragment, and it conveys to the reader a message that no writer wants to send: that the writer either is careless or—worse—has not mastered the language she is using. Language errors, such as fragments, misplaced commas, or shifts in verb tense send up little red flags in the reader's mind. The result is that the reader loses a little of his concentration on the issue being discussed. He becomes distracted and begins to wonder about the language competency of the writer. The writing loses effectiveness. Remember that whatever goal you set for your paper—whether you want it to persuade, describe, analyze, or speculate—you must also set another goal: to display language competence. Without it, your paper will not completely achieve its other aims. Language errors spread doubt like a virus; they jeopardize all the hard work you have done on your paper.

Credibility in the job market depends on language competence. Anyone who doubts this should remember the beating that Dan Quayle took in the press when he was vice president of the United States for misspelling the word potato at a Trenton, New Jersey, spelling bee. His error caused a storm of humiliating publicity for the hapless Quayle, and contributed to an impression of his general incompetence.

Although they may seem minor, these sorts of language errors—which are often called surface errors—can be extremely damaging in certain kinds of writing. Surface errors come in a variety of types, including misspellings, punctuation problems, grammar errors, and the inconsistent use of abbreviations, capitalization, and numerals. They are an affront to your reader's notion of correctness—and therein lies one of the biggest problems with surface errors. Different audiences tolerate different levels of correctness. You already know that you can get away with surface errors in, say, a letter to a friend, who will not judge you harshly for them, while those same errors in a job application letter might eliminate you from consideration for the job. Correctness depends to an extent on context.

Another problem is that the rules governing correctness shift over time. What would have been an error to your grandmother's generation—the splitting of an infinitive, for example, or the ending of a sentence with a preposition—is taken in stride today by most readers. So how do you write correctly when the rules shift from person to person and over time? Following are some tips.

2.1.1   Consider Your Audience

One of the great risks of writing is that even the simplest of choices you make regarding wording or punctuation can sometimes prejudice your audience against you in ways that may seem unfair. For example, look again at the old grammar "rule" forbidding the splitting of infinitives. After decades of counseling students to never split an infinitive (something this sentence has just done), composition experts now concede that a split infinitive is not a grammar crime. But suppose you have written a position paper trying to convince your city council of the need to hire security personnel for the library, and half of the council members—the people you wish to convince—remember their eighth-grade grammar teacher's outdated warning about splitting infinitives. How will they respond when you tell them, in your introduction, that "librarians are ordered to always accompany visitors to the rare book room because of the threat of vandalism"? How much of their attention have you suddenly lost because of their automatic recollection of a nonrule? It is possible, in other words, to write correctly and still offend your readers' notions of language competence.

Make sure that you tailor the surface features of your writing to the level of competency that your readers require. When in doubt, take a conservative approach. The same goes for the level of formality you should assume. Your audience might be just as distracted by contractions as by a split infinitive.

2.1.2   Aim for Consistency

When dealing with a language question for which there are different answers—such as whether to place a comma after the second item in a series of three ("The mayor's speech addressed taxes, housing for the poor, and the job situation.")—always use the same strategy. If, for example, you avoid splitting one infinitive, avoid splitting all infinitives in your paper.

2.1.3   Have Confidence in What You Already Know about Writing

It is easy for unpracticed writers to allow their occasional mistakes to discourage them about their writing ability. But most of what we know about writing is right. For example, we are all capable of writing sentences that are grammatically sound—even if we cannot identify the grammar rules by which we achieve coherence. Most writers who worry about their chronic errors have fewer than they think. Becoming distressed about errors makes writing more difficult. In fact, you already know more about grammar than you think you do. As various composition theorists have pointed out, the word *grammar* has several definitions. One meaning is "the formal patterns in which words must be arranged in order to convey meaning." We learn these patterns very early in life and use them spontaneously without thinking about them. Our understanding of grammatical patterns is extremely sophisticated, despite the fact that few of us can actually cite the rules that the patterns follow.

Hartwell (1985:111) tested grammar learning by asking native English-speakers of different ages and levels of education, including high school teachers, to arrange these words in natural order:

French the young girls four

Everyone he asked could produce the natural order for this phrase: "the four young French girls." Yet none of Hartwell's respondents said they knew the rule that governs the order of the words.

2.1.4   Eliminate Chronic Errors

The question then arises: If just thinking about our errors has a negative effect on our writing, how do we learn to write with greater accuracy? One important way is simply to write as often as possible. Give yourself practice in putting your thoughts into written shape, and get lots of practice in revising and proofing your work. And as you write and revise, be honest—and patient—with yourself. Chronic errors are like bad habits; getting rid of them takes time. You probably know of one or two problem areas in your writing that you could have eliminated but have not done so. Instead, you have "fudged" your writing at the critical points, relying on half-remembered formulas from past English classes or trying to come up with logical solutions to your writing problems. (Warning: Rules governing the English language are not always logical.) You may have simply decided that comma rules are unlearnable or that you will never understand the difference between the verbs *lay* and *lie*. And so you guess—and get the rule wrong a good part of the time. What a shame, when just a little extra work would give you mastery over those few gaps in your understanding and boost your confidence as well.

Instead of continuing with this sort of guesswork, instead of living with the gaps, why not face the problem areas now and learn the rules that have heretofore escaped you? What follows is a discussion of those surface features of a paper in which errors most commonly occur. You will probably be familiar with most—if not all—of the rules discussed, but there may be a few you have not yet mastered. Now is the time to do so.

2.2   SOME RULES OF PUNCTUATION AND GRAMMAR

2.2.1   Apostrophes

An apostrophe is used to show possession; when you wish to say that something belongs to someone or to another thing, you add either an apostrophe and an *s* or an apostrophe alone to the word that represents the owner.

When the owner is singular (a single person or thing), the apostrophe precedes an added *s:*

> According to Mr. Pederson's secretary, the board meeting has been canceled.
> The school's management team reduced crime problems last year.
> Somebody's briefcase was left in the classroom.

The same rule applies if the word showing possession is a plural that does not end in *s:*

> The women's club provided screening services for at-risk youth and their families.
> Professor Logan has proven himself a tireless worker for children's rights.

When the word expressing ownership is a plural ending in *s,* the apostrophe follows the *s:*

> The new procedure was discussed at the youth workers' conference.

There are two ways to form the possessive for two or more nouns:

1. To show joint possession (both nouns owning the same thing or things), the last noun in the series is possessive:

   Billy and Richard's first draft was completed yesterday.

2. To indicate that each noun owns an item or items individually, each noun must show possession:

   Professor Wynn's and Professor Camacho's speeches took different approaches to the same problem.

The apostrophe is important, an obvious statement when you consider the difference in meaning between the following two sentences:

Be sure to pick up the psychiatrist's things on your way to the airport.

Be sure to pick up the psychiatrists' things on your way to the airport.

In the first of these sentences, you have only one psychiatrist to worry about, while in the second, you have at least two!

2.2.2   Capitalization

When to capitalize.   Following is a brief summary of some hard-to-remember capitalization rules.

Rule 1: You may, if you choose, capitalize the first letter of the first word in a complete sentence that follows a colon (but remember to be consistent throughout your paper).

Our instructions are explicit: Do not allow anyone into the conference without an identification badge.

Rule 2: Capitalize proper nouns (nouns naming specific people, places, or things) and proper adjectives (adjectives made from proper nouns). A common noun following the proper adjective is usually not capitalized, nor is a common adjective preceding the proper adjective (such as *a, an,* or *the*):

Proper Nouns	**Proper Adjectives**
England	English sociologists
Iraq	the Iraqi educator
Shakespeare	a Shakespearean tragedy

Proper nouns include the following:

- *Names of famous monuments and buildings:* the Washington Monument, the Empire State Building, the Library of Congress
- *Historical events, eras, and certain terms concerning calendar dates:* the Civil War, the Dark Ages, Monday, December, Columbus Day

- *Parts of the country:* North, Southwest, Eastern Seaboard, the West Coast, New England (Note that when words like *north, south, east, west,* and *northwest* are used to designate direction rather than geographical region, they are not capitalized: "We drove east to Boston and then made a tour of the East Coast.")
- *Words referring to race, religion, and nationality:* Islam, Muslim, Caucasian, White (or white), Asian, African American, Black (or black), Slavic, Arab, Jewish, Hebrew, Buddhism, Buddhists, Southern Baptists, the Bible, the Koran, American
- *Names of languages:* English, Chinese, Latin, Sanskrit
- *Titles of corporations, institutions, businesses, universities, and organizations:* Dow Chemical, General Motors, the National Endowment for the Humanities, University of Tennessee, Colby College, Kiwanis Club, American Association of Retired Persons, the Oklahoma State Senate (Note: Some words once considered proper nouns or adjectives have, over time, become common: french fries, pasteurized milk, arabic numerals, italics, panama hat.)

Rule 3: Titles of individuals should be capitalized when they precede a proper name; otherwise, titles are usually not capitalized.

The committee honored Chairperson Furmanski.

The committee honored the chairperson from the sociology department.

We phoned Doctor MacKay, who arrived shortly afterward.

We phoned the doctor, who arrived shortly afterward.

A story on Queen Elizabeth's health appeared in yesterday's paper.

A story on the queen's health appeared in yesterday's paper.

Pope John Paul's visit to Colorado was a public relations success.

The pope's visit to Colorado was a public relations success.

When not to capitalize.   In general, do not capitalize nouns when your reference is nonspecific. For example, you would not capitalize the phrase *the senator,* but you would capitalize *Senator Smith.* The second reference is as much a title as it is a term of identification, while the first reference is a mere identifier. Likewise, there is a difference in degree of specificity between the phrase *the state treasury* and the *Texas State Treasury.*

Note that the meaning of a term may change somewhat depending on capitalization. What, for example, might be the difference between a Democrat and a democrat? (When capitalized, the word refers to a member of a specific political party; when not capitalized, the word refers to someone who believes in a democratic form of government.)

Capitalization depends to some extent on the context of your writing. For example, if you are writing a policy analysis for a specific corporation, you may capitalize words and phrases—Board of Directors, Chairperson of the Board, the Institute—that would not be capitalized in a paper written referring to boards of directors, chairpersons, and institutes in general. Likewise, in some contexts it is not unusual to see titles of certain powerful officials capitalized even when not accompanying a proper noun:

The President's visit to the Oklahoma City bombing site was considered timely.

In this case the reference is to a specific president, President Clinton.

2.2.3   Colons

There are uses for the colon that we all know. For example, a colon can separate the parts of a statement of time (4:25 A.M.), separate chapter and verse in a biblical quotation (John 3:16), and close the salutation of a business letter (Dear Senator Keaton:). But there are other uses for the colon that writers sometimes don't quite learn that can add an extra degree of flexibility to sentence structure.

The colon can introduce into a sentence certain kinds of material, such as a list, a quotation, or a restatement or description of material mentioned earlier in the paper.

> *List:* The committee's research proposal promised to do three things: (1) establish the extent of the problem; (2) examine several possible solutions; and (3) estimate the cost of each solution.

> *Quotation:* In his speech, the mayor challenged us with these words: "How will your council's work make a difference in the life of our city?"

> *Restatement or description:* Ahead of us, according to the senator's chief of staff, lay the biggest job of all: convincing our constituents of the plan's benefits.

2.2.4   Commas

The comma is perhaps the most troublesome of all punctuation marks, no doubt because its use is governed by so many variables, such as sentence length, rhetorical emphasis, and changing notions of style. Following are the most common problems.

Comma splices.   Joining two complete sentences by only a comma makes a comma splice. Examine the following examples of comma splices:

> An impeachment is merely an indictment of a government official, actual removal usually requires a vote by a legislative body.

> An unemployed worker who has been effectively retrained is no longer an economic problem for the community, he has become an asset.

> It might be possible for the city to assess fees on the sale of real estate, however, such a move would be criticized by the community of real estate developers.

In each of these passages, two complete sentences (also called independent clauses) have been "spliced" together by a comma. When a comma splice is taken out of context, it becomes easy to see what is wrong: The break between the two sentences is inadequate. Simply reading the draft through to try to "hear" the comma splices may not work, however, since the rhetorical features of your prose—its "movement"—may make it hard to detect this kind of sentence error.

There is one foolproof way to check your paper for comma splices. Locate the commas in your draft and then read carefully the structures on both sides of each comma to determine whether you have spliced together two complete sentences. If you find a complete sentence on both sides of a comma, and if the sentence following the comma does not begin with a coordinating conjunction (*and, but, for, nor, or, so, yet*), then you have found a comma splice.

There are five commonly used ways to correct comma splices:

1. Place a period between the two independent clauses

   Splice: A physician receives many benefits from his or her affiliation with clients, there are liabilities as well.

   Correction: A physician receives many benefits from his or her affiliation with clients. There are liabilities as well.

2. Place a comma and a coordinating conjunction (*and, but, for, or, nor, so, yet*) between the sentences:

   Splice: The chairperson's speech described the major differences of opinion over the departmental situation, it also suggested a possible course of action.

   Correction: The chairperson's speech described the major differences of opinion over the departmental situation, and it also suggested a possible course of action.

3. Place a semicolon between the independent clauses:

   Splice: Some people believe that the federal government should play a large role in establishing a housing policy for the homeless, many others disagree.

   Correction: Some people believe that the federal government should play a large role in establishing a housing policy for the homeless; many others disagree.

4. Rewrite the two clauses of the comma splice as one independent clause:

   Splice: Television programs play some part in the development of delinquent attitudes, however they were not found to be the deciding factor in determining the behavior of juvenile delinquents.

   Correction: Television programs were found to play a minor but not a decisive role in determining the delinquent behavior of juveniles.

5. Change one of the two independent clauses into a dependent clause by beginning it with a subordinating word. A subordinating word introducing a clause prevents the clause from being able to stand on its own as a complete sentence. Words that can be used as subordinators include *although, after, as, because, before, if, though, unless, when, which,* and *where.*

   Splice: The student meeting was held last Tuesday, there was a poor turnout.

   Correction: When the student meeting was held last Tuesday, there was a poor turnout.

Comma missing in a compound sentence.   A compound sentence is comprised of two or more independent clauses—two complete sentences. When these two clauses are joined by a coordinating conjunction, the conjunction should be preceded by a comma. (In the previous section, the second solution for fixing a comma splice calls for the writer to transform the splice into this sort of compound sentence.) The error is that writers sometimes fail to place the comma before the conjunction. Remember, the comma is there to signal the reader that another independent clause follows the coordinating conjunction. In other words, the comma is like a road sign, telling a driver what sort of road she is about to encounter. If the comma is missing, the reader does not expect to find the second half of a compound sentence and may be distracted from the text. As the following examples indicate, the missing comma is especially a problem in longer sentences or in sentences in which other coordinating conjunctions appear:

> *Missing comma:* The senator promised to visit the hospital and investigate the problem and then he called the press conference to a close.
>
> *With the comma added:* The senator promised to visit the hospital and investigate the problem, and then he called the press conference to a close.
>
> *Missing comma:* The water board can neither make policy nor enforce it nor can its members serve on auxiliary water committees.
>
> *With the comma added:* The water board can neither make policy nor enforce it, nor can its members serve on auxiliary water committees.

Notice how the comma sorts out the two main parts of the compound sentence, eliminating confusion. However, an exception to the rule must be noted. In shorter sentences, the comma may not be necessary to make the meaning clear:

> The mayor phoned and we thanked him for his support.

Placing a comma between the independent clauses after the conjunction is never wrong, however. If you are the least bit unsure of your audience's notions about what makes for "proper" grammar, it is a good idea to take the conservative approach and use the comma:

> The mayor phoned, and we thanked him for his support.

Missing comma or commas with a nonrestrictive element.   A nonrestrictive element is part of a sentence—a word, phrase, or clause—that adds information about another element in the sentence without restricting or limiting the meaning of that element. In other words, a nonrestrictive element simply says something about some other part of the sentence without changing radically our understanding of it. Although the information it carries may be useful, we do not have to have the nonrestrictive element for the sentence to make sense. To signal the nonessential nature of the element, we set it off from the rest of the sentence with commas.

Failure to indicate the nonrestrictive nature of an element by using commas can cause confusion. For example, see how the presence or absence of commas affects our understanding of the following sentence:

> The judge was talking with the police officer, who won the outstanding service award last year.
>
> The judge was talking with the police officer who won the outstanding service award last year.

Can you see that the comma changes the meaning of the sentence? In the first version of the sentence, the comma makes the information that follows it incidental: The judge was talking with the police officer, who happens to have won the service award last year. In the second version of the sentence, the information following the term *police officer* is important to the sense of the sentence; it tells us, specifically, which police officer—presumably there are more than one—the judge was addressing. The lack of a comma has transformed the material following the term *police officer* into a restrictive element—meaning one necessary to our understanding of the sentence. Be sure that in your paper you make a clear distinction between nonrestrictive and restrictive elements by setting off the nonrestrictive elements with commas.

Missing comma in a series.   A series is any two or more items of a similar nature that appear consecutively in a sentence. The items may be individual words, phrases, or clauses. One of the rules that we all learned a long time ago is that the items in a series of three or more items are separated by commas. In the following examples the series items are in italics:

> *The senator, the mayor,* and *the police chief* all attended the ceremony.

> Because of the new zoning regulations, *all trailer parks must be moved out of the neighborhood, all small businesses must apply for recertification and tax status,* and *the two local churches must repave their parking lots.*

The final comma, the one before the *and,* is sometimes left out, especially in newspaper writing. This practice, however, can make for confusion, especially in longer, complicated sentences like the second example. Here is the way the sentence would read without the final comma:

> Because of the new zoning regulations, all trailer parks must be moved out of the neighborhood, all small businesses must apply for recertification and tax status and the two local churches must repave their parking lots.

Notice how the second *and,* which is not set off from the sequence in front of it, seems at first to be an extension of the second clause in the series instead of the beginning of the third. This is the sort of ambiguous structure that can cause a reader to backtrack and lose concentration.

To avoid the possibility of causing this sort of confusion, it is a good idea always to include that final comma. And remember that if you do decide to include it, be consistent; make sure it appears in every series in your paper.

2.2.5   Misplaced Modifiers

A modifier is a word or group of words used to describe—to "modify" our understanding of—another word in the sentence. A misplaced modifier is one that appears either at the beginning or ending of a sentence and seems to describe some word other than the one the writer obviously intended. The modifier is disconnected from its intended meaning. Because the writer knows what she wishes to say, it is often hard for her to spot a misplaced modifier. But other readers find them, and the result can be disastrous for the sentence.

> *Incorrect:* Flying low over Washington, the White House was seen.
>
> *Correct:* Flying low over Washington, we saw the White House.
>
> *Incorrect:* Worried about the cost of the program, sections of the bill were trimmed in committee.
>
> *Correct:* Worried about the cost of the program, the committee trimmed sections of the bill.
>
> *Correct:* The committee trimmed sections of the bill because they were worried about the cost of the program.
>
> *Incorrect:* To lobby for prison reform, a lot of effort went into the TV ads.
>
> *Correct:* The lobby group put a lot of effort into the TV ads advocating prison reform.
>
> *Incorrect:* Stunned, the television network broadcast the defeated senator's concession speech.
>
> *Correct:* The television network broadcast the stunned senator's concession speech.

You will note that in the first two incorrect sentences, the confusion is largely due to the use of passive-voice verbs: the White House was seen, sections of the bill were trimmed. Often, though not always, the cause of a misplaced modifier is the fact that the actor in the sentence—*we* in the first example, *the committee* in the second—is either distanced from the modifier or obliterated by the passive-voice verb. It is a good idea to avoid passive voice unless you have a specific reason for using it.

One way to check for misplaced modifiers is to examine all modifiers at the beginnings or endings of your sentences. Look especially for *to be* phrases (to lobby) or for words ending in *–ing* or *–ed* at the start of the modifier. Then check to see whether the word being modified is in plain sight and close enough to the phrase to be properly connected.

2.2.6   Parallelism

Series of two or more words, phrases, or clauses within a sentence should be structured in the same grammatical way. Parallel structures can add power and balance to your writing by creating a strong rhetorical rhythm. Here is a famous example of parallelism from the U.S. Constitution. (The capitalization, preserved from the original document, follows eighteenth-century custom. Parallel structures have been italicized.)

Preamble to the Constitution

We the People of the United States, in Order to *form a more perfect Union, establish Justice, insure Domestic Tranquillity, provide for the Common Defense,*

> *promote the general Welfare,* and *secure the Blessings of Liberty to ourselves and our Posterity,* do ordain and establish this Constitution for the United States of America.

Note that there are actually two series in this sentence, the first composed of several phrases that each complete the infinitive phrase beginning with the word *to* (*to form,* [to] *Establish,* [to] *insure*), the second consisting of two verbs (*do ordain* and *establish*). These parallel series appeal to our love of balance and pattern, and give an authoritative tone to the sentence. We feel the writer has thought long and carefully about the subject, and has taken firm control of it.

We find a special satisfaction in balanced structures and so are more likely to remember ideas phrased in parallelisms than in less highly ordered language. For this reason—as well as for the sense of authority and control that they suggest—parallel structures are common in well-written speeches. Consider the following examples:

> We hold these truths to be self-evident, that all men are created equal, that they are endowed by their Creator with certain unalienable Rights, that among these are Life, Liberty, and the pursuit of Happiness.
>
> —Declaration of Independence

> But, in a larger sense, we can not dedicate—we can not consecrate—we can not hallow—this ground. The brave men, living and dead, who struggled here, have consecrated it, far above our poor power to add or detract. The world will little note, nor long remember what we say here, but it can never forget what they did here.
>
> —Abraham Lincoln, Gettysburg Address

> Let us never negotiate out of fear. But never let us fear to negotiate. . . . Ask not what your country can do for you; ask what you can do for your country.
>
> —John F. Kennedy, Inaugural Address

If the parallelism of a passage is not carefully maintained, the writing can seem sloppy and out of balance. To check for parallelism, scan your writing for any series of two or more items in a sentence. These items should be parallel in structure. In other words, if one item depends on an *–ing* construction, as in the second example following, so should its partners. Any lists in your paper should consist of items that are parallel in structure. Note the following examples of incorrect and correct constructions:

> *Incorrect:* The mayor promises not only to reform the police department, but also the giving of raises to all city employees.

> *Correct:* The mayor promises not only to reform the police department, but also to give raises to all city employees. [Connective structures such as *not only . . . but also* introduce elements that should be parallel.]

> *Incorrect:* The cost of doing nothing is greater than the cost to renovate the apartment block.

Correct: The cost of doing nothing is greater than the cost of renovating the apartment block.

Incorrect: Here are the items on the committee's agenda: (1) to discuss the new property tax; (2) to revise the wording of the city charter; and (3) a vote on the city manager's request for an assistant.

Correct: Here are the items on the committee's agenda: (1) to discuss the new property tax; (2) to revise the wording of the city charter; and (3) to vote on the city manager's request for an assistant.

2.2.7   Fused (Run-On) Sentences

A fused sentence is one in which two or more independent clauses (passages that can stand as complete sentences) have been joined together without the aid of any suitable connecting word, phrase, or punctuation; the sentences run together. As you can see, there are several ways to correct a fused sentence:

Incorrect: The council members were exhausted they had debated for two hours.

Correct: The council members were exhausted. They had debated for two hours. [The linked independent clauses have been separated into two sentences.]

Correct: The council members were exhausted; they had debated for two hours. [A semicolon marks the break between the two clauses.]

Correct: The council members were exhausted, having debated for two hours. [The second independent clause has been rephrased as a dependent clause.]

Incorrect: Our policy analysis impressed the committee it also convinced them to reconsider their action.

Correct: Our policy analysis impressed the committee by convincing them to reconsider their action. [The second clause has been rephrased as part of the first clause.]

Correct: Our policy analysis impressed the committee, and it also convinced them to reconsider their action. [The two clauses have been separated by a comma and a coordinating word.]

Although a fused sentence is easily noticeable to the reader, it can be maddeningly difficult for the writer to catch in proofreading. Unpracticed writers tend to read through the fused spots, sometimes supplying the break that is usually heard when sentences are spoken. To check for fused sentences, read the independent clauses in your paper carefully, making sure that there are adequate breaks among all of them.

2.2.8   Pronoun Errors

The difference between *its* and *it's*. Do not make the mistake of trying to form the possessive of it in the same way that you form the possessive of most nouns. The pronoun *it* shows possession by simply adding an *s:*

The prosecuting attorney argued the case on its merits.

The word *it's* is a contraction, meaning "it is":

It's the most expensive program ever launched by the prison.

What makes the *its/it's* rule so confusing is that most nouns form the singular possessive by adding an apostrophe and an *s:* The jury's verdict startled the crowd. When proofreading, any time you come to the word *it's,* substitute the phrase *it is* while you read. If the phrase makes sense, you have used the correct form. Consider the following examples:

If you have used the word *it's:*

The newspaper article was misleading in it's analysis of the election.

Then read *it's* as *it is:*

The newspaper article was misleading in it is analysis of the election.

If the phrase makes no sense, substitute *its* for *it's:*

The newspaper article was misleading in its analysis of the election.

Vague pronoun reference.   Pronouns are words that stand in place of nouns or other pronouns that have already been mentioned in your writing. The most common pronouns include *he, she, it, they, them, those, which,* and *who.* You must make sure that each pronoun reference is clear; in other words, that there is no confusion about the reference. Examine the following clear pronoun references:

The mayor said that he would support our bill if the city council would also back it.

The piece of legislation that drew the most criticism was the bill concerning housing for the poor.

The word that is replaced by the pronoun is called its *antecedent.* To check the accuracy of your pronoun references, ask yourself this question: To what does the pronoun refer? Then answer the question carefully, making sure that there is not more than one possible antecedent. Consider the following sentence:

Several special interest groups decided to defeat the new health care bill. This became the turning point of the government's reform campaign.

To what does the word *this* refer? The immediate answer seems to be the word *bill* at the end of the previous sentence. It is more likely the writer was referring to the attempt of the special interest groups to defeat the bill, but there is no word in the first sentence that refers specifically to this action. The reference is unclear. One way to clarify the reference is to change the beginning of the second sentence:

Several special interest groups decided to defeat the new health care bill. Their attack on the bill became the turning point of the government's reform campaign.

Here is another example:

When John F. Kennedy appointed his brother Robert to the position of U.S. Attorney General, he had little idea how widespread the corruption in the Teamsters Union was.

To whom does the word *he* refer? It is unclear whether the writer is referring to John or to Robert Kennedy. One way to clarify the reference is simply to repeat the antecedent instead of using a pronoun:

When President John F. Kennedy appointed his brother Robert to the position of U.S. Attorney General, Robert had little idea how widespread the corruption in the Teamsters Union was.

Pronoun agreement.   Remember that a pronoun must agree in gender and in number with its antecedent. This rule is generally easy for us to remember. Study the following examples of pronoun agreement:

Mayor Smith said that he appreciated our club's support in the election.

One reporter asked the senator what she would do if the President offered her a cabinet post.

Having listened to our case, the judge decided to rule on it within the week.

Engineers working on the housing project said they were pleased with the renovation so far.

The following words, however, can become troublesome antecedents. They may look like plural pronouns but are actually singular:

everybody	nobody	everyone
no one	somebody	each
someone	either	anyone

A pronoun referring to one of these words in a sentence must be singular, too. Pronoun agreement errors appear in the following examples:

Incorrect: Each of the women in the support group brought their children.

Correct: Each of the women in the support group brought her children.

Incorrect: Has everybody received their ballot?

Correct: Has everybody received his or her ballot? [The two gender-specific pronouns are used to avoid sexist language.]

Correct: Have all the delegates received their ballots? [The singular antecedent has been changed to a plural one.]

Shift in person. It is important to avoid shifting among first person (*I, we*), second person (*you*), and third person (*she, he, it, one, they*) unnecessarily. Such shifts can cause confusion:

> *Incorrect:* Most people [third person] who seek a job find that if you [second person] tell the truth during your interviews, you will gain the interviewers' respect.

> *Correct:* Most people who seek a job find that if they tell the truth during their interviews, they will win the interviewers' respect.

2.2.9 Quotation Marks

It can be difficult to remember when to use quotation marks and where they go in relation to other marks of punctuation. When faced with a gap in their knowledge of the rules, unpracticed writers often try to rely on logic rather than referring to a rule book. But the rules governing quotation marks do not always seem to us to rely on logic. The only way to make sure of your use of quotation marks is to memorize the rules. There are not many.

When to use quotation marks. Use quotation marks to enclose direct quotations, if they are four typed lines or less:

> In his farewell address to the American people, George Washington warned, "The great rule of conduct for us, in regard to foreign nations, is, in extending our commercial relations, to have with them as little political connection as possible." (U.S. Senate 1991)

Longer quotes are indented left and right and single-spaced—without quotation marks:

> Lincoln explained his motive for continuing the Civil War clearly in his response to Horace Greeley's open letter:
>
>> I would save the Union. I would save it the shortest way under the Constitution. The sooner the National authority can be restored, the nearer the Union will be the Union as it was. If there be those who would not save the Union unless they could at the same time save Slavery, I do not agree with them. If there be those who would not save the Union unless they could at the same time destroy Slavery, I do not agree with them. (Lincoln 1862)

Use single quotation marks to set off quotations within quotations:

> "I intend," said the professor, "to use in my lecture a line from Frost's poem, 'The Road Not Taken.'"

Note that when the interior quote occurs at the end of the sentence, both single and double quotation marks are placed outside the period. Use quotation marks to set off the following kinds of titles:

- The title of a short poem: "The Second Coming," by William Butler Yeats [But note that the title of a long poem published as a book does not appear in quotation marks; instead, it is italicized as a book would be: *The Dark Sister,* by Winfield Townley Scott]
- The title of a short story
- The title of an article or essay
- The title of a song
- An episode of a television or radio show

Use quotation marks to set off words or phrases used in special ways:

To convey irony: The so-called "liberal" administration has done nothing but cater to big business.

To set off a technical term: To have "charisma," Weber would argue, is to possess special powers. Many believe that John F. Kennedy had great charisma. [Note that once the term is defined, it is not placed in quotation marks again.]

Placement of quotation marks in relation to other punctuation.   Always place commas and periods inside closing quotation marks:

"My fellow Americans," said the President, "there are tough times ahead of us."

Place colons and semicolons outside closing quotation marks:

In his speech on voting, the sociologist warned against "an encroaching indolence"; he was referring to the middle class.

There are several victims of the government's campaign to "Turn Back the Clock": the homeless, the elderly, and the mentally impaired.

Place question marks, exclamation points, and dashes inside or outside closing quotation marks, depending on context. If the punctuation is part of the quotation, it goes inside the quotation mark:

"When will the tenure committee make up its mind?" asked the dean.

The demonstrators shouted, "Free the hostages!" and "No more slavery!"

If the punctuation is not part of the quotation, it goes outside the quotation mark:

Which president said, "We have nothing to fear but fear itself"?

Note that although the quote was a complete sentence, you do not place a period after it. There can only be one mark of "terminal" punctuation (punctuation that ends a sentence).

2.2.10   Semicolons

The semicolon is a little-used punctuation mark that is worth incorporating into your writing strategy because of its many potential applications. A semicolon can be used to correct a comma splice:

> *Incorrect:* The union representatives left the meeting in good spirits, their demands were met.
>
> *Correct:* The union representatives left the meeting in good spirits; their demands were met.
>
> *Incorrect:* Several guests at the fund-raiser had lost their invitations, however, we were able to seat them, anyway.
>
> *Correct:* Several guests at the fund-raiser had lost their invitations; however, we were able to seat them, anyway.

It is important to remember that conjunctive adverbs like *however, therefore,* and *thus* are not coordinating words (such as *and, but, or, for, so,* and *yet*) and cannot be used with a comma to link independent clauses. If the second independent clause begins with *however,* it must be preceded by either a period or a semicolon. As you can see from the second example, connecting the two independent clauses with a semicolon instead of a period preserves the suggestion that there is a strong relationship between the clauses.

Semicolons can separate items in a series. Usually commas separate items in a series:

> We ate breakfast, lunch, and dinner in the hotel.

But when the series items themselves contain commas, the items may be separated from one another with semicolons.

> The newspaper account of the rally stressed the march, which drew the biggest crowd; the mayor's speech, which drew tremendous applause; and the party afterwards in the park.

Avoid misusing semicolons. Do not use a semicolon to separate an independent clause from a dependent clause:

> *Incorrect:* Students from the college volunteered to answer phones during the pledge drive; which was set up to generate money for the new arts center.
>
> *Correct:* Students from the college volunteered to answer phones during the pledge drive, which was set up to generate money for the new arts center.

Although you can use a semicolon to separate two independent clauses, you should use a comma to separate an independent clause from a dependent clause. Do not overuse semicolons. Useful though semicolons are, if too many of them appear in your writing, they can distract your reader's attention. Avoid monotony by using semicolons sparingly.

2.2.11   Sentence Fragments

A fragment is a part of a sentence that is punctuated and capitalized as if it were an entire sentence. It is an especially disruptive kind of error, because it obscures the kinds of connections that the words of a sentence must make in order to complete the reader's understanding. Students sometimes write fragments because they are concerned that a particular sentence is growing too long and needs to be shortened. Remember that cutting the length of a sentence merely by adding a period somewhere along the way often creates a fragment. When checking your writing for fragments, it is essential that you read each sentence carefully to determine (1) whether there is a complete subject and a verb; and (2) whether there is a subordinating word preceding the subject and verb, making the construction a subordinate clause rather than a complete sentence.

Some fragments lack a verb:

Incorrect: The chairperson of our committee, having received a letter from the mayor. [It may look as if there is a verb in this passage, but the word *having,* which can be used as a verb, is used here as a gerund introducing a participial phrase. Watch out for words that look like verbs but are used in another way.]

Correct: The chairperson of our committee received a letter from the mayor.

Some fragments lack a subject:

Incorrect: Our study shows that there is broad support for improvement in the health care system. And in the unemployment system.

Correct: Our study shows that there is broad support for improvement in the health care system and in the unemployment system.

Some fragments are subordinate clauses:

Incorrect: After the latest edition of the newspaper came out. [This clause has the two major components of a complete sentence: a subject (*edition*) and a verb (*came*). Indeed, if the first word (*After*) were deleted, the clause would be a complete sentence. But that first word is a subordinating word, which acts to prevent the following clause from standing on its own as a complete sentence. Watch out for this kind of construction. It is called a subordinate clause, and it is not a sentence.]

Correct: After the latest edition of the newspaper came out, the mayor's press secretary was overwhelmed with phone calls. [A subordinate clause is connected in meaning to the independent clause either before or after it. A common method of revising a subordinate clause that has been punctuated as a complete sentence is to connect it to the complete sentence to which its meaning is most closely connected.]

Incorrect: Several members of Congress asked for copies of the Vice President's position paper. Which called for reform of the Environmental Protection Agency. [The clause beginning after the first period is a subordinate clause written as if it were a complete sentence.]

Correct: Several members of Congress asked for copies of the Vice President's position paper, which called for reform of the Environmental Protection Agency.

2.3   SPELLING

All of us have special spelling problems, words whose correct spelling we have not yet committed to memory. Most writers are not as bad at spelling as they believe themselves to be. Usually it is just a handful of words that the individual finds troubling. The most important thing to do when confronting your spelling problems is to be as sensitive as possible to those words with which you know you have trouble and keep a dictionary handy. No writer should be without a dictionary. There is no excuse for failing to look up a questionable spelling.

When using a computer to type your paper, take advantage of the "spell check" feature available with most word-processing software. It allows you to check those words listed in the program's dictionary. But do not rely entirely on your computer's spell checker. It will miss a variety of words that are properly spelled but are improperly used variants within a particular context. Notice that the mistakes in the following sentences would go unnoticed by a computer's spell checker:

> Wilbur wood rather dye than admit that he had been their. When he cited the bare behind the would pile, he thought,"Isle just lye hear until he goes buy."

Following are two lists of words that often give writers trouble. Read through the lists, looking for those words that tend to give you trouble.

2.3.1   Commonly Confused Words

The words in each pair listed below are often confused with each other. If you do not know the difference in a particular pair, consult your dictionary:

accept/except	complement/compliment
advice/advise	conscience/conscious
affect/effect	corps/corpse
aisle/isle	council/counsel
allusion/illusion	dairy/diary
an/and	descent/dissent
angel/angle	desert/dessert
ascent/assent	device/devise
bare/bear	die/dye
brake/break	dominant/dominate
breath/breathe	elicit/illicit
buy/by	eminent/immanent/imminent
capital/capitol	envelop/envelope
choose/chose	every day/everyday
cite/sight/site	fair/fare

formally/formerly
forth/fourth
hear/here
heard/herd
hole/whole
human/humane
its/it's
know/no
later/latter
lay/lie
lead/led
lessen/lesson
loose/lose
may be/maybe
miner/minor
moral/morale
of/off
passed/past
patience/patients
peace/piece
personal/personnel
plain/plane
precede/proceed
presence/presents
principal/principle
quiet/quite

rain/reign/rein
raise/raze
reality/realty
respectfully/respectively
reverend/reverent
right/rite/write
road/rode
scene/seen
sense/since
stationary/stationery
straight/strait
taught/taut
than/then
their/there/they're
threw/through
too/to/two
track/tract
waist/waste
waive/wave
weak/week
weather/whether
were/where
which/witch
whose/who's
your/you're

2.3.2 Commonly Misspelled Words

acceptable
accessible
accommodate
accompany
accustomed
acquire
against
a lot
annihilate
apparent

arguing/argument
authentic
before
begin/beginning
believe
bulletin
business
cannot
category
committee

condemn

courteous

definitely

dependent

desperate

develop

different

disappear

disappoint

easily

efficient

environment

equipped

exceed

exercise

existence

experience

fascinate

finally

foresee

forty

fulfill

gauge

guaranteed

guard

harass

hero/heroes

humorous

hurried/hurriedly

hypocrite

ideally

immediately

immense

incredible

innocuous

intercede

interrupt

irrelevant

irresistible

irritate

knowledge

license

likelihood

maintenance

manageable

meanness

mischievous

missile

necessary

nevertheless

no one

noticing/noticeable

nuisance

occasion/occasionally

occurred/occurrences

omit/omission

opinion

opponent

parallel

parole

peaceable

performance

pertain

practical

preparation

probably

process

professor

prominent

pronunciation

psychology

publicly

pursue/pursuing

questionnaire

realize

received/receipt

recession

recommend

referring   studying
religious   succeed/success/successfully
remembrance   susceptible
reminisce   suspicious
repetition   technical
representative   temporary
rhythm   tendency
ridiculous   therefore
roommate   tragedy
satellite   truly
scarcity   tyranny
scenery   unanimous
science   unconscious
secede/secession   undoubtedly
secretary   until
senseless   vacuum
separate   valuable
sergeant   various
shining   vegetable
significant   visible
sincerely   without
skiing   women
stubbornness   writing

FORMATS

Your format makes your paper's first impression. Justly or not, accurately or not, the format of your paper announces the level of your professional competence. A well-executed format implies that your paper is worth reading. More than that, however, a proper format brings information to your readers in a familiar form that has the effect of setting their minds at ease. Your paper's format should impress readers with your academic competence as a sociologist by following accepted professional standards. Like the style and clarity of your writing, format communicates messages that are often more readily and profoundly received than the content of the document itself.

The formats in this chapter are based on those endorsed by the American Sociological Association (ASA) and published in the ASA Style Guide (1997). These formats, structured for use by scholars sending papers to professional journals, conform to standards generally accepted in the discipline of sociology. Chapter 4 offers ASA-approved guidelines and models for citing and referencing sources used in a sociology paper. Unless your course instructor gives you special format instructions, follow the directions in this manual exactly.

This chapter contains format instructions for the following elements:

- General page format
- Title page
- Abstract
- Executive summary
- Outline page
- Table of contents
- List of tables and figures
- Tables
- Illustration and figures
- Text
- Headings and subheadings

- References
- Appendixes

Except for special guidelines from your instructor, follow the directions in this manual exactly.

3.1   GENERAL PAGE FORMAT

Sociology assignments should be typed or printed on 8 1/2 × 11 inch premium white bond paper, 20 pound or heavier. Do not use any other color or size except to comply with special instructions from your instructor, and do not use off-white or poor quality (draft) paper. Sociology that is worth the time to write and read is worth good paper.

Always submit to your instructor an original typed or computer-printed manuscript. Do not submit a photocopy! You should make a second copy for your own files in case the original is lost.

Unless your instructor gives special instructions, margins, except for theses and dissertations, should be one inch on all sides of the paper, and all papers should be double-spaced in a word-processing font scaled to 12, or typewriter pica, type. Typewriter elite type may be used if another is not available. Select a font that is plain and easy to read, such as Helvetica, Courier, Garamond, or Times Roman. Do not use script, stylized, or elaborate fonts.

Page numbers should appear in the upper-right-hand corner of each page, starting with the second page of the text and continuing consecutively through the paper. No page number should appear on the title page or on the first page of the text. Page numbers should appear one inch from the right side and one-half inch from the top of the page. You should use lowercase roman numerals (*i, ii, iii, iv, v, vi, vii, viii, ix, x,* and so on) for the pages, such as the title page, table of contents, and list of figures, that precede the first page of text. These roman numerals should begin with *ii* for the page that immediately follows the title page, and must be centered one-half inch from the bottom of the page.

Ask your instructor about bindings. In the absence of further directions, do not bind your paper or enclose it within a plastic cover sheet. Place one staple in the upper-left-hand corner, or use a paper clip at the top of the paper. Note that a paper to be submitted to a journal for publication should not be clipped, stapled, or bound in any form.

3.2   TITLE PAGE

This title page format differs slightly from the professional ASA format in order to allow for student information. Student writers should center the following information on the title page:

- Title of the paper
- Name of student (author)

- Course name, number, and section number
- Instructor
- Name of college or university
- Date

As the sample title page on page 65 shows, the title should clearly describe the problem addressed in the paper. If the paper discusses juvenile recidivism in Albemarle County jails, for example, the title "Recidivism in the Albemarle County Criminal Justice System" is professional, clear, and helpful to the reader. "Albemarle County," "Juvenile Justice," or "County Jails" are all too vague to be effective. Also, the title should not be "cute." A cute title may attract attention for a play on Broadway, but it will detract from the credibility of a paper in sociological science. "Inadequate Solid Waste Disposal Facilities in Denver" is professional. "Down in the Dumps" is not.

3.3   ABSTRACT

An abstract is a brief summary of a paper written primarily to allow potential readers to see if the paper contains information of sufficient interest for them to read. People conducting research want specific kinds of information, and they often read dozens of abstracts looking for papers that contain relevant data. Abstracts have the designation "Abstract" centered near the top of the page. Next is the title, also centered, followed by a summary of the paper's topic, research design, results, and discussion. The abstract should be written in one to three paragraphs totaling approximately 150 to 200 words. Remember, an abstract is not an introduction; instead, it is a brief summary, as demonstrated in the sample on page 66.

3.4   EXECUTIVE SUMMARY

An executive summary, like an abstract, summarizes the content of a paper but does so in more detail. A sample executive summary follows on pages 67–69. Whereas abstracts are read by people who are doing research, executive summaries are more likely to be read by people who need some or all of the information in the paper in order to make a decision. Many people, however, will read the executive summary to fix clearly in their mind the organization and results of a paper before reading the paper itself.

The length of the executive summary is dictated to some extent by the length of the document being summarized. For example, a 150- to 200-page grant report might be summarized in an 8- to 10-page executive summary, while a 25-page research paper might need only a page or two of summary. The lengthier executive summary might also contain headings and subheadings similar to those used in the actual report. By following the outline of the actual paper, the executive summary serves as a sort of summary of each of the sections in the much lengthier report.

Aspects of Social Stratification in the Florida Recount
of the 2000 Presidential Election

by

Blake C. Brown

for

Social Stratification 4443

Section 5023

Dr. Chelsea Johnson

Cornell University

October 1, 2004

Abstract

Female Body Image: A Multivariate Study

The recent upsurge in eating disorders has been linked to females' assessment of their bodies in relation to society's normative level. Evaluating the variables leading to body dissatisfaction provides information that can help women change their perspective. This study was designed to explore how female body image is associated with their age, self-esteem, locus of control, body ideal, perspective of their current weight, and perspective of men's ideal female body.

The results support the conclusion that the heavier a female perceives her current weight to be, the more negative her body image becomes. The current acceptance of an ideal that is not obtainable by the large majority of females compels women of all ages to strive for unrealistic goals. Women that affiliated their ideal with this reference were significantly less positive about their bodies than those with more reasonable models. The frustration associated with having a body type that yields little hope of achieving the "ideal" may provide a key in understanding how external locus of control was associated with negative body image in this study.

Low self-esteem was also associated with dissenting opinions of body. Negative societal reaction, allied with disapproving attitudes toward the endomorphic body type, often compels women to acquiesce to the master role of overweight female. This status is associated with an array of venomous characteristics, not the least of which is self-contempt.

Executive Summary

This summary of a Drug Assessment Study is written for practitioners who deal with drug-involved juvenile offenders repeatedly cycling through detention centers. The assessment process was initiated sometime after they were placed in detention. Two psychologists interviewed 198 youths over a six-month period and recorded the information they obtained on a specially designed "assessment" instrument. They also administered an instrument designed to measure the level of alcohol and other drug use, coupled with an unobtrusive measurement of denial and other underlying manifestations of substance abuse. The results of this study are summarized below.

One important finding had to do with interpersonal relationships. Those who used and abused alcohol and/or other drugs were generally friends of users and abusers. Those who did not use and abuse these substances almost always reported much less association with those who use and abuse drugs. Young people on probation and parole for substance-abuse-related offenses probably should be restrained by the court from association with those who have a serious alcohol and/or drug history.

The findings from this study support the hypothesis that when youths are distanced from the family in terms of communication, feelings, and disorganized relationships, their chances of alcohol and/or other drug involvement increase, at times dramatically. Significant progress in helping delinquents change and adjust might be attained by a serious commitment to family therapy and family development, especially with the cooperation and insistence of the court.

There is good reason to believe that significant differences exist between white and minority families with respect to child-rearing philosophy and practice. If this is true, it may well affect alcohol and/or other drug use, attitudes toward families and school, and other areas of juvenile misbehavior. It would follow that

SAMPLE EXECUTIVE SUMMARY (*CONT.*)

detention treatment plans, court-ordered probation, and aftercare alternatives should be differentiated, where feasible and legal, to respond to minority families at the point of their needs.

Findings from this study imply that for those youths who come in contact with the juvenile justice system, (1) blacks are much less addicted than either whites or other minorities, at least in very early adolescence; (2) black parents are significantly more concerned with their children's use of alcohol and/or other drugs when compared with white parents; (3) blacks report much more emotional support from their family members; and (4) there appears to be, at least on the surface, more dysfunctional family interaction among white families than black. Perhaps the juvenile justice system should develop neighborhood programs to provide positive support within the strong kinship networks already in place in the black culture; early intervention could reach black children before they fully enter the rebellious youth culture.

There is nothing in the data to support a connection between alcohol and/or other drug use on the part of black youth and the violent offenses they tend to commit when compared with white youth. They have fewer nondangerous options for acting out behavior than whites, and their families have fewer societal-economic support systems available to them. Older black youth from lower socioeconomic backgrounds are susceptible to self-enhancement through deviant activities. Court personnel might consider the realistic pressures on blacks, especially when many of these families lack adequate financial resources.

Although female detainees comprise only about 10 percent of the detention population, they have their own set of needs that must be addressed. They manifest lower self-concept, report more family dysfunction, and receive much less emotional support from family. This leads to significantly higher suicide attempts. Counselors should work hard for family resolution and restoration among the female population, perhaps developing special programs that address their unique circumstances.

SAMPLE EXECUTIVE SUMMARY (*CONT.*)

Educational and support groups are impacting low self-esteem and self-concept according to our Program Evaluation. Supporting these groups has been an excellent expenditure of grant funds. Certainly the guided group experience has the potential to enable youths to share feelings, give and receive positive feedback, and learn to feel better about themselves.

Finally, advocacy for success in school must be emphasized if delinquency and drug abuse are to be minimized. A positive link between the court and school systems needs to be forged. Otherwise, the juvenile court becomes a dumping ground for youths that encounter difficulty in school, bring drugs on campus, and act-out in a disruptive manner.

The body of literature cited in this report is fairly unified in asserting that common etiological roots cannot be shown between substance abuse and delinquency. Even the relationship between violent crime and substance abuse remains clouded (Inciardi 1981). A relationship between substance use and more serious delinquency appears to be developmental rather than causal (Huizinga et al. 1989). More than ever this suggests that attention should be given to the National Council of Juvenile and Family Court Judges' report, which argues from a systemic and holistic perspective (Criminal Justice Newsletter 1986). Drug use and abuse; child neglect; abandonment; sexual, physical, and emotional abuse; family violence; family dysfunction; and juvenile delinquency are interactive variables that cannot be clearly identified, diagnosed, or treated without addressing them together.

Our study supports a vast body of literature that suggests meaningful intervention in the lives of juveniles at risk should include, whenever possible, a holistic approach. Not only must each youth be requested to take responsibility for his or her behavior and work toward resolution of his or her problems, but also family members should be called to account for their responsibility, and compelled when necessary to participate in treatment.

3.5   OUTLINE PAGE

An outline page is a specific type of executive summary. Most often found in social policy analysis papers, an outline page provides more information about the organization of the paper than does an executive summary. The outline shows clearly the sections in the paper and the information in each. An outline page is an asset because it allows busy decision makers to understand the entire content of a paper without reading it or to refer quickly to a specific part for more information. Position papers and policy analysis papers are written for people in positions of authority who normally need to make a variety of decisions in a short period. Outline pages reduce the amount of time they need to understand a policy problem, the alternative solutions, and the author's preferred solution. Outline pages sequentially list the complete topic sentences of the major paragraphs of a paper, in outline form. In a position paper, for example, you will be stating a problem, defining possible solutions, and then recommending the best solution. These three steps will be the major headings in your outline. (See Chapter 1 for instructions on writing an outline.) Wait until you have completed the paper before writing the outline page. Take the topic sentences from the leading (most important) paragraph in each section of your paper and place them in the appropriate places in your outline. A sample outline page is presented on page 71.

3.6   TABLE OF CONTENTS

A table of contents does not provide as much information as an outline, but it does include the titles of the major divisions and subdivisions of a paper. Tables of contents are not normally required in student papers or papers presented at professional meetings but may be included. They are normally required, however, in books, theses, and dissertations. The table of contents should consist of the chapter or main section titles, the headings used in the text, with one additional level of titles, along with their page numbers, as the sample on page 72 demonstrates.

3.7   LIST OF TABLES AND FIGURES

A list of tables and figures contains the titles of the tables, illustrations, or figures in the paper, in the order in which they appear, along with their page numbers. If you have only a few figures, tables, or illustrations, you may list them together under the title "Figures" (and call them all "Figures" in the text). However, if you have more than a half-page of entries, you should have separate lists for tables, illustrations, and figures (and title them accordingly in the text). Each list should appear on a separate page somewhere following the title page and preceding the first page of text. An example of the format for such lists is presented on page 73.

SAMPLE OUTLINE PAGE

Outline of Contents

I.   The problem is that parking, picnic, and rest room facilities at Oak Ridge Community Park have deteriorated due to normal wear, adverse weather, and vandalism, and are inadequate to meet public demand.

A.   Only one major renovation has occurred since 1963, when the park opened.

B.   The Park Department estimates that 10,000 square feet of new parking space, 14 items of playground equipment, 17 new picnic tables, and repairs on current facilities would cost about $43,700.

II. Three possible solutions have been given extensive consideration:

A.   One option is to do nothing. Area residents will use the area less as deterioration continues, but no immediate outlay of public funds will be necessary.

B.   The first alternative solution is to make all repairs immediately. Area residents will enjoy immediate and increased use of facilities. $43,700 in funds will be needed. Sources include (1) Community Development Block Grant funds; (2) increased property taxes; (3) revenue bonds; and (4) general city revenues.

C.   A second alternative is to make repairs according to a priority list over a five-year period, using a combination of general city revenues and a $20,000 first-year bond issue. Residents will enjoy the most-needed improvements immediately. The bond issue will require City Council and voter approval.

III. The recommendation of this report is that alternative "C" be adopted by the City Council. The benefit/cost analysis demonstrates that residents will be satisfied if basic improvements are made immediately. The City Council should, during its May 15 meeting, (1) adopt a resolution of intent to commit $5,000 per year for five years from the general revenue fund, dedicated to this purpose; and (2) approve for submission to public vote in the November 2005 election a $25,000 bond issue.

Table of Contents

List of Figures

3.8   TABLES

Tables are used in the text to show relationships among data; they should help the reader come to a conclusion or understand a certain point. Tables that show simple results or "raw" data should not be included in the text of the paper. If you are required to include the data you have collected, tabulate and present it in an appendix.

Tables describe or summarize the data to say something new, and they stand on their own; they do not reiterate the content of the text. In other words, the reader should be able to understand the table without reading the text.

Tables should be numbered consecutively throughout the text. Clearly label the columns and rows in the table. Each word in the title (except articles, prepositions, and conjunctions) should be capitalized.

If the table is part of another work, the source from which you obtained the information should be shown immediately below the table, not in a footnote or endnote, with the complete citation included in your reference list at the end of the paper. A sample table is shown below.

SAMPLE TABLE

Projections of the Total Population of States, 1995 to 2025
(all population figures in thousands)

State	1995	2000	2005	2015	2025
Alabama	4,253	4,451	4,631	4,956	5,224
Alaska	604	653	700	791	885
Arizona	4,218	4,798	5,230	5,808	6,412
Arkansas	2,484	2,631	2,750	2,922	3,055
California	31,589	32,521	34,441	41,373	49,285
Colorado	3,747	4,168	4,468	4,833	5,188
Connecticut	3,275	3,284	3,317	3,506	3,739
Delaware	717	768	800	832	861
District of Columbia	554	523	529	594	655

Source: U.S. Bureau of the Census (2000)

3.9   ILLUSTRATIONS AND FIGURES

Illustrations are not normally inserted in the text of a sociology paper, nor even in an appendix, unless they are necessary to explain the content. If illustrations are necessary, do not paste or tape photocopies of photographs or similar materials to the text or the appendix. Instead, photocopy each one on a separate sheet of paper and center it, along with its typed title, within the normal margins of the paper. The format of illustration titles should be the same as that for tables and figures.

Figures in the form of charts and graphs may be very helpful in presenting certain types of information, as the example below shows.

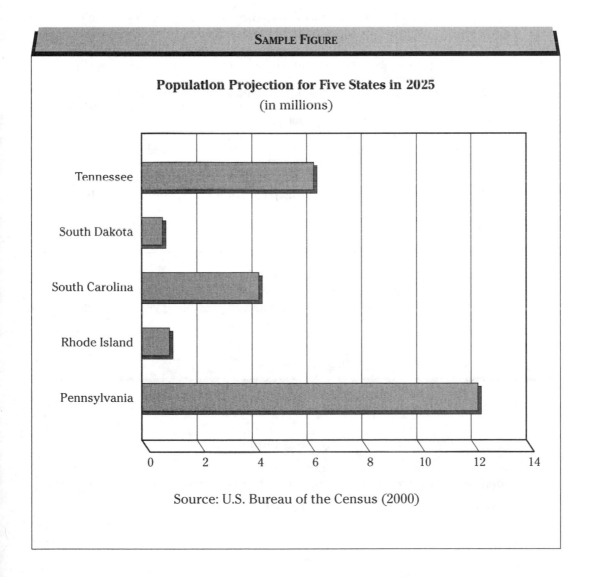

SAMPLE FIGURE

Population Projection for Five States in 2025
(in millions)

Source: U.S. Bureau of the Census (2000)

3.10   TEXT

Ask your instructor for the number of pages required for the paper you are writing. The text should follow the directions explained in Chapters 1 and 2. Part III of this manual describes several types of papers that are commonly assigned in sociology classes. The text in each varies with the goal of the project. Headings and subheadings also vary with the assignment. Procedures for applying headings and subheadings to your text are described in the following section.

3.11   HEADINGS AND SUBHEADINGS

Your papers should include no more than three levels of headings. The following description gives the appropriate listing for each level:

1. Primary headings should be printed in all caps and either centered or aligned at the left margin.
2. Secondary headings should be printed in italics and either centered or aligned at the left margin. The first letter in each word (except articles, prepositions, and conjunctions) should be capitalized.
3. Tertiary headings should be printed in italics (with only the first word and proper nouns capitalized and with a period at the end), and should be run-in heads, indented at the beginning of the paragraph.

The illustration at the base of this page shows the proper use of headings:

3.12   REFERENCES

The format for listing references in ASA style is discussed in detail in Chapter 4. Some instructors prefer papers to be structured in article format, with everything presented as tightly compressed and succinct as possible. If your instructor favors

---

SAMPLE HEADINGS

REVIEW OF LITERATURE

Number of Children and Marital Satisfaction

Families with more than two children. Although many people believe that large families lead to increased marital satisfaction, the results of . . .

this system, your reference section should immediately follow (after a double space) the last line of your discussion section. Other instructors prefer the references to be listed on a separate page. Ask your instructor which system you should follow. See the sample reference listing on page 98.

3.13 APPENDIXES

Appendixes are reference materials provided for the convenience of the reader at the back of the paper, after the reference list. Providing information that supplements the important facts in the text, they may include maps, charts, tables, and selected documents like questionnaires. Do not place materials that are merely interesting or decorative in your appendix. Use only items that will answer questions raised by the text or are necessary to explain the text.

Follow the formatting guidelines for illustrations, tables, and figures when adding material in an appendix. At the top center of the page, label your first appendix "Appendix A," your second appendix "Appendix B," and so on. If you are only appending one item, it should be labeled "Appendix," with no letter indicating sequence. Do not append an entire government report, journal article, or other publication, but only the portions of such documents that are necessary to support your paper. The source of the information should always be evident on the appended pages.

The example on page 78 illustrates how you might append the questionnaire in a survey paper.

Appendix

Questionnaire

The following statements are concerned with your feelings about your marriage. To the left of each question, please put the number that indicates the degree to which your marriage possesses each of the following qualities. The number 1 represents the least degree and 5 represents the greatest degree.

Least Degree   1   2   3   4   5   Greatest Degree

_____   1.   Spend time doing things together.

_____   2.   Are very committed to each other.

_____   3.   Have good communication (talking, sharing feelings).

_____   4.   Deal with crises in a positive manner.

_____   5.   Express appreciation to each other.

_____   6.   Have a very close relationship.

_____   7.   Have a very happy relationship.

_____   8.   My spouse makes me feel good about myself.

_____   9.   I make my spouse feel good about himself or herself.

_____   10.   If I could, I would marry my current spouse again.

Please give the following information:

AGE: _____   SEX: _____male   _____female

Number of years married to current spouse: _____

Number of children: _____

Have you ever had an extramarital affair?   _____yes   _____no

THANKS FOR YOUR HELP!

Source: Modified from Stinnett and DeFrain (1985)

CITING SOURCES

One of your most important jobs as a research writer is to document your use of source material carefully and clearly. Failure to do so will cause your reader confusion, damage the effectiveness of your paper, and perhaps make you vulnerable to a charge of plagiarism. Proper documentation is more than just good form; it is a powerful indicator of your own commitment to scholarship and the sense of authority that you bring to your writing. Good documentation demonstrates your expertise as a researcher and increases the reader's trust in you and your work; it gives credibility to what you are writing.

Unfortunately, as anybody who has ever written a research paper knows, getting the documentation right can be a frustrating, confusing job, especially for the novice writer. Positioning each element of a single reference citation accurately can require what seems an inordinate amount of time spent thumbing through the style manual. Even before you begin to work on specific citations, there are important questions of style and format to answer.

4.1 PRELIMINARY CONSIDERATIONS

Direct quotes must always be credited, as must certain kinds of paraphrased material. Information that is basic—important dates, and facts or opinions universally acknowledged—need not be cited. Information that is not widely known, whether fact or opinion, should be documented.

What if you are unsure whether or not a certain fact is widely known? You are, after all, very probably a newcomer to the field in which you are conducting your research. If in doubt, supply the documentation. It is better to overdocument than to fail to do justice to a source.

Although the question of which documentation style to use may be decided for you in some classes by your instructor, others may allow you to choose.

There are several styles available, each designed to meet the needs of writers in particular fields. The citation and reference systems approved by the Modern Language Association (MLA) and the American Psychological Association (APA) are often used in the humanities and social sciences.

The American Sociological Association (ASA) has its own system that is widely used by sociology students and professionals. The ASA has adopted a modification of the style elaborated in the *Chicago Manual of Style* (CMS), perhaps the most universally approved of all documentation authorities. One of the advantages of using the ASA style, which is outlined in a pamphlet entitled *ASA Style Guide* (1997), is that it is designed to guide the professional sociologist in preparing a manuscript for submission to a journal. The ASA style is required for all papers submitted to the *American Sociological Review,* the official journal of the ASA and the most influential sociology journal in publication. It is also required for all the leading journals in sociology and many of the less prestigious ones.

4.2   CITING SOURCES IN ASA FORMAT

A parenthetical reference or citation is a note placed within the text, near where the source material occurs. In order not to distract the reader from the argument, the citation is as brief as possible, containing just enough information to refer the reader to the full reference listing that appears in the bibliography or reference section following the text. Usually the minimum information necessary is the author's last name—meaning the name by which the source is alphabetized in the references at the end of the paper—and the year of the publication of the source. As indicated by the following models, this information can be given in a number of ways. Models for listing bibliographical entries that correspond to parenthetical citations are given in the next section of this chapter.

4.2.1   Text Citations

Citations within the text should include the author's last name and the year of publication. Page numbers should be included only when quoting directly from a source or referring to specific passages. Subsequent citations of the same source should be identified the same way as the first. The following examples identify the *ASA Style Guide*'s (1997) citation system for a variety of possibilities.

When the author's name is in the text, it should be followed by the publication year in parentheses:

Freedman (2004) postulates that when individuals . . .

When the author's name is not in the text, the last name and publication date should be enclosed in parentheses:

. . . encourage more aggressive play (Perrez 1999).

As noted previously, the page number should be included when the material referred to is quoted directly, or when you wish to refer the reader to a specific page of the source text. However, some instructors prefer page numbers for all citations in order to check for plagiarism. Ask your instructor what system you should follow. When the page number is included, it should follow the publication year and be preceded by a colon, with no space between the colon and the page number:

Thomas (1999:741) builds on this scenario . . .

When the publication has two authors, cite both last names:

. . . establish a sense of self (Holmes and Watson 1872:114–116).

When a publication has three authors, cite all three last names in the first citation, with *et al.* (in roman type) used for subsequent citations in the text. Thus a first citation would read:

. . . found the requirements very restrictive (Mollar, Querley, and McLarry 1926).

Thereafter, the following form is sufficient:

. . . proved to be quite difficult (Mollar et al. 1926).

For more than three authors, list the first author's last name and use *et al.* (in roman type) for the remaining authors in all citations.

When citing two authors with the same last name, use a first initial to differentiate between them.

. . . the new budget cuts (K. Grady 1994).
. . . stimulate economic growth (B. Grady 1993).

When citing two works by the same author, in the same note, place a comma between the publication dates of the works.

George (1996, 2004) argues for . . .

If the two works were published in the same year, differentiate between them by adding lowercase letters to the publication dates. Be sure to add the letters to the references in the bibliography, too.

. . . the city government (Estrada 2002a, 2002b).

Direct quotes of fewer than four lines should be placed in the text, with quotation marks at the beginning and end. The citation should include the page number in one of the following formats:

The majority of these ads promote the notion that "If you are slim, you will also be beautiful and sexually desirable" (Rockett and McMinn 1999:278).

Smith and Hill (1997) found that "women are far more likely to obsess about weight" (p. 127).

Direct quotes of four lines or more should be indented, single spaced, and presented in a smaller font or type when possible. They should be blocked—no tab set for the first line—with no quotation marks, as follows:

According to Brown (2005):

There are few girls and women of any age or culture raised in white America, who do not have some manifestation of the concerns discussed here, i.e., distortion of body image, a sense of being "out-of-control" in relationship to food, addiction to dieting, binging, or self-starvation. (P. 61)

Note that in the block quote the author, date, and/or page number follows the period at the end, and that the *P* for *page* is capitalized when the page number appears alone without the author and date, as in this example.

Sometimes information is obtained from a source that is cited in a secondary source. Although it is always best to locate and cite the original source, sometimes this is not possible. When citing a source that is itself cited in a secondary source, refer in your parenthetical citation to the original source, and not to the later source in which the original is quoted. For example, if you wish to cite a passage from a 1999 article by John Smith that you found cited in a 2003 article by Arleen Michaels, your citation should look like this:

. . . the promise of a subsequent generation (Smith 1999).

See "Article Cited in a Secondary Source" on page 92 for information on how to list this citation in your references.

The *ASA Style Guide* only briefly discusses reference formats for works published anonymously. Section 17.34 of the *Chicago Manual of Style* (2003) indicates that if the authorship of an anonymous work is known, the name is given in brackets:

([Morey, Cynthia] 1977)

According to section 17.32 of the *Chicago Manual of Style,* if the name of the author of an anonymous work cannot be ascertained, the reference begins with the title of the work. The first of the following models refers to a magazine article, the second to a book. Note that in the case of the book title, the initial article "The" is moved to the end of the title.

("The Case for Prosecuting Deadbeat Dads" 1996:36–38)

(*Worst Way to Learn: The Government's War on Education, The* 2003)

Section 17.41 of the *Chicago Manual of Style* recommends including the name of an editor, compiler, or translator, without an abbreviation such as "ed.," "comp.," or "trans.," when there is no author's name given.

Cite chapters, tables, appendixes, and the like as follows:

. . . (Johnson 1995, chap. 6).
. . . (Blake 2005, table 4:34).
. . . (Shelby 1976, appendix C:177).

When citing a work reprinted from an earlier publication, give the earliest date of publication in brackets, followed immediately by the date of the version you have used:

. . . Baldwin ([1897] 2002) interpreted this . . .

When citing more than one source, separate the citations by a semicolon and order them in a manner of your choice. You may arrange them in alphabetical order, date order, or order of importance to your argument, but whatever order you choose, use it consistently throughout your paper:

. . . are related (Harmatz 1999:48; Marble et al. 1996:909; Powers and Erickson 2001:48; Rackley et al. 1988:10; Thompson and Thompson 2000:1067).

Give the date for dissertation and unpublished papers. When the date is not available, use "n.d." (no date) in place of the date. Use the word "forthcoming" when materials cited are unpublished but scheduled for publication.

Studies by Barkley (forthcoming) and Jorden (n.d.) lend support . . .

When citing National Archives or other archival sources, abbreviate the citations. The *Chicago Manual of Style* (section 17.324) suggests that the parenthetical citation should include the record group (RG) as well, leaving other information for the citation in the reference section:

(NA, RG 43)

Classic texts.   When citing classic texts, such as the Bible, standard translations of ancient Greek texts, or numbers of the Federalist Papers, you may use the systems by which they are subdivided. Since any edition of a classic text employs the standard subdivisions, this reference method has the advantage of allowing your reader to find the source passage in any published edition of the text. It is not necessary to include a citation for a classic text in the reference section.

You may cite a biblical passage by referring to the particular book, chapter, and verse, all in roman type, with the translation given after the verse number:

"But the path of the just is as the shining light, that shineth more and more unto the perfect day" (Proverbs 4:18 King James Version).

The Federalist Papers are numbered:

Madison addresses the problem of factions in a republic (Federalist 10).

Newspapers.   According to the *Chicago Manual of Style* (2003, section 17.191), references to material in daily newspapers should be handled within the syntax of your sentence:

> In an August 10, 1999, editorial, the *New York Times* painted the new regime in glowing colors.

> An article entitled "Abuse in Metropolis," written by Harry Black and published in the *Daily News* on December 24, 2001, took exception to the mayor's remarks.

According to the *Chicago Manual of Style,* references to newspaper items are not usually included in the reference list or bibliography. If you wish to include newspaper references, however, there is a model of a bibliographical entry in the next section of this chapter.

Public documents.   When citing a public/government document or one with institutional authorship, you should supply the minimum identification:

> . . . (U.S. Bureau of the Census 1993:223).

Since the *ASA Style Guide* gives formats for only two types of government publications, the following models are based not only on practices from the ASA guide but also on formats found in the *Chicago Manual of Style* (sections 17.290–355). Corresponding bibliography entries appear in the next section.

Parenthetical text references to both the *Senate Journal* and the *House Journal* start with the journal title in place of the author, the session year, and, if applicable, the page:

> (*Senate Journal* 1997:24)

Congressional debates are printed in the daily issues of the *Congressional Record,* which are bound biweekly and then collected and bound at the end of the session. Whenever possible, you should consult the bound yearly collection instead of the biweekly compilations. Your parenthetical reference should begin with the title *Congressional Record* (or *Cong. Rec.*) in place of the author's name and include the year of the congressional session, the volume and part of the *Congressional Record,* and finally the page:

> (*Cong. Rec.* 1930, 72, pt. 8:9012)

References to congressional reports and documents, which are numbered sequentially in one- or two-year periods, include the name of the body generating the material, the year, and the page:

> (U.S. Congress 1997:12)

Note that any reference that begins with *U.S. Senate* or *U.S. House* may omit the *U.S.* if it is clear from the context that you are referring to the United States.

Whichever form you use, be sure to use it consistently, in both the notes and the bibliography.

Bills and resolutions. According to the *Chicago Manual of Style* (section 17.309), bills and resolutions, which are published in pamphlets called slip bills, on microfiche, and in the *Congressional Record,* are not always given a parenthetical text reference and a corresponding bibliography entry. Instead, the pertinent reference information appears in the syntax of the sentence. If, however, you wish to cite such information in a text reference, the form depends on the source from which you took your information. If citing to a slip bill, use one of these forms:

(U.S. Senate 1996)

(*Visa Formalization Act of 1996*)

You may cite either the body that authored the bill or the title of the work itself. Whichever method you choose, remember to begin your bibliography entry with the same material. Here is a model for citing to the *Congressional Record:*

(U.S. Senate 1996:S7658)

The number following the date and preceded by an *S* (for Senate; *H* for House) is the page in the *Congressional Record.*

As with bills and resolutions, laws (also called statutes) are not necessarily given a parenthetical text reference and a bibliography entry. Instead, the identifying material is included in the text. If you wish to make a formal reference for a statute, you must structure it according to the place where you found the law published. Initially published separately in pamphlets, as slip laws, statutes are eventually collected and incorporated, first into a set of volumes called *U.S. Statutes at Large* and later into the *U.S. Code,* a multivolume set that is revised every six years. You should use the latest edition. When citing to a slip law, you should either use *U.S. Public Law* (in roman type) and the number of the piece of legislation, or the title of the law:

(U.S. Public Law 678:16–17)

(*Library of Congress Book Preservation Act of 1997:*16–17)

When citing to the *Statutes at Large,* use this form:

(*Statutes at Large* 2005:466)

The following form is for citing to the *U.S. Code:*

(*Library of Congress Book Preservation Act of 1997, U.S. Code,* Vol. 38, sec. 1562)

United States Constitution. According to the *Chicago Manual of Style* (section 17.321), references to the United States Constitution include the number of the article or amendment, the section number, and the clause, if necessary:

(U.S. Constitution, art. 3, sec. 3)

It is not necessary to include the Constitution in the bibliography.

A reference to a report, bulletin, circular, or any other type of material issued by the Executive Department starts with the name of the agency issuing the document, although you may use the name of the author, if known:

(Department of Labor 2004:334)

United States Supreme Court. As with laws, Supreme Court decisions are rarely given their own parenthetical text reference and bibliography entry but are instead identified in the text. If you wish to use a formal reference, however, you may place within the parentheses the title of the case, in italics, followed by the source (for cases after 1875 this is the *United States Supreme Court Reports,* abbreviated U.S.), which is preceded by the volume number and followed by the page number. You should end the first reference to the case that appears in your paper with the date of the case, in brackets. You need not include the date in subsequent references:

(*State of Nevada v. Goldie Warren* 324 U.S. 123 [1969])

Before 1875, Supreme Court decisions were published under the names of official court reporters. The reference below is to William Cranch, *Reports of Cases Argued and Adjudged in the Supreme Court of the United States, 1801–1815,* 9 vols. (Washington, D.C., 1804–1817). The number preceding the clerk's name is the volume number; the last number is the page:

(1 Cranch 137)

For most of these parenthetical references, it is possible to move some or all of the material outside the parentheses simply by incorporating it in the text:

In 1969, in *State of Nevada v. Goldie Warren* (324 U.S. 123), the judge ruled that an observer of a traffic accident has an obligation to offer assistance to survivors.

Lower courts. Decisions of lower federal courts are published in the *Federal Reporter.* The note should give the volume of the *Federal Reporter* (F.); the series, if it is other than the first (2d, in the model below); the page; and, in brackets, an abbreviated reference to the specific court (the example below is to the Second Circuit Court) and the year:

(*United States v. Sizemore,* 183 F. 2d 201 [2d Cir. 1950])

Government commissions. According to the *Chicago Manual of Style* (section 17.320), references to bulletins, circulars, reports, and study papers that are issued by various government commissions should include the name of the commission, the date of the document, and the page:

(Securities and Exchange Commission 1985:57)

Because government documents are often credited to a corporate author with a lengthy name, you may devise an acronym or a shortened form of the name and indicate in your first reference to the source that this name will be used in later citations:

(*Bulletin of Labor Statistics* 1997, 1954; *hereafter BLS*)

The practice of using a shortened name in subsequent references to any corporate author, whether a public or private organization, is sanctioned in most journals and approved in the *Chicago Manual of Style* (section 17.47). Thus, if you refer often to the *U.N. Monthly Bulletin of Statistics,* you may, after giving the publication's full name in the first reference, use a shortened form of the title—perhaps an acronym such as *UNMBS*—in all later citations.

Local government.   According to the *Chicago Manual of Style* (section 17.323), references to state and local government documents are similar to those for the corresponding national government sources:

(Oklahoma Legislature 1995:24)

The *Chicago Manual of Style* restricts bibliographical information concerning state laws or municipal ordinances to running text or notes. (See section 17.312 for examples of note citations.)

Interviews.   According to the *Chicago Manual of Style* (sections 17.205, 17.208), in the author-date system, citations to interviews should be handled by references within the text—in the syntax of a sentence—rather than in parentheses:

In a March 1997 interview with O. J. Simpson, Barbara Walters asked questions that seemed to upset and disorient the former superstar.

For published or broadcast interviews, no parenthetical reference is necessary, but there should be a complete citation under the interviewer's name in the bibliography.

An unpublished interview conducted by the writer of the paper should also be cited in the syntax of the sentence:

In an interview with the author on April 23, 2003, Dr. Kennedy expressed her disappointment with the new court ruling.

If you are citing material from an interview that you conducted, identify yourself as "the author" and give the date of the interview. Cite the interview by placing the date in parentheses following the name of the person whom you interviewed:

> Marsha Cummings (2000), Director of the Children's Hospital in Oklahoma City, was interviewed by the author on November 14, 2000.

4.2.2   References

Parenthetical citations in the text point the reader to the fuller source descriptions at the end of the paper known as the references or bibliography. This reference list, which always directly follows the text under the heading REFERENCES, is arranged alphabetically according to the first element in each citation. As stated in Chapter 3, some instructors prefer papers to be structured in article format, with everything presented as tightly compressed and succinct as possible. If your instructor favors this system, your reference section should immediately follow (after a double space) the last line of your discussion section. Other instructors prefer the references to be listed on a separate page. Ask your instructor which system you should follow.

As with most alphabetically arranged bibliographies, there is a kind of reverse-indentation system: After the first line of a citation, all subsequent lines are indented five spaces. The entire references section is double-spaced.

The ASA uses standard, or "headline style," capitalization for titles in the reference list. In this style, all first and last words in a title, and all other words except articles (*a, an, the*), coordinating words (*and, but, or, for, nor*), and prepositions (*among, by, for, of, to, toward,* and so on) are capitalized.

Remember that every source cited in the text, with those exceptions noted in the examples below, must have a corresponding entry in the references section. Do not include references to any work not cited in the text of your paper.

Most of the following formats are based on those given in the *ASA Style Guide* (1997). Formats for bibliographical situations not covered by the ASA guide are taken from the *Chicago Manual of Style* (2003).

Books

ONE AUTHOR.   First comes the author's name, inverted, then the date of publication, followed by the title of the book, the place of publication, and the name of the publishing house. Use first names for all authors or initials if no first name is provided. Add a space after each initial, as in the example below. For place of publication, always identify the state unless the city is New York. Use postal abbreviations to denote states (OK, MA, and so on).

Periods divide most of the elements in the citation, although a colon separates the place of publication from the name of the publisher. Custom dictates that the main title and subtitle be separated by a colon, even though a colon may not appear in the title as printed on the title page of the book.

> Northrup, A. K. 2002. *Living High off the Hog: Recent Pork Barrel Legislation in the Senate.* Cleveland, OH: Johnstown.

TWO AUTHORS.   Only the name of the first author is reversed, since it is the one by which the citation is alphabetized. Note that there is no comma between the first name of the first author and the *and* following:

Spence, Michelle and Kristen Ruell. 1996. *Hiring and the Law.* Boston, MA: Tildale.

THREE OR MORE AUTHORS.   The use of *et al.* is not acceptable in the references section; list the names of all authors of a source. While the ASA style places commas between all names in the text citation—(Moore, Rice, and Traylor 2002)—it deletes the comma separating the next-to-last and last names in the bibliographical reference. Note also that the ASA does not advocate abbreviating the word University in the name of a press, as indicated in the model below.

Moore, J. B., Allen Rice and Natasha Traylor. 2002. *Down on the Farm: Culture and Folkways.* Norman, OK: University of Oklahoma Press.

ANONYMOUS SOURCE.   Section 17.34 of the *Chicago Manual of Style* states that if you can ascertain the name of the author when that name is not given in the work itself, place the author's name in brackets:

[Morey, Cynthia]. 1977. *How We Mate: American Dating Customs, 1950–2000.* New York: Putney.

Do not use *anonymous* to designate an author whose name you cannot determine; instead, according to section 17.32 of the *Chicago Manual of Style,* begin your reference entry with the title of the book, followed by the date. You may move initial articles (*a, an, the*) to the end of the title:

Worst Way to Learn: The Government's War on Education, The. 1997. San Luis Obispo, CA: Blakeside.

EDITOR, COMPILER, OR TRANSLATOR AS AUTHOR.   When no author is listed on the title page, begin the citation with the name of the editor, compiler, or translator:

Trakas, Dylan, comp. 1998. *Making the Road-Ways Safe: Essays on Highway Preservation and Funding.* El Paso, TX: Del Norte Press.

EDITOR, COMPILER, OR TRANSLATOR WITH AUTHOR

Pound, Ezra. 1953. *Literary Essays.* Edited by T. S. Eliot. New York: New Directions.

Stomper, Jean. 2000. *Grapes and Rain.* Translated by John Picard. New York: Baldock.

UNTRANSLATED BOOK.   If your source is in a foreign language, it is not necessary, according to section 17.64 of the *Chicago Manual of Style,* to translate the title into English. Use the capitalization format of the original language.

Picon-Salas, Mariano. 1950. *De la Conquesta a la Independencia.* Mexico, DF: Fondo de Cultura Económica.

If you wish to provide a translation of the title, do so in brackets or parentheses following the title. Set the translation in roman type, and capitalize only the first word of the title and subtitle, proper nouns, and proper adjectives:

Wharton, Edith. 1916. *Voyages au front* (Visits to the Front). Paris, France: Plon.

TWO OR MORE WORKS BY THE SAME AUTHOR.   If you wish you may replace the author's name in all citations after the first by a three-em dash (six strokes of the hyphen):

Russell, Henry. 1978. *Famous Last Words: Notable Supreme Court Cases of the Last Five Years.* New Orleans, LA: Liberty Publications.

———. 1988. *Great Court Battles.* Denver, CO: Axel and Myers.

CHAPTER IN A MULTIAUTHOR COLLECTION

Gray, Alexa North. 1998. "Foreign Policy and the Foreign Press." Pp. 188–204 in *Current Media Issues,* edited by Barbara Bonnard and Luke F. Guinness. New York: Boulanger.

The parenthetical text reference may include the page reference:

(Gray 1998:195–197)

You must repeat the name if the author and the editor are the same person:

Farmer, Susan A. 1995. "Tax Shelters in the New Dispensation: How to Save Your Income." Pp. 58–73 in *Making Ends Meet: Strategies for the Nineties,* edited by Susan A. Farmer. Nashville, TN: Burkette and Hyde.

AUTHOR OF A FOREWORD OR INTRODUCTION.   According to section 17.46 of the *Chicago Manual of Style,* there is no need to cite the author of a foreword or introduction in your bibliography, unless the foreword or introduction is of major significance. In that case, list the bibliography entry under the name of the author of the work itself. Place the name of the author of the foreword or introduction after the title of the work:

Givan, Basil. 2000. *Marital Stress among the Professoriat: A Case Study,* with foreword by Carla Farris. New York: Galapagos.

The parenthetical text reference cites the name of the author of the foreword or introduction, not the author of the book:

(Farris 2000)

SUBSEQUENT EDITIONS.   If you are using an edition of a book other than the first, you must cite the number of the edition or the status, such as *Rev. ed.* for *Revised edition,* if there is no edition number:

Hales, Sarah. 2002. *The Coming Water Wars.* 3d ed. Pittsburgh, PA: Blue Skies.

MULTIVOLUME WORK.   If you are citing a multivolume work in its entirety, use the following format:

Graybosch, Charles. 1988–1989. *The Rise of the Unions.* 3 vols. New York: Starkfield.

If you are citing only one of the volumes in a multivolume work, use the following format:

Graybosch, Charles. 1988. *The Beginnings.* Vol. 1 of *The Rise of the Unions.* New York: Starkfield.

REPRINTS

Adams, Sterling R. [1964] 2001. *How to Win an Election: Promotional Campaign Strategies.* New York: Starkfield.

CLASSIC TEXTS.   According to the *Chicago Manual of Style* (sections 17.247, 17.250), references to classic texts such as sacred books and Greek verse and drama are usually confined to the text and not given citations in the bibliography.

Periodicals

JOURNAL ARTICLES.   Journals are periodicals, usually published either monthly or quarterly, that specialize in serious scholarly articles in a particular field.

Journal with Continuous Pagination.   Most journals are paginated so that each issue of a volume continues the numbering of the previous issue. The reason for such pagination is that most journals are bound in libraries as complete volumes of several issues; continuous pagination makes it easier to consult these large compilations:

Hunzecker, Joan. 2002. "Teaching the Toadies: Cronyism in Municipal Politics." *Review of Local Politics* 4:250–262.

Johnson, J. D., N. E. Noel and J. Sutter-Hernandez. 2000. "Alcohol and Male Acceptance of Sexual Aggression: The Role of Perceptual Ambiguity." *Journal of Applied Social Psychology* 30:1186–1200.

Note that the name of the journal, which is italicized, is followed without punctuation by the volume number, which is itself followed by a colon and the page numbers. There should be no space between the colon and the page numbers, which are inclusive. Do not use *p.* or *pp.* to introduce the page numbers.

Journal in Which Each Issue Is Paginated Separately.   The issue number appears in parentheses immediately following the volume number.

Skylock, Browning. 1991. "'Fifty-Four Forty or Fight!': Sloganeering in Early America." *American History Digest* 28(3):25–34.

Entwisle, Doris, Karl Alexander and Linda Olson. 2000. "Urban Youth, Jobs, and High School." *American Sociological Review* 65(2):279–297.

Article Published in More Than One Journal Issue

Crossitch, Vernelle. 1997. "Evaluating Evidence: Calibrating Ephemeral Phenomena," parts 1–4. *Epiphanic Review* 15:22–29; 16:46–58; 17:48–60.

Articles Published in Foreign-Language Journals

Sczaflarski, Richard. 2001. "The Trumpeter in the Tower: Solidarity and Legend" (in Polish). *World Political Review* 32:79–95.

Article Cited in a Secondary Source.   When referencing a source that has itself been cited in a secondary source, first list the complete citation of the source you cited, followed by the words *cited in,* and a listing of the source from which you obtained your citation.

Johnson, William A. and Richard P. Rettig. 1999. "Drug Assessment of Juveniles in Detention." *Social Forces* 28(3):56–69, cited in John Duncan and Mary Ann Hopkins. 2004. "Youth and Drug Involvement: Families at Risk." *British Journal of Addiction* 95:45.

Gonzalez, Tim, Lucy Hammond, Fred Luntz and Virginia Land. 2002. "Free Love and Nickel Beer: On Throwaway Relationships." *The Journal of Sociology and Religion* 12(2):14–29, cited in Emanuel Hiddocke, Cheryl Manson and Ruth Mendez. 2005. *The Death of the American Family.* Upper Saddle River, NJ: Prentice Hall, p. 107.

MAGAZINE ARTICLES.   Magazines, which are usually published weekly, bimonthly, or monthly, appeal to the popular audience and generally have a wider circulation than journals. *Newsweek* and *Scientific American* are examples of magazines.

Monthly Magazine

Stapleton, Bonnie and Ellis Peters. 1981. "How It Was: On the Trail with Og Mandino." *Lifetime Magazine,* April, pp. 23–24, 57–59.

Weekly or Bimonthly Magazine

Bruck, Connie. 1997. "The World of Business: A Mogul's Farewell." *The New Yorker,* October 18, pp. 12–15.

NEWSPAPER ARTICLES

Everett, Susan. 2002. "Beyond the Alamo: How Texans View the Past." *The Carrollton Tribune,* February 16, D1, D4.

Sources stored in archives.   According to the *ASA Style Guide,* if you refer to a number of archival sources, you should group them in a separate part of the references section and name it *Archival Sources.* A sample entry follows:

Clayton Fox Correspondence, Box 12. July–December 1903. File: Literary Figures 2. Letter to Edith Wharton, dated September 11.

According to the *Chicago Manual of Style* (section 17.324), materials housed in the National Archives or in one of its branches are cited according to their record group (RG) number. The citation may also include title, subsection, and file number:

> National Archives. RG 43. Records of the National Committee on Poverty and
>   Aging. File 78A-M22.

Public documents.   Since the *ASA Style Guide* gives formats for only two types of government publications, the following bibliographical models are based not only on practices from the ASA guide but also on formats found in the *Chicago Manual of Style* (sections 17.290–355).

CONGRESSIONAL JOURNALS.   References to either the *Senate Journal* or the *House Journal* begin with the journal's title and include the years of the session, the number of the Congress and session, and the month and day of the entry:

> *U.S. Senate Journal.* 1997. 105th Cong., 1st sess., 10 December.

The ordinal numbers *second* and *third* may be represented as *d (52d, 103d)* or as *nd* and *rd,* respectively.

CONGRESSIONAL DEBATES

> *Congressional Record.* 1930. 71st Cong., 2d sess. Vol. 72, pt. 8.

CONGRESSIONAL REPORTS AND DOCUMENTS

> U.S. Congress. 1997. House Subcommittee on the Study of Governmental/Public
>   Rapport. *Report on Government Efficiency as Perceived by the Public.* 105th
>   Cong., 2d sess., pp. 11–26.

BILLS AND RESOLUTIONS

Slip Bill.   The abbreviation *S. R.* in the first model below stands for *Senate Resolutions,* and the number following is the bill or resolution number. For references to House bills, the abbreviation is *H. R.* Notice that the second model refers the reader to the more complete first entry. The choice of formats depends upon the one you used in the parenthetical text reference.

> U.S. Senate. 1996. *Visa Formalization Act of 1996.* 105th Cong., 1st sess. S. R. 1437.
>
> *Visa Formalization Act of 1996.* See U.S. Senate. 1996.

CONGRESSIONAL RECORD

> Senate. 1997. *Visa Formalization Act of 1997.* 105th Cong., 1st sess., S. R. 1437. *Congressional Record* 135, no. 137, daily ed. (10 December): S7341.

LAWS

Slip Law

U.S. Public Law 678. 105th Cong., 1st sess., 4 December 1997. *Library of Congress Book Preservation Act of 1997.*

Library of Congress Book Preservation Act of 1997. U.S. Public Law 678. 105th Cong., 1st sess., 4 December 1997.

Statutes at Large

Statutes at Large. 1998. Vol. 82, p. 466. *Library of Congress Book Preservation Act of 1997.*

Library of Congress Book Preservation Act of 1997. Statutes at Large 82:466.

United States Code

Library of Congress Book Preservation Act of 1997. U.S. Code, Vol. 38, sec. 1562.

UNITED STATES CONSTITUTION.   According to the *Chicago Manual of Style,* the Constitution is not listed in the bibliography.

EXECUTIVE DEPARTMENT DOCUMENT

Department of Labor. 1998. *Report on Urban Growth Potential Projections.* Washington, D.C.: GPO.

The abbreviation for the publisher in the above model, GPO, stands for the Government Printing Office, which prints and distributes most government publications. According to the *Chicago Manual of Style* (section 17.295), you may use any of the following formats to refer to the GPO:

Washington, D.C.: U.S. Government Printing Office, 2004.

Washington, D.C.: Government Printing Office, 2004.

Washington, D.C.: GPO, 2004.

Washington, 2004.

Washington 2004.

Remember to be consistent in using the form you choose.

LEGAL REFERENCES

Supreme Court.   Federal court decisions are only rarely listed in bibliographies. If you do wish to include such an entry, here is a suitable format:

State of Nevada v. Goldie Warren. 1969. 324 U.S. 123.

For a case prior to 1875, use the following format:

Marbury v. Madison. 1803. 1 Cranch 137.

Lower Courts

United States v. Sizemore. 1950. 183 F. 2d 201 (2d Cir.).

PUBLICATIONS OF GOVERNMENT COMMISSIONS

U.S. Securities and Exchange Commission. 1984. *Annual Report of the Securities and Exchange Commission for the Fiscal Year.* Washington, D.C.: GPO.

PUBLICATIONS OF STATE AND LOCAL GOVERNMENTS.   Remember that references for state and local government publications are modeled on those for corresponding national government documents:

Oklahoma Legislature. 1991. *Joint Committee on Public Recreation. Final Report to the Legislature,* 1995, Regular Session, on Youth Activities. Oklahoma City.

Interviews.   According to section 17.205 of the *Chicago Manual of Style,* interviews need not be included in the bibliography, but if you or your instructor wants to list such entries, here are possible formats:

PUBLISHED INTERVIEW

Untitled Interview in a Book

Jorgenson, Mary. 1998. Interview by Alan McAskill. Pp. 62–86 in *Hospice Pioneers,* edited by Alan McAskill. Richmond, VA: Dynasty Press.

Titled Interview in a Periodical

Simon, John. 1997. "Picking the Patrons Apart: An Interview with John Simon," by Selena Fox. *Media Week,* March 14, pp. 40–54.

INTERVIEW ON TELEVISION

Snopes, Edward. 2002. Interview by Klint Gordon. *Oklahoma Politicians.* WKY Television, June 4.

UNPUBLISHED INTERVIEW

Kennedy, Melissa. 1997. Interview by author. Tape recording. Portland, ME, April 23.

Unpublished sources

PERSONAL COMMUNICATIONS.   According to section 17.208 of the *Chicago Manual of Style,* references to personal communications may be handled completely in the text of the paper:

In a letter to the author, dated July 16, 1997, Mr. Bentley admitted the organizational plan was flawed.

If, however, you wish to include a reference to an unpublished communication in the bibliography, you may do so using one of the following models:

Bentley, Jacob. 1997. Letter to author, July 16.

Duberstein, Cindy. 2003. Telephone conversation with the author, June 5.

Timrod, Helen. 1997. E-mail to author, April 25.

THESES AND DISSERTATIONS

Hochenauer, Klint. 1999. "Populism and the Free Soil Movement." Ph.D. dissertation, Department of Sociology, Lamont University, Cleveland.

PAPER PRESENTED AT A MEETING

Zelazny, Kim and Ed Gilmore. 2005. "Art for Art's Sake: Funding the NEA in the Twenty-First Century." Presented at the annual meeting of the Conference of Metropolitan Arts Boards, June 15, San Francisco.

UNPUBLISHED MANUSCRIPTS

Borges, Rita V. 1993. "Mexican-American Border Conflicts, 1915–1970." Department of History, University of Texas at El Paso, El Paso. Unpublished manuscript.

WORKING AND DISCUSSION PAPERS

Blaine, Emory and Ralph Cohn. 2004. "Analysis of Social Structure in Closed Urban Environments." Discussion Paper No. 312, Institute for Sociological Research, Deadwood College, Deadwood, SD.

Electronic sources

ON-LINE SOURCES.   The need for a reliable online citation system continues to grow, but attempts to establish one are hampered by a number of factors. For one thing, there is no foolproof method of clearly reporting even such basic information as the site's author(s), title, or date of establishment. Occasionally authors identify themselves clearly; sometimes they place a link to their home page at the bottom of the site. But it is not always easy to determine exactly who authored a particular site. Likewise, it can be difficult to determine whether a site has its own title or instead exists as a subsection of a larger document with its own title. Perhaps the biggest problem facing online researchers is the instability of Internet sites. Although some sites may remain in place for weeks or months, many either move to another site—not always leaving a clear path for you to find it—or disappear.

The ASA Style Guide (1997:37–38) lists only a few models for electronic sources. Therefore,until such time as an authoritative ASA citation system for the Internet is available, we suggest the following simple formats, based in part on the models found in the *ASA Style Guide.*

On-Line Journal Article.   The *retrieval date* in the models below is the most recent date on which you accessed the source for your research project.

> Bucknell, Vespasia. 2003. "Servitude as a Way of Life: Religious Denominations in Middle America." *Skeptic's Journal* 4:22–37. Retrieved February 21, 2005 (http://www.religiosk.org/protesta.buck.html).

On-Line Newpaper Article

> Squires, Amanda. 2000. "Hard Times for Social Workers, Says Mayor." *El Paso Sun Times,* July 14, p. 2. Retrieved November 12, 2000 (http://www.elpasosun.com/2000-12/12.html).

The question of whether to break a lengthy site address at the end of a line is not discussed in the *ASA Style Guide,* but one of the guide's models does make such a line break. Other sources suggest breaking a site address only after a slash (/). Do not place a hyphen following the slash. Remember, the one thing that is absolutely required in order to find a site on the Internet is the site address, so make sure that you copy it accurately.

E-Mail Document.   Due to the ephemeral nature of e-mail sources, most researchers recommend not including citations to e-mail in the bibliography. Instead, you may handle e-mail documentation within the text of the paper.

> In an e-mail dated March 22, 1997, Bennett assured the author that the negotiations would continue.

If, however, you would like to include an e-mail citation in your references section, here is a possible format:

> Bennett, Suzanne. sbb@mtsu.socka.edu. 15 March 1997. RE: Progress on education reform petition [E-mail to Courtney Cline (coline@usc.cola.edu)].

The name of the author of the e-mail message is placed first, followed by the author's e-mail address and the date of the message. Next comes a brief statement of the subject of the message, followed by the recipient's name and e-mail address, in brackets.

CD-ROM.   The publisher of a CD-ROM can usually be identified in the same way as a book's publisher. The following model is for a source with an unascertainable author. Note that it is still necessary to include the latest date on which you accessed the database.

> *Dissertation Abstracts Ondisc.* 1861–1994. CD-ROM: UMI/Dissertation Abstracts Ondisc. Retrieved December 15, 1996.

A sample reference page is shown on page 98.

References

Entwisle, Doris, Karl Alexander and Linda Olson. 2000. "Urban Youth, Jobs, and High School." *American Sociological Review* 65(2):279–297.

Johnson, J. D., N. E. Noel and J. Sutter-Hernandez. 2000. "Alcohol and Male Acceptance of Sexual Aggression: The Role of Perceptual Ambiguity." *Journal of Applied Social Psychology* 30(6):1186–1200.

Johnson, William A. and Richard P. Rettig. 1999. "Drug Assessment of Juveniles in Detention." Social Forces 28(3):56–69, cited in John Duncan and Mary Ann Hopkins. 2004. "Youth and Drug Involvement: Families at Risk." *British Journal of Addiction* 95:45.

Moore, J. B., Allen Rice and Natasha Traylor. 1998. *Down on the Farm: Culture and Folkways.* Norman, OK: University of Oklahoma Press.

Sczaflarski, Richard. 2001. "The Trumpeter in the Tower: Solidarity and Legend" (in Polish). *World Political Review* 32:79–95.

Squires, Amanda. 2000. "Hard Times for Social Workers, Says Mayor." *El Paso Sun Times,* July 14, p. 2. Retrieved November 12, 2000 (http://www.elpasosun.com/2000-12/12.html).

Stapleton, Bonnie and Ellis Peters. 1981. "How It Was: On the Trail with Og Mandino." *Lifetime Magazine,* April, pp. 23–24, 57–59.

Stomper, Jean. 2000. *Grapes and Rain.* Translated by John Picard. New York: Baldock.

PART II

CONDUCTING RESEARCH IN SOCIOLOGY

ORGANIZING THE RESEARCH PROCESS

5.1   GAINING CONTROL OF THE RESEARCH PROCESS

The research paper is where all your skills as an interpreter of details, an organizer of facts and theories, and a writer of clear prose come together. Building logical arguments with facts and hypotheses is the way things get done in sociology, and the most successful social scientists are those who master the art of research.

Students new to writing research papers sometimes find themselves intimidated. After all, the research paper adds what seems to be an extra set of complexities to the writing process. As any other expository or persuasive paper does, a research paper must present an original thesis using a carefully organized and logical argument. But a research paper often investigates a topic that is outside the writer's own experience. This means that the writer must locate and evaluate information that is new to him, in effect educating himself as he explores his topic. A beginning researcher sometimes feels overwhelmed by the basic requirements of the assignment or by the authority of the source material.

In the beginning it may be difficult to establish a sense of control over the different tasks you are undertaking in your research project. You may have little notion which direction to take in searching for a thesis, or even where the most helpful sources of information might be located. If you fail to monitor your own work habits carefully, you may unwittingly abdicate responsibility for the paper's argument by borrowing it wholesale from one or more of your sources.

Who is in control of your paper? The answer must be you—not the instructor who assigned you the paper, and certainly not the published writers whose opinions you solicit. If all your paper does is paste together the opinions of others, it has little use. It is up to you to synthesize an original idea through the evaluation of your source material. At the beginning of your research project, there will be many elements of your paper about which you are unsure—you will probably not yet have a definitive thesis sentence, for example, or even much understanding of the shape of your argument. You can establish a measure of control over the process you will go through to complete the paper. And if you work regularly and systematically, keeping yourself open to new ideas as they present themselves, your sense of control will grow. The following are some suggestions to help you establish and maintain control of your paper.

5.1.1   Understand Your Assignment

A research assignment can fall short simply because the writer did not read the assignment carefully. Considering how much time and effort you are about to put into your project, it is a very good idea to make sure you have a clear understanding of what it is you are to do. Be sure to ask your instructor about any aspect of the assignment that is unclear to you—but only after you have thought about it carefully. Recopying the assignment instructions in your own handwriting is a good way to start, even though your instructor may have given them to you in writing.

5.1.2   Establish Your Topic

It may be that the assignment gives you a great deal of specific information about your topic, or that you are allowed considerable freedom in establishing one for yourself. In a social problems class in which you are studying issues affecting American society, your professor might give you a very specific assignment—for example, a paper examining the difficulties of establishing viable community policy in the wake of significant changes in the urban family structure—or she may allow you to choose for yourself the issue that your paper will address. You need to understand the terms, set up in the assignment, by which you will design your project.

5.1.3   Ascertain Your Purpose

Whatever the degree of latitude you are given in the matter of your topic, pay close attention to the way in which your instructor has phrased the assignment. Is your primary job to describe a current social issue or to take a stand on it? Are you to compare social systems, and if so, to what end? Are you to classify, persuade, survey, or analyze? Look for such descriptive terms in the assignment directions to determine the purpose of the project.

5.1.4   Understand Who Your Audience Is

Your own orientation to the paper is profoundly affected by your conception of the audience for whom you are writing. Granted, your number-one reader is your instructor, but who else would be interested in your paper? Are you writing for the citizens of a community? A group of professionals? A city council? A paper that describes the complex changes in the urban family may justifiably contain much more technical jargon for an audience of sociology professionals than for a citizens group made up of local business and civic leaders.

5.1.5   Determine the Kind of Research You Are Doing

In your paper you will do one or both of two kinds of research, primary and secondary. Primary research requires you to discover information firsthand, often by conducting interviews, surveys, or polls. In primary research, you are collecting and sifting through raw data—data that have not already been interpreted by researchers—that you will study, select, arrange, and speculate on. This raw data may be the opinions of experts or people on the street, historical documents, the theoretical speculations of a famous sociologist, or material collected from other researchers. It is important to carefully set up the method(s) by which you collect your data. Your aim is to gather the most accurate information possible, from which sound observations may be made later, either by you or by other writers using the material you have uncovered.

Secondary research makes use of secondary sources—that is, published accounts of primary materials. Although the primary researcher might poll a community for its opinion on the outcome of a recent bond election, the secondary researcher will use the material from the poll to support a particular thesis. In other words, secondary research focuses on interpretations of raw data. Most of your college papers will be based on your use of secondary sources.

5.1.6   Keep Your Perspective

Whichever type of research you perform, you must keep your results in perspective. There is no way in which you, as a primary researcher, can be completely objective in your findings. It is not possible to design a questionnaire that will net you absolute truth, nor can you be sure that the opinions you gather in interviews reflect the accurate and unchanging opinions of the people you question. Likewise, if you are conducting secondary research, you must remember that the articles and journals you are reading are shaped by the aims of their writers, who are interpreting primary materials for their own ends. The farther you get from a primary source, the greater the possibility for distortion. Your job as a researcher is to be as accurate as possible, and that means keeping in view the limitations of your methods and their ends.

5.2   EFFECTIVE RESEARCH METHODS

5.2.1   Establish Effective Procedures

In any research project there will be moments of confusion, but establishing effective procedures can prevent confusion from overwhelming you. You need to design a schedule for the project that is as systematic as possible, yet flexible enough so that you do not feel trapped by it. A schedule will help keep you from running into dead-ends by always showing you what to do next. At the same time, it will help you to retain the presence of mind necessary to spot new ideas and new strategies as you work.

5.2.2 Give Yourself Plenty of Time

There may be reasons why you feel like putting off research: unfamiliarity with the library, the pressure of other tasks, or a deadline that seems comfortably far away. Do not allow such factors to deter you. Research takes time. Working in a library often seems to speed up the clock, so that the hour you expected it to take to find certain sources becomes two hours. You should allow yourself time not only to find material, but to read, assimilate, and set it in context with your own thoughts.

The schedule that follows lists the steps of a research project in the order in which they are generally accomplished. Remember that each step is dependent on the others, and that it is quite possible to revise earlier decisions in light of later discoveries. After some background reading, for example, your notion of the paper's purpose may change, which may, in turn, alter other steps. One of the strengths of a good schedule is its flexibility. The general schedule lists tasks for both primary and secondary research; you should use only those steps that are relevant to your project.

Research Schedule

Task	Date of Completion
Determine topic, purpose, and audience	_____
Do background reading in reference books	_____
Narrow your topic; establish a tentative hypothesis	_____
Develop a working bibliography	_____
Consult alternative sources of information, if necessary	_____
Read and evaluate written sources, taking notes	_____
Determine whether to conduct interviews or surveys	_____
Draft a thesis and outline	_____
Write a first draft	_____
Obtain feedback (show draft to instructor, if possible)	_____
Do more research, if necessary	_____
Revise draft	_____
Correct bibliographical format of paper	_____
Prepare final draft	_____
Proofread	_____
Proofread again, looking for characteristic errors	_____
Deadline for final draft	_____

5.2.3   Do Background Reading

Whether you are doing primary or secondary research, you need to know what kinds of work have already been done in your field of study. A good way to start is by consulting general reference works, though you do not want to overdo it (see the following paragraph). Chapter 6 lists specialized reference works focusing on topics of interest to sociologists. You might find help in such volumes even for specific, local problems, such as how to restructure a juvenile treatment program or plan an antidrug campaign aimed at area schools.

Be very careful not to rely too exclusively on material taken from general encyclopedias. You may wish to consult one for an overview of a topic with which you are unfamiliar, but students new to research are often tempted to import large sections—if not entire articles—from such volumes, and this practice is not good scholarship. One major reason that your instructor has required a research paper from you is to have you experience the kinds of books and journals in which the discourse of sociology is conducted. General reference encyclopedias, such as *Encyclopaedia Britannica* or *Colliers Encyclopedia,* are good places for instant introductions to subjects; some encyclopedias even include bibliographies of reference works at the ends of their articles. But you will need much more detailed information about your subject to write a useful paper. Once you have gotten some general background information from an encyclopedia, move on.

A primary rule of source hunting is to use your imagination. Determine which topics relevant to your study might be covered in general reference works. For example, if you are looking for introductory readings to help you with the aforementioned research paper on antidrug campaign planning, you might look into such specialized reference tools as the *Encyclopedia of Social Work.* Remember to check articles in such works for lists of references to specialized books and essays.

5.2.4   Narrow Your Topic and Establish a Working Thesis

Before beginning to explore outside sources, it would be a good idea for you to examine what you already know or think about your topic, a job that can only be accomplished well in writing. You might wish to use one or more of the prewriting strategies described in Chapter 1. You might be surprised by what you know—or don't know—about the topic. This kind of self-questioning can help you discover a profitable direction for your research.

For a research paper on a course in social problems, Emily Faucet was given the general topic of studying grassroots attempts to legislate morality in American society. She chose the topic of textbook censorship. Here is the path her thinking took as she looked for ways to limit the topic effectively and find a thesis:

General Topic	Textbook Censorship
Potential topics	How a local censorship campaign gets started
	Funding censorship campaigns
	Reasons behind textbook censorship
	Results of censorship campaigns

Working thesis	It is disconcertingly easy in our part of the state to launch a textbook censorship campaign.

It is unlikely that you will come up with a satisfactory thesis at the beginning of your project. You need to guide yourself through the early stages of research toward a main idea in a way that is both useful and manageable. Having in mind a working thesis—a preliminary statement of your purpose—can help you select material that is of greatest interest to you as you examine potential sources. The working thesis will probably evolve as your research progresses, and you need to be ready to accept such change. You should not fix on a thesis too early in the research process, or you may miss opportunities to refine it.

5.2.5   Develop a Working Bibliography

As you begin your research, you will look for published sources—essays, books, articles, and interviews with experts in the field—that may help you with your project. This list of potentially useful sources is your working bibliography. There are many ways to discover items for the bibliography. You can search the cataloging system in your library, as well as the specialized published bibliographies in your field, for titles. (Some of these bibliographies are listed in Chapter 6.) The general reference works you consulted for your background reading may also list such sources, and each specialized book or essay you find will have a bibliography of sources its writer used that may be useful to you.

From your working bibliography you can select items for the final bibliography, which will appear in the final draft of your paper. Early in your research you may not know which sources will help you and which will not. It is important to keep an accurate description of each entry in your working bibliography to tell clearly which items you have investigated, which you will need to consult again, and which you will discard. Building the working bibliography also allows you to practice using the required bibliographical format for the final draft. As you list potential sources, include all the information about each source needed for your format, and place the information in the correct order, using the proper punctuation.

The American Sociological Association's bibliographical format—the one most often required for sociology papers—is described in detail in Chapter 4 of this manual.

5.2.6   Consult Alternative Sources of Information

In the course of your research you may need to consult a source that is not immediately available to you. For example, while working on the antidrug campaign paper, you might find that a packet of potentially useful information is available from a government agency or a public interest group at the state or federal level. Maybe an essential book is not held by your university library or by any other local library. Or perhaps a successful antidrug program has been implemented in the school system of a city comparable in size to yours but located in another state.

In such situations, it may be tempting to disregard potential sources because of the difficulty of obtaining them. If you ignore the existence of material important to your project, however, you are not doing your job.

It is vital that you take steps to acquire the needed material. In the first situation, you can simply write to the agency or public interest group; in the second, you may use your library's interlibrary loan procedure to obtain a copy of the book; in the third, you can track down the council that manages the antidrug campaign, by e-mail, mail, or phone, to ask for information. Remember that many businesses and government agencies want to share their information with interested citizens; some even have employees or entire departments whose job is to facilitate communication with the public. Be as specific as possible when asking for information by mail. It is a good idea to briefly outline your project—in no more than a few sentences—in order to help the respondent determine the type of information you need. Also, be sure to begin the job of locating and acquiring long-distance source material as soon as possible, to allow for the various delays that often occur while conducting a search at a distance.

5.2.7   Evaluate Written Sources

Few research experiences are more frustrating than half-remembering something worth using from a source that you can no longer identify. Establish an efficient method of examining and evaluating the sources listed in your working bibliography that will leave you with an accurate written record of your examination. The following are some suggestions for using written sources.

Determine quickly the potential usefulness of a source. For books, you can read through the prefatory material (the introduction, foreword, and preface), looking for the author's thesis; you can also examine chapter headings, dust jackets, and indexes. A journal article should announce its intention in its abstract or introduction, which in most cases will be a page or less in length. This preliminary examination should tell you whether a more intensive examination is worthwhile. Note that whatever you decide about the source, you should photocopy the title page of the book or journal article, making sure that all important publication information (including title, date, author, volume number, and page numbers) is included. Write on the photocopied page any necessary information that is not printed there. Without such a record, later in your research you might forget that you had looked at that text, and you may find yourself examining it again.

When you have determined that a potential source is worth closer inspection, explore it carefully. If it is a book, determine whether you should invest the time it will take to read it in its entirety. Whatever the source, make sure you understand not only its overall thesis, but also each part of the argument that the writer sets up to illustrate or prove the thesis. Get a feel for the shape of the writer's argument, for how the subtopics mesh to form a logical defense of her main point. What do you think of her logic? Her examples? Coming to an accurate appraisal may take more than one reading.

As you read, try to get a feel for the larger argument in which this source takes its place. References to other writers will give you an indication of where else to look for source material as well as of the general shape of scholarly opinion concerning your subject. If you can see the article you are reading as only one element of an ongoing dialogue instead of an attempt to have the last word on the subject, then you can place the argument of the paper in perspective. The same goes for book-length treatments.

5.2.8   Use Photocopies

Periodicals and most reference works cannot be checked out of the library. Before the widespread placement of photocopy machines, students could use these materials only by sitting in the library, reading sources, and jotting down information on note cards. Although there are advantages to using the note-card method, photocopying saves you time in the library and allows you to take the source information in its original shape home, where you can decide how to use it at your convenience, perhaps shaping the material at your computer keyboard.

If you decide to make copies of source material, you should do the following:

- Follow all copyright laws.
- Have the exact change for the photocopy machines.
- Record all necessary bibliographical information on the photocopy. If you forget to do this, you may find yourself making an extra trip to the library just to get an accurate date of publication or set of page numbers.

Remember that photocopying a source is not the same thing as examining it. You will still have to spend time going over the material, assimilating it in order to use it accurately. It is not enough merely to have the information close at hand or even to read it through once or twice. You should understand it thoroughly. Be sure to give yourself time for this kind of evaluation.

5.2.9   Determine Whether to Conduct Interviews or Surveys

If your project calls for primary research, you may need to interview experts on your topic or to conduct a survey of opinions among a select group using a questionnaire. Be sure to prepare yourself as thoroughly as possible for any primary research. Following are some tips for conducting an interview.

Establish a purpose for each interview, bearing in mind the requirements of your working thesis. In what ways might your discussion with the subject benefit your paper? Write down your formulation of the interview's purpose. Estimate the length of time you expect the interview to take and inform your subject. Arrive for your scheduled interview on time and dressed appropriately. Be courteous.

Learn as much as possible about your topic by researching published sources. Use this research to design your questions. If possible, learn something about the people you interview. This knowledge may help you establish rapport with your subjects and will also help you tailor your questions. Take a list of pre-pared questions to the interview. However, be ready to depart from your list of questions to follow any potentially useful direction that the interview takes.

Take notes during the interview and bring along extra pens. The use of a tape recorder may inhibit some interviewees. If you wish to use audiotape, ask for permission from your subject. Follow up your interview with a thank-you letter and, if feasible, a copy of the published paper in which the interview is used.

If your research requires a survey or questionnaire, see Chapter 11 for in-structions on designing and conducting surveys, polls, and questionnaires.

5.3   ETHICAL USE OF SOURCE MATERIAL

Your goal is to integrate the source material skillfully into the flow of your writ-ten argument, using it as effectively as possible. This means that sometimes you will need to quote from a source directly, while at other times you should recast (paraphrase) source information into your own words.

5.3.1   Quoting

When should you quote? You should directly quote from a source when the orig-inal language is distinctive enough to enhance your argument, or when rewording the passage would lessen its impact. You should also quote a passage to which your paper will take exception. In the interest of fairness, it is important to let a writer taking an opposing view state his case in his own words. Rarely, however, should you quote a source at great length (longer than two or three paragraphs). Nor should your paper, or any lengthy section of it, be merely a string of quoted passages. The more quotations you take from others, the more disruptive they are to the rhetorical flow of your own language. Too much quot-ing creates a "cut-and-paste" paper, a choppy patchwork of varying styles and bor-rowed purposes in which the sense of your own control over the material is lost.

Acknowledge quotations carefully.   Failing to signal the presence of a quota-tion skillfully can lead to confusion or choppiness:

> The U.S. Secretary of Labor believes that worker-retraining programs have failed because of a lack of trust within the American business culture. "The American business community does not visualize the need to invest in its workers" (Winn 1992:11).

The phrasing of the first sentence in this passage seems to suggest that the quote following it comes from the Secretary of Labor. Note how this revision clar-ifies the attribution:

> According to reporter Fred Winn (1992), the U.S. Secretary of Labor believes that worker-retraining programs have failed because of a lack of trust within the

American business culture. Summarizing the Secretary's view, Winn writes, "The American business community does not visualize the need to invest in its workers" (p. 11).

The origin of each quote must be signaled (cited) within your text at the point where the quote occurs, as well as in the list of works cited (references) that follows the text. Chapter 4 describes documentation formats set forth by the American Sociological Association and the *Chicago Manual of Style*.

Quote accurately.   If your quotation introduces careless variants of any kind, you are misrepresenting your source. Proofread your quotations very carefully, paying close attention to such surface features as spelling, capitalization, italics, and the use of numerals. Occasionally, either to make a quotation fit smoothly into a passage, to clarify a reference, or to delete unnecessary material from a quotation, you may need to change the original wording slightly. You must signal any such change to your reader by using brackets:

"Several times in the course of his speech, the attorney general said that his stand [on gun control] remains unchanged" (McAffrey 1995:2).

Ellipses may be used to indicate that words have been left out of a quote:

"The last time voters refused to endorse one of the senator's policies . . . was back in 1982" (Laws 1992:143).

When you integrate quoted material with your own prose, it is unnecessary to begin the quote with ellipses:

Benton raised eyebrows with his claim that "nobody in the mayor's office knows how to tie a shoe, let alone balance a budget" (Williams 1990:12).

5.3.2   Paraphrasing

Your writing has its own rhetorical attributes, its own rhythms and structural coherence. Inserting too many quotations into a section of your paper can disrupt the patterns you establish in your prose and diminish the effectiveness of your own language. Paraphrasing, or recasting source material in your own words, is one way of avoiding the risk of creating a choppy hodgepodge of quotations. Paraphrasing allows you to communicate ideas and facts from a source in your own prose, thereby keeping intact the rhetorical characteristics that distinguish your writing.

Remember that the salient fact about a paraphrase is that its language is yours. It is not a near copy of the source writer's language. Merely changing a few words of the original does justice to no one's prose and frequently produces stilted passages. This sort of borrowing is actually a form of plagiarism. To fully integrate the material you wish to use into your writing, use your own language.

Paraphrasing may actually increase your comprehension of source material; recasting a passage requires you to think carefully about its meaning—more carefully, perhaps, than you might if you merely copied it word-for-word.

5.3.3   Avoiding Plagiarism

Paraphrases require the same sort of documentation that direct quotes do. The words of a paraphrase may be yours, but the idea is someone else's. Failure to give that person credit, in the form of references within the text and in the bibliography, may make you vulnerable to a charge of plagiarism.

What kind of paraphrased material must be acknowledged? Basic material that you find in several sources need not be acknowledged by a reference. For example, it is unnecessary to cite a source for the information that Franklin Delano Roosevelt was elected to a fourth term as President of the United States shortly before his death, because this is a commonly known fact. However, Professor Smith's opinion, published in a recent article, that Roosevelt's winning of a fourth term hastened his death is not a fact, but a theory based on Smith's research and defended by her. If you wish to make use of Smith's opinion in a paraphrase, you need to give her credit for it, as you should the judgments and claims of any other source. Any information that is not widely known, whether factual or open to dispute, should be documented. This includes statistics, graphs, tables, and charts taken from a source other than your own primary research.

Plagiarism is the using of someone else's words or ideas without giving that person credit. Although some plagiarism is deliberate, produced by writers who understand that they are guilty of a kind of academic thievery, much of it is unconscious, committed by writers who are not aware of the varieties of plagiarism or who are careless in recording their borrowings from sources. Plagiarism includes the following:

- Quoting directly without acknowledging the source
- Paraphrasing without acknowledging the source
- Constructing a paraphrase that closely resembles the original in language and syntax

One way to guard against plagiarism is to keep careful records in your notes of when you have quoted source material directly and when you have paraphrased—making sure that the wording of the paraphrase is yours. Make sure that all direct quotes in your final draft are properly set off from your own prose, either with quotation marks or in indented blocks.

SOURCES OF INFORMATION

Where we get our information is extremely important. The ability to locate valid and reliable information efficiently is vitally important when you are writing papers in sociology. For most papers written in college, the library is the place to find most—if not all—of the information needed. Mastering effective information gathering will help you to be more productive in your research and writing. Further, effective library research skills enable you to practice lifelong learning using information sources available at most libraries.

This chapter highlights methods of information retrieval for major sources in sociology. To give a specific example, let's assume you have been assigned a paper or want information on the traditional American family. With the materials introduced in this chapter, you should be able to find a concise definition of "traditional family," lists of articles and books written about the topic, theories about its impact upon American society, reviews of books to provide a balanced coverage, and government and other statistical sources that help document historical change of the American family—while associating it with a variety of variables, such as age, geographic region, race, and socioeconomic status.

In some cases, someone in a public agency or private organization has probably already conducted significant research on your topic. If you can find the right person, you may be able to secure much more information in much less time than you can by looking in the local library by yourself.

Did you know, for example, that the members of the U.S. Senate and House of Representatives constantly use the services of the Congressional Research Service (CRS), and that, upon request to your congressperson or senator, materials from the CRS may be sent to you on the topic of your choice? Further, every agency of government on the local, state, and national levels employs people who are responsible primarily for the purpose of gathering information that is needed to help their managers make decisions. Much of the research that is done by these employees is available upon request.

This chapter is divided into sections, each describing a type of reference tool. The sections are arranged so that you can become familiar with the nature and uses of general reference works first, and then with the nature and uses of specialized studies. Bibliographic examples were selected according to the following criteria: All are available in English, most are available in college libraries, and all are examples of sources potentially useful to sociology students. Publications that may seem unusually dated often represent the inaugural issue of the document or publication being described.

6.1   GUIDES TO SOCIOLOGICAL LITERATURE

Guides to the literature are books or articles that identify sources that enable students to search for information on individual topics. Some guides focus exclusively on the two principal categories of reference works: finding aids, such as bibliographies and periodical indexes; and content reference works, such as handbooks, yearbooks, subject dictionaries, and subject encyclopedias.

6.1.1   General Guides

Some guides include discussions of various types of research materials, such as government publications, while others include lists of important book-length studies on topics in a subject field. Students can identify sociological reference publications by consulting a guide that covers a wide spectrum of fields related to their areas of interest. There are several general guides that can be of great benefit. The following is an example of such guidebooks:

> Fargis, Paul, ed. 2002. *The New York Public Library Desk Reference.* 4th ed. New York: Hungry Minds, Inc. This reference book includes commonly needed material on a vast range of topics—some of interest to social science students, such as the addresses of national, state, county, and city government consumer protection agencies; forms of addressing government and military personnel; brief accounts of events in world history; and descriptions of international organizations. There is an index.

6.1.2   Specialized Guides

For most academic disciplines, there are specialized guides to the literature. Given an unfamiliar topic in sociology or a related field, a student can consult a guide that focuses on sociology or the social sciences for titles of content reference works containing information on the topic. The following is an example:

> Aby, Stephen H., James Nalen and Lori Fielding. 2005. *Sociology: A Guide to Reference and Information Sources.* 3d ed. Littleton, CO: Libraries Unlimited. Part of the Reference Sources in the Social Sciences Series (No. 1), this excellent guide is divided into three sections: (1) works of use to all social sciences; (2) individual social science resources of use to sociologists; and (3) sociological sources, including general works and a section on resources especially useful in twenty-two subdivisions of sociology.

Sometimes there are guides that reference all available information on a given subject or constellation of subjects. The following is an example of such a guidebook:

Selth, Jefferson P. 1985. *Alternative Lifestyles: A Guide to Research Collections on Intentional Communities, Nudism, and Sexual Freedom.* Westport, CT: Greenwood Publishing Group. This book describes thirty research collections on intentional communities, nudism, and sexual freedom in the United States, that total 120,000 volumes, 15,000 periodicals, 125,000 audiovisual items, over 3 million photographs, and many ephemeral materials.

6.1.3 Handbooks

A handbook is a compact fact book designed for quick reference. It usually deals with one broad subject area, and emphasizes generally accepted data rather than recent findings. In the latter respect, handbooks differ from yearbooks, although these reference tools overlap in the way they are used and the information they include. Two types of handbooks useful to sociologists are: (1) statistical handbooks, that provide data about a number of demographic and social characteristics; and (2) subject handbooks, that offer a comprehensive summary of research findings and theoretical propositions for broad substantive areas in a discipline.

Statistical handbooks. Containing data gathered from numerous sources, statistical handbooks provide students with information necessary for the description and analysis of social trends and phenomena. Among the many statistical handbooks useful to sociologists are the following:

U.S. Bureau of the Census. Annual. *County and City Data Book.* Washington, D.C.: Government Printing Office. This handbook contains statistics on population, housing, income, education, and employment for counties, standard metropolitan statistical areas, cities, urbanized areas, and unincorporated places. Since there is no subject index, the only subject access to the tables is through the "Outline of Tabular Subject Content" located in the front of the volume. This handbook is published irregularly.

U.S. Bureau of the Census. 1971. *Historical Statistics of the United States: Colonial Times to 1970.* 2 vols. Washington, D.C.: Government Printing Office. This two-volume work contains statistics on a wide spectrum of social and economic developments from the colonial period to 1970. The tables are accompanied by explanatory notes and references to additional sources of statistical information. To use this work effectively, you may turn to the table of contents, which provides a broad subject access; the subject index, which offers a more narrow topical approach to the data; or the time period index, which provides access to statistics on major topics for individual decades.

Gutierrez, Lynda, Andrea Yurasits, Angela Hurdle, and Michele Franklin, eds. 1999. *Demographics USA: County Addition.* New York: Trade Dimensions. The information in this guide is organized within a geographic hierarchy by region, state, metropolitan area, and county. Summaries are provided for each geographic area. You will find information dealing with the area's total population, its percentage of the U.S. total, and listings by age, sex, number of households, number of persons in household, and so on.

By following the guidelines in Chapter 7, students can access many statistical handbooks on the Internet.

Subject handbooks.   Subject handbooks in sociology provide a summary and a synthesis of concepts, research, and theoretical approaches of specific topical areas within the discipline—such as formal organizations, socialization, and social psychology. Students who want a brief overview of well-established information or an explanation of major concepts in one substantive area—such as women's studies—will find that the following subject handbook is a convenient source.

> Howard, Angela M. and Frances M. Kavenik, eds. 2000. *Handbook of American Women's History.* New York: Sage Publications. This book is the result of networking among women's history and women's studies colleagues. It offers introductory and fundamental information necessary for a general understanding of the field. It was designed to assist both students and teachers who wanted to research basic information regarding sources and materials.

Other subject handbooks available to sociology students can be accessed on the Internet by following the guidelines in Chapter 7.

6.1.4   Yearbooks

Although in many cases they contain a good deal of background information, yearbooks are fact books that focus on the developments and events of a given year. Unlike handbooks, they emphasize current information. Like handbooks, there are two types of yearbooks most useful for sociology students: (1) statistical yearbooks, which provide the most recent data on social and demographic characteristics; and (2) subject yearbooks, which review current theory and research.

Statistical yearbooks.   You can turn to the most recent yearbook for the latest data available on topics such as population composition, fertility, and economic activity, and you can also use back issues to collect data for previous time periods. This is especially true in cases where no handbook presents data for a specific geographical or topical area. Among the general statistical yearbooks often used by sociologists are the following:

> *Statistical Yearbook.* Annual. New York: United Nations/Statistical Office. In this annual publication, prepared by the Statistical Office of the United Nations, tables cover population, workforce, agriculture, production, mining construction, consumption, transportation, external trade, wages and prices, national income, finance, social statistics, education, and culture. Normally, each series covers a ten-to-twenty-year span. The table of contents is the only subject access to this book. Sources are cited. Textual material, including indexes, is in French and English.

Statistical Yearbook. Annual. Paris: UNESCO. The statistical charts in this annual publication are printed in three languages, and cover aspects of education, science, and culture in 200 member nations of UNESCO. The data are generated from questionnaires given to a wide variety of respondents. There is no index.

Government Finance Statistics Yearbook. Annual. Washington, D.C.: International Monetary Fund. This annual reference volume publishes tables that document revenues and spending by governments around the world. There is no index.

Vital Statistics of the United States. Annual. 2 Vols. Hyattville, MD: U.S. Department of Health and Human Services. This yearly series is published annually. Volume 1 presents the year's birth statistics at the national and local levels, and Volume 2 covers death statistics.

Stanley, Harold W. and Richard G. Niemi, eds. 2000. *Vital Statistics on American Politics, 1999–2000.* Washington, D.C.: Congressional Quarterly. The charts and tables in this guide cover a wide range of topics related to American politics, including the media (newspaper endorsements of presidential candidates from 1932 to 1988 are graphed), interest groups, and the geographical and ethnic composition of political bodies. An index is included.

Statistical yearbooks focusing on a special subject are often useful to sociologists interested in specific problems. Two yearbooks focusing on specific subjects are the following:

Demographic Yearbook. Annual. New York: United Nations/Statistical Office. This annual contains demographic statistics for over two hundred separate geographic areas. Population and vital statistics appear in each annual volume, but the subject matter of the other statistical compilations varies from year to year. Each volume includes an introduction that defines terms and describes the tables. The table of contents lists tables by broad categories. A cumulative index in each volume identifies the annual volumes in which statistics on individual topics are to be found and indicates the time span of the statistics in individual volumes.

U.S. Federal Bureau of Investigation. Annual. *Uniform Crime Reports for the United States.* Washington, D.C.: Government Printing Office. This annual report contains statistics on crimes, offenders, and law enforcement personnel. Tables include statistics by type of offenses, geographical divisions, age groups, trends, and police employment. The table of contents provides the only subject access to the tables.

Subject yearbooks.   The subject yearbook (also known as the *annual review*) is particularly useful because it contains articles that give a brief overview of recent major developments in the field. These articles, based on the latest published research, allow a student beginning a research project to define and clarify the subject matter. The bibliographies appended to the articles can provide useful leads for further reading. The subject yearbook for sociology is the following:

Annual Review of Sociology. Annual. Palo Alto, CA: Annual Reviews. New developments in the field of sociology are discussed in approximately sixteen essays covering ten broad subject areas in this annual. Areas covered include formal organizations, social processes, urban sociology, and institutions. The essays average twenty-five to thirty pages in length and include extensive bibliographies. Each volume, beginning with the second, contains cumulative indexes that list essays by author and broad subject area.

6.1.5   Subject Dictionaries and Encyclopedias

Subject dictionaries.   The primary purpose of a dictionary is to supply meanings and give accurate spellings of words. The words that are included, and the exhaustiveness of their definitions, depend on the type of dictionary. This discussion focuses on subject dictionaries.

Virtually all academic disciplines have their own specialized language. The function of a subject dictionary is to explain briefly the words—whether terms or names—that make up a particular subject's specialized jargon. Such a source lists terms unfamiliar in common usage, as well as rather ordinary terms that have taken on specialized and technical meanings within the context of a subject discipline.

Sociology is a broad field encompassing every aspect of human social behavior. Many concepts or terms that have a common usage take on a specialized meaning in sociology. The term *norm* is an example. In common usage the word refers to something common or "normal." In sociology, however, *norm* refers to the rules or sets of expectations that guide social behavior.

In addition to defining concepts, subject dictionaries are also useful for locating brief descriptions of methodological techniques or tests and definitions of major theories. When students are unsure of the exact meaning of a concept or theory, or of the function of a specific methodological technique, they can consult a sociology dictionary or a broader dictionary of the social sciences. The following are examples, some of which are designed for specific areas within the discipline of sociology.

> Abel, E. L. 1984. *A Dictionary of Drug Abuse Terms and Terminology.* Westport, CT: Greenwood.
>
> Cockerham, William C. and Ferris J. Ritchey. 1997. *Dictionary of Medical Sociology.* New York:Greenwood.
>
> Harris, D. K. 1988. *Dictionary of Gerontology.* New York: Greenwood.
>
> Johnson, Allan G. 2000. *The Blackwell Dictionary of Sociology: A User's Guide to Sociological Language.* 2d ed. New York: Blackwell Publishers.
>
> Marshall, Gordon. 1998. *A Dictionary of Sociology.* New York: Oxford University Press.
>
> Mills, J. 1992. *Womanwords: A Dictionary of Words about Women.* New York: Free Press.
>
> Richter, A. 1993. *Dictionary of Sexual Slang.* New York: Wiley.
>
> Rothenberg. R. 1997. *Race, Class, Gender: A Dictionary.* New York: St. Martin's Press.

Encyclopedias.   While dictionaries contain brief definitions of terms, encyclopedias include summary essays about individual topics. There are two types of encyclopedias: general encyclopedias, which are wide-ranging in topical coverage, and subject encyclopedias, which focus on topics within an individual subject discipline or a group of related disciplines. This discussion focuses on subject encyclopedias.

The essays in subject encyclopedias are often written by recognized scholars. They include bibliographies listing major topical studies and cross-references listing other essays that may contain useful additional information. You can use a subject encyclopedia in several ways—as an introduction to a topic, as a means of viewing a topic in a wider context, or as the starting point for research. You may find an essay on the topic helpful for clarification and definition of your research project, and the bibliography can provide valuable leads for further reading. The following three subject encyclopedias are especially useful to sociology majors:

International Encyclopedia of the Social Sciences. 1968. 17 vols. New York: Macmillan. This seventeen-volume set contains articles covering the subject matter of the following fields, as well as some of the most important contributors in their development: anthropology, economics, geography, history, law, political science, psychiatry, psychology, sociology, and statistics. The treatment of individual topics is often divided into more than one essay, each approaching the topic from the perspective of a different social science. Although the encyclopedia is arranged alphabetically by subject, the articles are lengthy and cover broad areas. To find a specific topic, you should consult the index in the last volume. There is also a useful Classification of Articles section in the last volume. The essays themselves are carefully cross-referenced, and the bibliographies accompanying the articles—some of which are extensive, although dated—remain useful.

Tierney, H., ed. 1989–1991. *Women's Studies Encyclopedia: Views from the Inside.* 3 vols. New York: Greenwood. This is an excellent resource for students interested in this area. The major focus of this three-volume work is on the American experience. There is no single feminist perspective informing the entries. Contributors had the widest possible latitude in developing their articles.

Borgatta, E. F. and M. L. Borgatta, eds. 1992. *Encyclopedia of Sociology.* 4 vols. New York: Macmillan. This four-volume set is a comprehensive general sociology encyclopedia intended for a broad audience. It contains 370 lengthy articles written by 339 sociologists, each two to eighteen pages in length, which conclude with bibliographies.

Among others, the *Encyclopedia of Philosophy,* the *Encyclopedia of Psychology,* and the *Encyclopedia of Religion* can also be very helpful referencing tools for sociology students. The following is a short list of encyclopedias covering specific areas within sociology:

Clark, Robin E., Judith F. Clark, Christine A. Adamec and Richard C. Gelles, eds. 2001. *The Encyclopedia of Child Abuse.* 2d. ed. New York: Facts on File.

DiCanio, M. 1993. *The Encyclopedia of Violence: Origins, Attitudes, Consequences.* New York: Facts on File.

Kaplan, Jeffery. 2000. *Encyclopedia of White Power: A Sourcebook on the Radical Racist Right.* New York: AltaMira Press.

Lerner, Richard M. and Jacqueline Lerner, eds. 2001. *Adolescence in America: An Encyclopedia.* New York: ABL-CLIO, Inc.

Maddox, George L., ed. 2001. *The Encyclopedia of Aging: A Comprehensive Resource in Gerontology and Geriatrics.* New York: Springer.

6.1.6   Indexes and Abstracts

Indexes contain lists of citations of articles printed in journals, magazines, and other periodicals. The standard citation for articles in indexes includes the author's name, the date of the issue in which the article appears, the article title, the name of the journal, the volume and/or issue number, and page numbers. Abstracts contain short summaries of articles or books. Indexes and abstracts are important because the articles in scholarly journals often update information found in books, or in some cases constitute the only published treatments of certain topics.

On-line database systems.   Specialized indexes and abstracts list articles published in scholarly journals by subject and author. Most are now retrievable through computer on-line database systems located in the library. These CD-ROM networks index thousands of professional and popular articles in most academic areas. The most useful databases for sociology are stored in Sociofile, which indexes over 1,900 international journals in sociology and related fields that are stored in two print indexes titled *Sociological Abstracts* (1974–present) and *Social Sciences Index* (1983–present). *Social Sciences Index* indexes journals in most of the social sciences, including anthropology, area studies, economics, environmental science, geography, law, and political science.

Other databases that offer potential sources for your sociology studies are the following:

> *ERIC,* an education database (1966–present) consisting of the *Resources in Education* file and the *Current Index to Journals in Education* file, compiling journal article citations with abstracts from over 750 professional journals.

> *Psyclit,* a psychology database (1974–present) that compiles summaries for literature in psychology and related disciplines and corresponds to *Psychological Abstracts,* which indexes about 1,300 professional journals in twenty-seven languages.

> *Readers' Guide to Periodical Literature,* a popular and general interest database (1983–present) that provides citations from more than 900 journals and magazines in the popular press.

> *United States Government Periodical Index,* a government periodicals database (November 1994–present) that indexes approximately 180 U.S. government sources covering a wide variety of subjects. The reference department in many libraries also allows you to access over forty other databases on FIRSTSEARCH.

Discipline indexes.   Discipline indexes identify articles in journals by the discipline or group of related disciplines (such as social sciences) rather than by the topic, while other indexes identify journal articles according to broad topical areas without a discipline focus. An example of a discipline index that indexes by subject articles in social science, economics, and anthropology journals as well as those in sociology is the following:

> *Social Sciences Index.* Annual. New York: H. W. Wilson. A quarterly publication with annual cumulations, this index organizes—by subject and author—articles

in over 260 journals in anthropology, sociology, law, and criminology. A helpful feature is the separate Book Reviews index at the back of each issue.

Topical indexes.   An important topic often becomes the focus of an index, which is generated to make all articles relevant to that topic available to researchers, regardless of field or discipline. Examples of topical indexes frequently used by sociologists are the following:

Population Index. Annual. Princeton, NJ: Office of Population Research, Princeton University, and Population Association of America. This quarterly indexes books, journals, and government publications. The annotated entries are arranged by broad subjects—such as mortality, internal migration, and spatial distribution. Each issue also contains several articles on topics of current interest. Geographical, author, and statistical indexes cumulate annually.

Statistical Reference Index Annual Abstracts. Annual. Bethesda, MD: Congressional Information Service. This annual volume is a guide to American statistical publications produced by private organizations and state governments. Contents are organized by the type of organization publishing the reports, each of which is briefly described. An accompanying volume includes four indexes: subject and name, category, issuing sources, and title.

Other topical indexes of interest to sociology students are the following:

Gallup, George and George Gallup, Jr. 1999. *The Gallup Poll Cumulative Index: Public Opinion, 1935–1997.* New York: Scholarly Resources, Inc.

Inventory of Marriage and Family Literature. 1994. vol. 19. St. Paul, MN: National Council on Family Relations.

Kaiser Index to Black Resources, 1948–1986. 1992. Brooklyn, NY: Carlson.

Sanders-May, Susan. 1966. *Family Violence: Index of New Information and Bibliography.* Washington, D.C.: Abbe Publications Association.

Women's Studies Index, 1999. 2000. Detroit, MI: Gale Group.

Citation indexes.   A third type of index, the citation index, lists articles that have referred to previous research by a particular author. When a researcher knows of one article—or author of articles—on a particular topic, newer, related materials can be found by locating articles that cite the original work or author. Thus you can find articles without depending on any subject classification system. This type of index is useful for determining the quality of a specific key research paper, or for tracing the developments in theory and methods that were stimulated by this key paper. A student can determine the number of times a key article has been used, as well as the names of the sociologists who have cited it. A citation index useful to sociologists follows:

Social Sciences Citation Index. Annual. Philadelphia, PA: Institute for Scientific Information. This service enables the user to identify recent articles that refer to earlier works. Each issue is divided into three parts. The Citation Index, arranged alphabetically by cited author, lists articles in which a particular work was cited. The Source Index lists alphabetically the authors who are citing the original work and gives bibliographic information for each article that cites the original work.

The Permaterm Subject Index lists articles by all the significant words in the titles. The index is issued three times a year and cumulates annually.

General abstracts.   Like indexes, abstracts provide a complete citation for each article and include a brief summary of its contents. Abstracts enable researchers to determine whether an article is useful without having to locate and read it. This can be important when students are working in a library with a small periodical collection and must depend on interlibrary loans to acquire articles. A general abstract covering topics in the field of sociology is the following:

> *Sociological Abstracts.* Annual. New York: Sociological Abstracts. This source indexes and summarizes over 6,000 books and journal articles each year. Within broad subject areas—such as group interaction, social differentiation, and feminist studies—abstracts are arranged alphabetically by author. The last issue of each year contains cumulative author and subject indexes. The abstract is currently issued five times a year.

Specialized abstracts.   A specialized abstract covers a particular topic in greater detail than general abstracts and cites research that is published outside the field of sociology. A particularly useful one to sociologists is the following:

> *Criminal Justice Abstracts.* Annual. Hackensack, NJ: National Council on Crime and Delinquency. This quarterly (entitled *Crime and Delinquency Literature* through 1976) abstracts books and journals in the area of crime and delinquency. Abstracts are arranged under broad subject areas, such as correction and law enforcement. There is a detailed subject index. Each issue also contains a review of current developments in one area, such as aid to victims, employee theft, and delinquency prevention.

Examples of other specialized abstracts within the broader discipline of sociology include the following:

> *Abstracts in Social Gerontology.* Annual. Newbury Park, CA: Sage.
>
> *Child Development Abstracts and Bibliography.* Annual. Chicago, IL: University of Chicago Press.
>
> *Sage Family Studies Abstracts.* Annual. Beverly Hills, CA: Sage.
>
> *Sage Race Relations Abstracts.* Annual. Beverly Hills, CA: Sage.
>
> *Women's Studies Abstracts.* Annual. New York: Rush.

6.1.7 Bibliographies

Bibliographies constitute a particularly important category of finding aids. An individual bibliography might list any or all of the following: books, periodicals, periodical articles, published documents, unpublished documents, or unpublished manuscripts. Our focus is on bibliographies as finding aids for articles and for books other than reference books. Whenever you use a bibliography that does not list journal articles, you must also consult a periodical index or abstract in order to compile a thorough reading list on the topic.

Some bibliographies provide only citations for the books and articles they list; others provide annotations as well. Standard bibliographic citation form for journal articles includes author, title, journal name, volume and sometimes number, and date of publication. Usually, the information is sufficiently complete to locate the item. Annotated bibliographies provide more information, helping you decide if an individual title might be useful. An annotation is a brief summary of the article or book's content along with a comment on its quality.

Bibliographies come in two formats: Some are short and are appended to articles or books, and others are book length.

Appended bibliographies.   Appended bibliographies identify titles that are either cited in the article or book or are relevant to the topic being discussed. You can use a bibliography appended to a reliable book or article as a guide to your readings on the topic. To identify appended bibliographies on a particular topic, you may consult the following:

> *Bibliographic Index.* Annual. New York: H. W. Wilson. Published in April and August and in a cumulated annual volume in December, this work lists, by subject, bibliographies with fifty or more entries that are published separately or as parts of books or periodicals in English and West European languages. Citations specify whether the bibliographies are annotated. Each volume begins with a prefatory note that briefly explains the forms used in the entries.

Book-length bibliographies.   Bibliographic indexes also identify book-length bibliographies. Their scope is ordinarily wider than that of appended bibliographies. Some book-length bibliographies are published only once and are retrospective in nature. Here is an example of this type:

> Aldous, Joan. *International Bibliography of Research in Marriage and the Family, 1900–1964.* 1967. St. Paul, MN: Family Social Science, University of Minnesota.

Others are published periodically, sometimes annually, and are called *current bibliographies.* Each new edition lists titles that have appeared since the previous edition. However, most current bibliographies have a one- to two-year lag time between the publication of a book and its citation.

Some useful current bibliographies cover a particular academic discipline, such as sociology, or a group of related disciplines, such as social sciences. Generally, the coverage includes articles as well as books, and the scope is international. The following is an example:

> *International Bibliography of Sociology.* Annual. London, UK: Tavistock. One of a set entitled *International Bibliography of the Social Sciences,* this volume attempts to provide comprehensive coverage of scholarly publications in the field, regardless of country of origin, language, or type. Three to five thousand citations are arranged in a detailed classification scheme, with author and subject indexes providing complete access. Citations are not annotated. All information is given in French and English. Although the volume is published each year, there is a one- to two-year lag time.

National libraries, such as the British Library or the Library of Congress, have copies of most of the important books on all subjects that are available in that country. Therefore, the subject catalog of the Library of Congress, available in most U.S. college and university libraries, can be used as a reasonably comprehensive current bibliography on most topics:

> U.S. Library of Congress. Annual. *Subject Catalog: A Cumulative List of Works Represented by Library of Congress Printed Cards.* Washington, D.C.: Library of Congress. Published in quarterly, yearly, and five-year cumulative editions since 1950, the *Subject Catalog* lists books cataloged by the Library of Congress and other major libraries in the United States. Each edition offers the single most comprehensive bibliography of works on every subject (excluding works of fiction), and from all parts of the world, that have become available during the period it covers. Subject headings are cross-referenced.

The following bibliographies contain materials with potential use for students of sociology:

> Aday, R. H. 1988. *Crime and the Elderly: An Annotated Bibliography.* New York: Greenwood.
>
> De Young, Mary. 1987. *Child Molestation: An Annotated Bibliography.* Jefferson, NC: McFarland.
>
> Engeldinger, E. A. 1986. *Spouse Abuse: An Annotated Bibliography of Violence between Mates.* Metuchen, NJ: Scarecrow.
>
> Ghorayshi, P. 1990. *The Sociology of Work: A Critical Annotated Bibliography.* New York: Garland.
>
> Kinlock, G. C. 1987. *Social Stratification: An Annotated Bibliography.* New York: Garland.
>
> Norquest, Joan. 1988. *The Homeless in America: A Bibliography.* Santa Cruz, CA: Reference and Research Services.
>
> ———. 1988. *Substance Abuse I: Drug Abuse: A Bibliography.* Santa Cruz, CA: Reference and Research Services.
>
> ———. 1990. *Substance Abuse II: Alcohol Abuse: A Bibliography.* Santa Cruz, CA: Reference and Research Services.
>
> ———. 1991. *The Elderly in America: A Bibliography.* Santa Cruz, CA: Reference and Research Services.

6.2   GENERAL PERIODICALS AND NEWSPAPERS

6.2.1   *General Periodicals*

General periodicals contain articles on a range of topics intended to attract general readers with varied interests. News magazines, hobby or recreational magazines, and a host of publications such as the *Saturday Review* and the *New Yorker* are all classified as general periodicals. A student can find information on specific topics covered in general periodicals by consulting the *Readers' Guide to Periodical Literature* in printed format on the library shelf, going back for several decades, or on the CD-ROM Database Network going back to 1983.

In addition to broadening a student's knowledge and outlook, general periodicals can also serve a legitimate research function for sociologists. Many general periodicals include regular features on important social problems (such as poverty, unemployment, or busing) and public opinion (attitudes toward marijuana smoking, abortion, and so on). Among the major general periodicals that are nonsociological but that emphasize social and political affairs are the *New York Times Magazine, Atlantic Monthly, Newsweek, U.S. News and World Report, Time,* and *Harper's.* General periodicals reporting current events and issues of interest to the sociologist usually do not analyze them from a sociological perspective. However, one general periodical that does is the following:

> *Society* (formerly *Transaction: Social Science and Modern Society*). Annual. New Brunswick, NJ: Rutgers University Press. Written for the layperson by well-known sociologists and other social scientists, this periodical covers a wide variety of topics in the areas of government, housing, welfare, law, race relations, and education. It is issued monthly.

Other examples of similar utility are *Business Week, Psychology Today,* and *Library Journal.* These periodicals cover professional news, trends, developments, and other events for the professions. Articles are often written by professionals in the field.

6.2.2   Newspapers

Newspapers are regularly issued publications (daily, weekly, semiweekly) that report events and discuss topics of current interest. The types of information that sociologists may find useful include news items comprising factual reporting of events; editorials, representing the editors' thinking on current issues; feature articles, presenting an investigation of a topic; and columns, including comments or reports on current events or issues by journalists. In newspapers you can find factual information on topics such as crime or intergroup conflict. Also, you can identify attitudes of people toward important social issues.

Among the newspapers distinguished for the extensive coverage they give to national affairs are the *Washington Post* and the *New York Times.* You can find articles that cover specific topics in the *New York Times* by consulting its index:

> *New York Times Index.* Annual. New York: New York Times. This index provides subject access to *New York Times* news stories, editorials, and other features. Published every two weeks, it is cumulated annually. Each entry begins with a subject, followed by references to other sections in the index (if there are any). Then the article is summarized. For the sake of brevity, the citation identifies each month by one or two letters, followed by the date, a roman numeral for a section, an arabic page number, and sometimes a column number, prefaced by a colon. The year is always identified on the cover and title page and is essential information to record when copying citations. One important item to note

in using this index is that the cross-references that directly follow the subject in each entry must be checked in the index to obtain a complete citation. You cannot identify the exact location of the articles noted in this section without doing so.

The following major newspapers have indexes available either in print or on microfilm:

Chicago Tribune
Houston Post
Los Angeles Times
National Observer
New Orleans Times-Picayune
New York Times
Times of London
Wall Street Journal
Washington Post

You may need coverage of an important topic from a number of different perspectives. In such a research project, a local newspaper or the *New York Times* would not suit your needs. For example, you may want to compare the coverage of right-to-work laws presented in a Southwestern newspaper to those presented in a Northern newspaper. For that type of project you should consult the following:

NewsBank. Annual. Greenwich, CT: Urban Affairs Library. This publication not only indexes articles on subjects from over 150 daily and weekly urban newspapers, but also includes the articles themselves on microfiche. The index is divided into thirteen subject sections—Business and Economic Development, Consumer Affairs, Government Structure, Social Relations, Welfare and Poverty, Housing and Urban Renewal, Law and Order, Education, Political Development, Health, Transportation, Environment, and Employment—each contained in a separate binder. The microfiche copies of the articles are located in the back of each binder. Note that there is a separate binder containing an Introduction, a Guide to the Index, and an overall Name Index. The Guide to the Index section is designed as an aid to determine in which of the thirteen major subject categories a particular topic is covered. A cumulative subject index for each topical area is provided annually.

6.3   ACADEMIC JOURNALS

Articles in scholarly journals, written by specialists and critically evaluated by other scholars prior to being accepted for publication, represent the most recent additions to an academic discipline's shared store of knowledge or to its debate on a particular topic. Students who are interested in compiling a well-rounded and up-to-date reading list on a topic should always consult the scholarly journals.

Most journals contain a book review section in which scholars in the field present critiques of recently published books. These reviews usually give an accurate assessment of the book's quality from the field's standpoint. When faced with a choice of several books, you can save time by reading book reviews to select the most useful, authoritative sources.

Sociologists publish numerous journals, some rather general in scope, and some devoted to a particular subfield within the discipline, such as family studies. As a sociology student, you should be familiar with the following journals:

American Journal of Sociology. Annual. Chicago, IL: University of Chicago Press. This bimonthly journal, first published in 1895, reports research and fieldwork on a variety of topics in sociology. The articles range from twelve to fifty pages, though the average length is approximately twenty-seven pages. Short papers that summarize recent empirical research are included in the Research Notes section. Each issue also contains a comprehensive book review section with evaluative reviews.

American Sociological Review. Annual. Washington, D.C.: American Sociological Association. The official journal of the American Sociological Association, this bimonthly publication, first published in 1936, contains articles that cover all areas of sociology. The average length of articles is twelve pages. The journal also reports the activities of the Association and contains a section for comments and discussions of previous articles.

Social Forces. Annual. Chapel Hill, NC: University of North Carolina Press. This quarterly, first published in 1922, contains articles averaging twenty pages in length, includes papers on all aspects of sociology. The journal is international in scope, but articles about the United States predominate. Each issue contains a number of authored book reviews. Special issues, in which all the articles focus on a specific topic, appear at least once a year.

These major sociology journals represent a small fraction of the scholarly periodicals published by sociologists. Students can find a brief description of other scholarly journals within sociology and other academic disciplines by consulting the following:

Katz, Bill, Linda S. Katz, William A. Katz, and Barry G. Richards, eds. 2000. *Magazines for Libraries.* 3d ed. New York: Bowker. This work contains publication information and descriptive and evaluative annotations for over 6,500 periodicals and newspapers. Titles are organized into approximately one hundred subject areas, such as Aeronautics Space Science, Africa, Business Education, General Magazines, Government Magazines, History, Newspapers, and Opinion Magazines. Because of this topical organization, the volume's index is particularly useful for locating individual titles.

The list starting on page 126 is a list of professional journals of interest to sociologists, political scientists, and other social scientists. Some are refereed—that is, the articles they contain are sent out to scholars for review before publication—while others are not. But all contain articles with potential use for sociology students.

Addiction

Addictive Behaviors

Administration and Society

Administration in Social Work

Administrative Science Quarterly

Adolescence

Age and Aging

Aging and Society

AIDS and Public Policy Journal

Alcohol Health and Research World

Alcoholism Treatment Quarterly

American Anthropologist

American Behavioral Scientist

American Demographics

American Economic Review

American Educational Research Journal

American Ethnologist

American Indian Culture and Research Journal

American Journal of Community Psychology

American Journal of Drug and Alcohol Abuse

American Journal of Economics and Sociology

American Journal of Education

American Journal of Family Therapy

American Journal of Orthopsychiatry

American Journal of Physical Anthropology

American Journal of Political Science

American Journal of Psychiatry

American Journal of Psychoanalysis

American Journal of Psychology

American Journal of Psychotherapy

American Journal of Public Health

American Journal of Sociology

American Political Science Review

American Politics Quarterly

American Psychologist

American Sociological Review

American Sociologist

Annals of the American Academy of Political and Social Science

Annual Review of Anthropology

Annual Review of Psychology

Annual Review of Sociology

Anthropological Quarterly

Applied Psycholinguistics

Archive of Sexual Behavior

Australian and New Zealand Journal of Sociology

Australian Journal of Anthropology

Australian Journal of Politics and History

Australian Journal of Social Issues

Behavior Research and Therapy

Behavior Research Methods, Instruments, and Computers

Behavior Science Research

Behavior Therapy

Behavioral Health Management

Behavioral Neuroscience

Behavioral Science

Black Scholar

British Journal of Clinical Psychology

British Journal of Criminology

British Journal of Educational Psychology

British Journal of Law and Society

British Journal of Political Science

British Journal of Psychology

British Journal of Social Psychology

British Journal of Sociology

Cambridge Journal of Education

Canadian Journal of Behavioral Science

Canadian Journal of Criminology

Canadian Journal of Economics

Canadian Journal of Experimental Psychology

Canadian Journal of Political Science

Canadian Journal of Psychiatry

Canadian Journal of Psychology

Canadian Psychologist

Canadian Psychology

Canadian Review of Sociology and Anthropology

Child Abuse and Neglect

Child and Adolescent Social Work Journal

Child Development

Child Psychiatry and Human Development

Child Study Journal

Child Welfare

Clinical Social Work Journal

Cognitive Psychology

Communication Quarterly

Communication Reports

Communication Research

Communication Theory

Communist Affairs

Communist and Post-Communist Studies

Communities

Community Development Journal

Community Mental Health Journal

Comparative Education Review

Comparative Political Studies

Comparative Politics

Comparative Studies in Society and History

Conflict Studies

Contemporary Drug Problems

Contemporary Economic Policy

Contemporary Education

Contemporary Sociology

Counseling Psychologist

Crime and Delinquency

Criminal Justice and Behavior

Criminal Justice Ethics

Criminal Justice Review

Criminology

Critical Quarterly

Critical Review

Critical Studies in Mass Communication

Cultural Anthropology

Current Sociology

Day Care and Early Education

Death Studies

Demography

Developmental Psychology

Dissertation Abstracts International, A: The Humanities and Social Sciences

Drugs and Society

Economic Development and Cultural Change

Economic History Review

Economic Inquiry

Economic Journal

Economist

Economy and Society

Education

Education and Urban Society

Educational and Psychological Measurement

Educational Gerontology

Educational Psychology Review

Educational Review

Educational Studies

Educational Theory

Environment and Behavior

Environmental Ethics

Environmental Policy and Law

Environmental Politics

Ethics

Ethnic and Racial Studies

Ethnic Groups

Ethnohistory

Ethnology

Ethnology and Sociobiology

European Economic Review

European Journal of Political Research

European Journal of Political Science

European Studies Review

Experimental Study of Politics

Families in Society

Family and Community Health

Family Economics Review

Family Planning Perspectives

Family Process

Family Relations

Feminist Issues

Feminist Studies

Forum of Applied Research and Public Policy

Free Inquiry in Creative Sociology

Futurist

Gender and Society

Gerontologist

Global Political Assessment

Global Risk Assessment: Issues, Concepts and Applications

Growth and Change

Harvard Educational Review

Health and Social Work

Higher Education Quarterly

Hispania

Hispanic Journal of Behavioral Sciences

History and Political Economy

History and Theory

History of Political Thought

History of the Human Sciences

Human Communication Research

Human Ecology

Human Ecology Forum

Human Organization

Human Relations

Human Rights

Human Rights Quarterly

Human Rights Review

Humanist

Impact of Science in Society

Individual Psychology

Industrial and Labor Relations Review

Industrial Relations

Information Sciences

Innovation Higher Education

Inter-American Economic Affairs

International Affairs

International Criminal Justice Review

International Development Review

International Economic Review

International Interactions

International Journal of Aging and Human Development

International Journal of Comparative Sociology

International Journal of Eating Disorders

International Journal of Group Psychotherapy

International Journal of Health Services

International Journal of Offender Therapy and Comparative Criminology

International Journal of Political Education

International Journal of Public Administration

International Journal of Social Psychiatry

International Journal of Sociology of Law

International Journal of Sociology of the Family

International Journal of Urban and Regional Research

International Labour Review

International Migration Review

International Organization

International Political Science Review

International Relations

International Review of Education

International Review of Social History

International Security

International Social Science Journal

International Social Science Review

International Social Work

International Studies

International Studies Quarterly

Interpretation: Journal of Political Philosophy

Journal for the Scientific Study of Religion

Journalism Quarterly

Journal of Abnormal Child Psychology

Journal of Abnormal Psychology

Journal of Addictive Diseases

Journal of Adolescence

Journal of Adolescent Chemical Dependency

Journal of Adolescent Health

Journal of Adolescent Research

Journal of Advertising

Journal of African Studies

Journal of Aging and Social Policy

Journal of Aging Studies

Journal of American History

Journal of American Indian Education

Journal of Anthropological Research

Journal of Applied Behavior Analysis

Journal of Applied Behavioral Science

Journal of Applied Communication Research

Journal of Applied Gerontology

Journal of Applied Psychology

Journal of Applied Social Psychology

Journal of Asian and African Studies

Journal of Asian Studies

Journal of Behavior Therapy and Experimental Psychiatry

Journal of Black Psychology

Journal of Black Studies

Journal of Business Communication

Journal of Child and Family Studies

Journal of Child Psychology and Psychiatry and Allied Disciplines

Journal of Clinical Child Psychology

Journal of Clinical Psychology

Journal of Communication

Journal of Community Health

Journal of Comparative and Physiological Psychology

Journal of Comparative Economics

Journal of Comparative Family Studies

Journal of Comparative Psychology

Journal of Conflict Resolution

Journal of Consumer Research

Journal of Contemporary Ethnography

Journal of Contemporary History

Journal of Counseling Psychology

Journal of Creative Behavior

Journal of Criminal Justice

Journal of Criminal Law and Criminology

Journal of Cross-Cultural Psychology

Journal of Democracy

Journal of Developing Areas

Journal of Development Economics

Journal of Development Studies

Journal of Divorce and Remarriage

Journal of Drug Education

Journal of Drug Issues

Journal of Econometrics

Journal of Economic History

Journal of Economic Issues

Journal of Economic Literature

Journal of Economic Perspectives

Journal of Economic Theory

Journal of Education

Journal of Educational Measurement

Journal of Educational Research

Journal of Elder Abuse and Neglect

Journal of Environmental Economics and Management

Journal of Environmental Management

Journal of Ethnic Studies

Journal of Experimental Child Psychology

Journal of Experimental Education

Journal of Experimental Social Psychology

Journal of Family History

Journal of Family Issues

Journal of Family Law

Journal of Family Psychology

Journal of Family Violence

Journal of Gambling Studies

Journal of General Education

Journal of General Psychology

Journal of Genetic Psychology

Journal of Gerontological Social Work

Journal of Gerontology

Journal of Group Psychotherapy, Psychodrama, and Sociometry

Journal of Health and Social Behavior

Journal of Health Politics, Policy, and Law

Journal of Homosexuality

Journal of Housing

Journal of Housing and Community Development

Journal of Humanistic Psychology

Journal of Human Resources

Journal of InterAmerican Studies and World Affairs

Journal of Interdisciplinary History

Journal of Interdisciplinary Studies

Journal of International Affairs

Journal of Interpersonal Violence

Journal of Japanese Studies

Journal of Labor Research

Journal of Latin American Studies

Journal of Law and Economics

Journal of Law and Politics

Journal of Legal Studies

Journal of Leisure Research

Journal of Libertarian Studies

Journal of Management

Journal of Management Studies

Journal of Marital and Family Therapy

Journal of Marriage and the Family

Journal of Medical Ethics

Journal of Memory and Language

Journal of Modern African Studies

Journal of Modern History

Journal of Near Eastern Studies

Journal of Negro Education

Journal of Nonverbal Behavior

Journal of Offender Rehabilitation

Journal of Parapsychology

Journal of Peace Research

Journal of Peace Science

Journal of Peasant Studies

Journal of Pediatric Psychology

Journal of Personal Assessment

Journal of Personality

Journal of Personality and Social Psychology

Journal of Police Science and Administration

Journal of Policy Analysis and Management

Journal of Political and Military Sociology

Journal of Political Economy

Journal of Political Science

Journal of Politics

Journal of Popular Culture

Journal of Primary Prevention

Journal of Psychiatric Research

Journal of Psychohistory

Journal of Psychology

Journal of Psychosomatic Research

Journal of Public Administration Research and Theory

Journal of Public Policy

Journal of Rehabilitation

Journal of Research and Development in Education

Journal of Research in Crime and Delinquency

Journal of School Psychology

Journal of Sex Research

Journal of Social History

Journal of Social Issues

Journal of Social Policy

Journal of Social, Political, and Economic Studies

Journal of Social Psychology

Journal of Social Work Education

Journal of Special Education

Journal of Specialists in Group Work

Journal of Sport and Social Issues

Journal of Studies on Alcohol

Journal of Substance Abuse Treatment

Journal of the American Academy of Child and Adolescent Psychiatry

Journal of the American Geriatrics Society

Journal of the American Oriental Society

Journal of the American Planning Association

Journal of the American Society for Information Science

Journal of the Experimental Analysis of Behavior

Journal of the History of Ideas

Journal of the History of the Behavioral Sciences

Journal of Theoretical Politics

Journal of the Philosophy of Sport

Journal of the Royal Anthropological Institute

Journal of the Royal Society of Health

Journal of Third World Studies

Journal of Traumatic Stress

Journal of Urban Affairs

Journal of Urban Analysis

Journal of Urban History

Journal of Verbal Learning and Verbal Behavior

Journal of Youth and Adolescence

Journals of Gerontology

Journals of Gerontology (Series B: Psychological and Social Sciences)

Language

Language Learning

Latin American Research Review

Law and Contemporary Problems

Law and Philosophy

Law and Policy Quarterly

Law and Society Review

Learning and Motivation

Linguistic Inquiry

Linguistics and Education

Literature and Psychology

Man-Environment Systems

Management Communication Quarterly

Management Science

Marriage and Family Review

Mathematical Social Sciences

Media, Culture, and Society

Micropolitics

Mid-American Review of Sociology

Middle East Journal

Middle Eastern Studies

Modern Asian Studies

Modern Language Journal

Monographs for the Society for Research in Child Development

Multivariate Behavioral Research

New Political Science

New Politics

Papers on Language and Literature

Peace Research

Perspectives on Political Science

Philosophical Quarterly

Philosophical Review

Philosophy and Phenomenological Research

Philosophy and Public Affairs

Philosophy and Rhetoric

Philosophy and Science

Philosophy of the Social Sciences

Policy and Politics

Political Anthropology

Political Behavior

Political Communication

Political Communication and Persuasion

Political Geography Quarterly

Political Psychology

Political Quarterly

Political Research Quarterly

Political Science

Political Science Quarterly

Political Science Review

Political Science Reviewer

Political Studies

Political Theory

Politics

Politics and Society

Politics and the Life Sciences

Polity

Population and Development Review

Population Bulletin

Proceedings of the Academy of Political Science

Professional Psychology, Research, and Practice

Psychiatric Quarterly

Psychiatry

Psychoanalytic Review

Psychobiology

Psychological Assessment

Psychological Bulletin

Psychological Record

Psychological Reports

Psychological Science

Psychology and Aging

Psychology in the Schools

Psychology of Women Quarterly

Psychophysiology

Psychosomatic Medicine

Public Administration

Public Administration Review

Public Health Reports

Public Law

Public Management

Public Opinion Quarterly

Public Policy

Public Relations Quarterly

Public Relations Review

Public Welfare

Quarterly Journal of Economics

Race and Class

Radical America

Radical History Review

Research in Education

Research in Higher Education

Research on Aging

Review of Black Political Economy

Review of Economics and Statistics

Review of Economic Studies

Review of Educational Research

Review of International Studies

Review of Law and Social Change

Review of Metaphysics

Review of Politics

Revolutionary World

Rural Sociology

Sage

Science

Science and Public Affairs

Science and Public Policy

Science and Society

Sciences, The

Sex Roles

Simulation

Simulation and Games

Simulation and Gaming

Skeptical Inquirer

Small Group Research

Social Action

Social and Economic Studies

Social Behavior and Personality

Social Biology

Social Casework

Social Forces

Social History

Social Indicators Research

Social Justice

Social Philosophy and Policy

Social Policy

Social Problems

Social Psychology Quarterly

Social Research

Social Science and Medicine

Social Science Information

Social Science Journal

Social Science Quarterly

Social Science Research

Social Science Review

Social Theory and Practice

Social Work

Social Work Education

Social Work with Groups

Socialism and Democracy

Socialists Review

Society

Sociological Analysis and Theory

Sociological Inquiry

Sociological Methods and Research

Sociological Perspectives

Sociological Quarterly

Sociological Review

Sociology

Sociology and Social Research

Sociology of Education

Sociology of Religion

Sociology of Sport Journal

Southern Economic Journal

Studies in Comparative Communism

Studies in Conflict and Terrorism

Studies in Family Planning

Studies in Philosophy and Education

Suicide and Life-Threatening Behavior

Survey

Technological Forecasting and Social Change

Technology and Culture

Terrorism

Theory and Decision

Theory and Society

Third World

Urban Affairs Quarterly

Urban Affairs Review

Urban and Social Change Review

Urban Anthropologist

Urban Anthropology and Studies of Cultural Systems and World Economic Development

Urban Education

Urban Review

Urban Studies

Victimology

Violence and Victims

War and Society

Western Journal of Communications

Western Political Quarterly

Women and Environments

Women and Politics: A Quarterly Journal of Research and Policy Studies

Women and Work

Women's Studies International Forum

Women's Studies Quarterly

World Affairs

World Development

World Marxist Review

World Policy Journal

World Politics

Youth and Society

6.4   RESEARCHING BOOKS

Academic books, along with articles from professional journals, will usually form the greater part of the sociology student's reading list on an individual research topic. If the sources of information used in book research are unreliable, the results will be unsatisfactory. There are two principal paths for a student to take in evaluating a book-length study: Rely on book reviews, or examine the bibliographic character of the book itself.

6.4.1   Book Review Sources

Since 1975, reviews appearing in most of the major sociology journals have been indexed in the book review section of the Social Sciences Index (see the previous discussion of indexes). The reviews are indexed by the name of the author of the book; the journal, volume, and date; and the page of the review. There is a time lag, however—sometimes more than a year—between a book's publication and the appearance of a review in a scholarly journal. The need for more current reviews led to a new type of journal, consisting entirely of scholarly book reviews. The journal for sociologists is the following:

> *Contemporary Sociology: A Journal of Reviews.* Annual. Washington, D.C.: American Sociological Association. This journal reviews books published in every area of sociology, plus many in related fields, such as education. Each issue also contains feature essays that review several books on related topics or the works of one major author. The reviews are arranged by broad subject areas, and each issue also contains a list of new publications.

For reviews of books on the popular market, along with many very academic selections, the *New York Review of Books* (1976–present) and the *New York Times Book Review* (1923–present) are two reliable sources.

6.4.2   Bibliographic Character of the Work

By examining a book closely, you can usually assess the quality of information presented. The preface and introduction give clues to who the author is, why the work was written, and what methodology and research tools were used in the book's preparation. If the author is an acknowledged authority in the field, this fact will often be mentioned in the preface or the foreword.

The footnotes, the in-text references, and the extent and quality of the bibliography (or in some cases, the lack of one) can also serve as clues about the reliability of the work. If few or no original documents have been used, or if major works in the field have not been cited and evaluated, you have reason to question the quality of the book.

Finally, the reputation of the publisher or organization that sponsors a particular book says something about its value. Some publishers have rigid standards of scholarship and others do not. For example, the requirements of university presses are generally very high, and the major ones—such as Cambridge, Chicago, Michigan, and Harvard—are discriminating publishers of studies in sociology.

6.5   U.S. GOVERNMENT PUBLICATIONS

6.5.1   General Publications

U.S. government publications comprise all the printed public documents of the federal government. The materials include, for example, the official records of the meetings of Congress; the text of laws, court decisions, and public hearings and rulings of administrative and regulatory agencies; studies of economic and social issues commissioned by official agencies; and the compilation of statistics on a number of social and demographic characteristics of the U.S. population.

Federal publications provide sociologists with material for research in many subfields in sociology. You can find government publications that cover such topics as the educational attainment of minorities, sex discrimination, drug abuse, and a number of other social issues. However, the fact that a document is "official" is no automatic guarantee of the accuracy of the information or data it might contain; accuracy depends on the methods of information and data collection the agency used. Therefore, the use of these publications—like the use of any other source material—requires good judgment. You can identify relevant late nineteenth- and twentieth-century federal government publications by consulting the following:

U.S. Superintendent of Documents. Annual. *Monthly Catalog of United States Government Publications.* Washington, D.C.: Government Printing Office. This catalog, first published in 1885, is the most complete listing of federal documents available. The detailed indexes—subject, author/agency, and title—identify individual items by entry number. Entries identify individual author (if any), pagination, date, illustration notes, series title, and serial number, and include reference to any other publication superseded by this item as well as the Superintendent of Documents number. (U.S. documents are catalogued by this number in many libraries—especially those that are depositories.)

Cumulative Subject Index to the Monthly Catalog of United States Government Publications, 1900–1971. 1973. Washington, D.C.: Carrollton Press. This is a comprehensive subject index to more than 1 million publications listed in the *Monthly Catalog* from 1900 through 1971. To discover what has been published on a given subject, one first finds the topic and then goes to the appropriate subheading. This will be followed by one or more years in parentheses, each followed by one or more entry numbers, such as "(65) 14901." Then researchers must turn to the *Monthly Catalog* for the specified year (in this case, 1965) and locate the entry number (in this case, 14901) to find a complete citation for the publication.

6.5.2 U.S. Census Bureau Publications

U.S. Census Bureau publications are important resources. They allow sociology students to summarize social and demographic characteristics of various population groups in the United States by using descriptive statistics. We frequently think of the Census Bureau as a government agency that collects census data every ten years. There are actually ten categories of censuses, and data are collected and reported at different intervals. In addition to collecting data on national and state populations, the Census Bureau studies subpopulations that are of special interest. These studies are generally published in *Current Population Reports*. Recent reports, for example, have focused on the characteristics of blacks, persons of Hispanic origin, and poverty-level families.

Because the Census Bureau analyzes and publishes data, sociology students can locate relevant census materials by consulting guides and indexes to statistical reports published by the government. The following comprehensive volume indexes statistical studies by all government agencies. It can be used to locate a variety of statistics on a given topic:

> *American Statistics Index.* Annual. Washington, D.C.: Congressional Information Service. This commercially produced abstract has become an important source for identifying statistical publications of the U.S. government. It indexes and abstracts statistics on numerous topics from the publications of many government agencies, describes these publications, and has the material available on microfiche. This source is issued monthly in two sections—indexes and abstracts—and is cumulated annually. The index volume contains four separate indexes that list the publications by subject and name; by geographic, economic, and demographic categories; by title; and by agency report numbers. The abstract volume gives brief descriptions of the publications and their content.

The Census Bureau publishes an index to its own publications. If you require information on a topic that is routinely studied by the Census Bureau, you should consult the following:

> U.S. Bureau of the Census. Annual. *Bureau of the Census Catalog.* Washington, D.C.: Government Printing Office. An indispensable guide, first published in 1790, to materials issued by the Bureau of the Census and publications from other agencies that contain statistics, this catalog is published quarterly, updated with monthly supplements, and has annual cumulations. The basic volume is retrospective, covering the years 1790–1945 in Part I and 1946–1972 in Part II. The arrangement differs in each part. The material includes annotated lists of census publications for the years covered, followed by subject and geographical indexes. The annual cumulation lists and annotates only those publications issued during that year.

A number of reports or volumes published by the Census Bureau are useful to sociology students doing research. Two of these publications—*County and City Data Book* and *Historical Statistics of the United States*—have been discussed previously under other subheadings. These publications summarize many of the important findings of past censuses as well as more recent ones.

In addition to the population census, the Bureau also conducts surveys of housing, business, and manufacturing. A student who wants information about the structural or industrial characteristics of the United States can use these decade censuses to find past and current statistics. These censuses have the advantages and disadvantages discussed earlier.

Census publications provide, at little cost to the researcher, much descriptive information on various components of the American population. However, you should be aware of some serious problems with census data. Because most data are compiled every five or ten years, often a researcher must either find more current information or use the somewhat dated statistics published by the Census Bureau. Also, the design of the census survey does not always include the type of questions or issues that are of interest to sociology students. For example, a student comparing the educational or employment status of blacks with that of persons of Hispanic origin for a period between 1970 and 1990 would not be able use 1970 census data because the 1970 census of population did not ask persons of Hispanic origin to identify their racial or ethnic background. Another disadvantage of census publications is that they use only descriptive statistics to summarize the data. Their analysis does not indicate the relevance or meaning of trends. You can determine social and demographic differences within populations, but must look elsewhere for the causes of these differences.

INTERNET RESOURCES AND DISTANCE LEARNING

7.1 INTERNET RESOURCES FOR WRITING WELL

The preceding chapters of this book have given you much information about research and writing, but the Internet offers even more. Particularly good places to start your Internet search for help in writing are Web sites known as OWLs (Online Writing Labs), such as the Purdue University OWL at (http://owl.english.purdue.edu/). Several universities now offer their own OWLs, and you may want to check your own college's home page to see if it provides one. At the Purdue University OWL home page you will find a lot of helpful information. First, for people in the Purdue community, the Purdue OWL offers the following:

- One-on-one tutorials
- In-lab and in-class workshops
- Study materials for English as a Second Language
- Conversation groups for English practice
- A grammar hotline
- A collection of reference materials
- Computers and a printer
- A quiet space to study

Second, for everyone who visits the site, the OWL offers:

- *The Writing Lab Newsletter* (including on-line archives of back issues)
- resources for teachers on using the Writing Lab and OWL, including using OWL in the new English 106/108 course
- Writing Across the Curriculum resources

The Virginia Tech OWL (http://athena.english.vt.edu/~owl/index.htm) offers similar sources, including the following:

- GRAM—The Grammar Hotline is an e-mail based service open to the public. Come ask GRAM Owl a question!
- KIO—The "Know-It Owl," a self-help environment, is also open to the public.
- ETE—The Electronic Tutoring Environment is a one-on-one tutoring environment. Sorry, this area is restricted to Virginia Tech students, faculty, and staff. Note: if you need to make an appointment for the face-to-face writing center, you need to visit this page for details. This is only for on-line appointments.
- Links—The links lead to other places around Virginia Tech and the world that might be of interest to writers of all levels.

7.2   SOCIOLOGY RESOURCES ON THE INTERNET

Even large catalogs cannot now hold all the potential Internet resources for sociology. Fortunately, many Internet sites specialize in creating lists of links to excellent resources. Our purpose in this chapter is to help you get started in your Internet sociology research by providing you with a list of sites that will, when you follow their links to other sites and then follow the links you find there, lead you to thousands of sources of information for your research projects. As you have probably already discovered, your college library probably offers you on-line access to books, journal articles, and many other resources on-line.

For students using a text from one of the Pearson publishers (Prentice Hall, Longman, and others), *Research Navigator*™ (www.researchnavigator.com) may be the best first stop for information related to sociology. As stated on their Web page: Pearson's *Research Navigator*™ is the easiest way for students to start a research assignment or research paper. Complete with extensive help on the research process and four exclusive databases of credible and reliable source material, including the EBSCO Academic Journal and Abstract Database, *New York Times* Search by Subject Archive, "Best of the Web" Link Library, and *Financial Times* Article Archive and Company Financials, *Research Navigator*™ helps students quickly and efficiently make the most of their research time. Access to *Research Navigator*™ is free when purchased with many new Pearson textbooks.

Melissa Payton's (2004) booklet entitled *The Prentice Hall Guide to Evaluating Online Resources* (with *Research Navigator*™): *Sociology 2004*, is an excellent resource for Internet research in sociology. She deals with: how to find and evaluate on-line sources in sociology; and how to use *Research Navigator*™ with ContentSelect, The *New York Times* Search, Link Library; and the World Wide Web in sociology. This booklet—a $10 retail value—is free with adoption of any Pearson Publishing text in sociology, and students also receive free access to *Research Navigator*™ with the booklet.

Perhaps a mandatory stop for any serious student of sociology is the Web page of the American Sociological Association (www.asanet.org/), which offers links to state and international organizations involved in sociological services, along with a wide array of sociological resources.

You may not be aware that often a good starting place for research in sociology is your own college library or sociology department home page. Many colleges and universities have established sociology resource pages that are constantly changing to provide you with updated resources. Some of them are also highly entertaining and creative. The resources page entitled Sociology in Cyberspace (http://www.trinity.edu/~mkearl/), sponsored by the Sociology Department at Trinity University in San Antonio, Texas, provides a good example. Sociology in Cyberspace was established by Professor Michael C. Kearl of Trinity University's Department of Sociology and Anthropology. On the site's home page, Professor Kearl states:

> I am most interested in the potential of this cyberspace medium to inform and to generate discourse, to enhance information literacy, and to truly be a "theater of ideas." This site features commentary, data analyses (hey, we've become a "factoid" culture), occasional essays, as well as the requisite links, put together for courses taught by myself and my colleagues. Additions and updates are made daily.

Among the information available on Professor Kearl's site is the following:

- General sociology resources
- Sociological theory
- Data resources and some useful Web tools
- Methods and statistics
- Guide to writing research papers
- Exercising the imagination: Subject-based Inquiries
- Op-Ed
- Search engine for site—improved for the new millennium
- Sociology of Death and Dying. The premier tour.
- The Times of Our Lives: Social Contours of the Fourth Dimension. This path takes you just about everywhere, from circadian rhythms to the implications of historical ignorance.
- A Sociological Social Psychology. Another far-ranging tour, from the nature-nurture controversy to history's thumbprint on generations.
- Marriage & Family Life. On life's home base.
- Social Gerontology. We're in the midst of an aging revolution whose impacts will be felt for centuries to come.
- Social Inequality. Reflecting on the growing gap between America's haves and have-nots.
- Gender & Society. Have gender inequalities decreased or increased with social evolution?
- Race & Ethnicity. How well is the American melting pot dissolving inequalities between racial and ethnic groups?
- Sociology of Knowledge. To what extent are different types of knowledge socially constructed?
- Demography. Are social processes ultimately demographically determined?

Sociology students may now access international resources much more easily than in the past. The United Kingdom, for example, offers a wide array of resources, including The Social Science Information Gateway (http://sosig.ac.uk/). The Gateway's home page describes its services as follows:

- *What Is SOSIG?* The Social Science Information Gateway (SOSIG) is a freely available Internet service that aims to provide a trusted source of selected, high-quality Internet information for students, academics, researchers and practitioners in the social sciences, business, and law. It is part of the UK Resource Discovery Network.

- *SOSIG Internet Catalogue* The SOSIG Internet Catalogue is an on-line database of high-quality Internet resources. It offers users the chance to read descriptions of resources available over the Internet and to access those resources directly. The catalogue points to thousands of resources, and each one has been selected and described by a librarian or academic. The catalogue is browsable or searchable by subject area.

- *Social Science Search Engine* This is a database of over 50,000 Social Science Web pages. Whereas the resources found in the SOSIG Internet Catalogue have been selected by subject experts, those in the Social Science Search Engine have been collected by software called a "harvester" (similar mechanisms may be referred to as "robots" or "Web crawlers"). All the pages collected stem from the main Internet catalogue. This provides the equivalent of a social science search engine.

- *Social Science Grapevine* Grapevine is the "people oriented" side of SOSIG, offering a unique on-line source of career development opportunities for social science researchers in all sectors. Grapevine carries details of relevant training and development opportunities from employers and training providers. Researchers can also make their CVs available on-line and freely accessible to all visitors to the site. Grapevine's Likeminds section provides a forum for exchange of ideas and information about potential research opportunities and partnerships. If you want to find contacts in your field you can also check the social science departmental database.

7.3 A GUIDE TO DISTANCE LEARNING

7.3.1 *For Students Considering Distance Learning*

Perhaps you are apprehensive about taking a distance learning course, or perhaps you want to take one but simply do not know where to begin. In either case, this introduction will help you. You will have some important questions to ask before you sign up, and this section will address some of them.

Are distance learning courses effective? Initial studies indicate that if the amount of material learned is a valid criterion for effectiveness, then the answer is yes! After reviewing more than four hundred studies of the effectiveness of distance learning courses, Thomas L. Russell, Director Emeritus of Instructional Telecommunications at North Carolina State University, concluded that distance learning and classroom courses were equally effective (Young 2000).

This does not mean, however, that the two methods are the same in every respect. When they compared distance learning and classroom introductory psychology courses, Texas Tech psychology professors Ruth S. Maki and William S. Maki found that distance learning students scored from 5 to 10 percent higher on tests of knowledge, but that they expressed less satisfaction with their courses (Carr 2000). Furthermore, whereas students in classroom courses appreciated having more contact with their professors, their distance learning counterparts observed that on-line courses required more work than their comparable classroom experiences.

If you are a bit uneasy about taking a course in which your only contact with people will be through e-mail or over the Internet, you have a lot of company. New experiences are almost always a bit unsettling, and you may not be as comfortable with a computer as some of your friends are. The good news is that institutions that provide distance learning have gone to a lot of trouble to make your introduction to their courses as trouble-free as possible. After entering their Web sites, you will find easy-to-follow, step-by-step instructions and other sources of help on every aspect of your new education experience.

You may want to visit such a site to see what it is like. A good example is World Campus 101 (WC101), established by Penn State University and located at the following Web address: www.worldcampus.psu.edu. World Campus sociology course offerings include the following:

- Rural Organization
- Introductory Sociology
- Sociology of Aging
- Social Influence and Small Groups (On-Line Individual: one-semester delivery)
- Work and Occupations
- Gender, Occupations, and Professions

Are you likely to succeed in distance learning courses? The answer to this question depends on a number of factors, and every student will react to distance learning situations at least a little differently than any other. Among the factors that will influence your chances of success, however, are how comfortable you are with the following:

- Working alone
- Communicating with people without seeing them
- Accomplishing tasks without reminders from others
- Using computers
- Solving occasional technical problems on computers
- Learning how to use new software

How is distance learning different from classroom courses? Everything considered, distance learning and classroom courses are probably more alike than they are different. Like classroom courses, distance learning courses have an actual, living person as an instructor; actual, living people as students; and printed or printable course materials. In both classroom and distance learning, individual initiative and responsibility are required for success, and in both set-tings the quality of the course depends in large part on the competence of the instructor.

The primary differences are that in distance courses you will work alone on a computer and spend your course-related time according to your own schedule, rather than attending classes. While in classroom courses other students and the instructor have a physical presence, in distance learning your contact with others is in electronic form. Interestingly, many students report spending more time on their distance learning courses than on their classroom courses.

Distance learning, therefore, offers several advantages over regular class-room courses. You don't need to commute or relocate; your learning schedule can vary from day-to-day and week-to-week; you can connect on a whim or wait until something awakens you at 2 A.M. and you are unable to get back to sleep. In ad-dition, the interaction with other students in on-line courses is often more sat-isfying than you might first suspect. As messages start streaming back and forth, each student's personality is revealed. Some students send photos of themselves so that others have a better idea of who they are.

There is also a down side to on-line learning. The one factor that seems to ir-ritate distance learners most is that they cannot get instant feedback; you can't just raise your hand and receive an immediate answer to your questions, as you can in a classroom. A related drawback, subtle but profound, is that the non-verbal responses that students unwittingly come to count on in a classroom are missing from an on-line course. Is your on-line instructor frowning or smiling as she makes a certain comment? In other words, the act of communication is some-times more complex than we think. In addition, sometimes on-line course in-structions are not sufficiently focused or specific, and it may take several communications to understand an assignment.

Another potential difficulty with distance learning is that on-line students are less likely to appreciate their options than students in classrooms. Rather than welcome the chance to make their own choices, they tend to want to do ex-actly what the instructor wants.

Other problems occasionally appear in on-line courses. Sometimes course materials provide ambiguous instructions and out-of-date hyperlinks. Testing can be complicated and may require special passwords. Some students must go to their local community college to take examinations, but other on-line colleges simply remind students of their academic integrity statements. If you are social by nature, you may suffer from feelings of isolation. You may find that it takes longer to establish rapport with on-line students with whom you have little in common. There may be some initial confusion as you learn how to run the sys-tem and interact effectively, or you may have difficulty interpreting messages from other students. And, a problem you may encounter with your on-line teacher may also arise with your classmates: Lack of visual contact means a loss of in-flection. Humor and sarcasm are more difficult to detect in written communica-tions. Finally, you may face what seems at times to be an overwhelming volume of e-mail featuring a lot of repetition (Hara and King 1999).

This brief survey of characteristics of distance learning may help you deal with a range of on-line situations as they arise. All in all, if you assess your own personality correctly, your chances of success in distance learning are substantial.

7.3.2   Sociology Distance Learning Courses and Distance Learning Resources On-Line

New distance learning courses are appearing daily. In 1998, in its second survey of distance education programs, the U.S. Department of Education (1998) identified 1,680 programs offering 54,000 on-line courses and enrolling 1.6 million students. These figures represent a 72 percent increase in distance learning activity from 1995 to 1998. The number of sociology courses offered on-line, however, is not extensive, but here are some tips for locating those that do exist.

Your local bookstore (as well as amazon.com and barnesandnoble.com) offers several guides to distance learning. Your Internet search for a suitable course may take some time, since offerings change continuously. You can find links to many colleges and universities at Web U.S. Universities, by State (www.utexas. edu/world/univ/state/). You will also find that Western Governors University (www.wgu.edu) provides a list of sociology courses available at several other colleges. The list of general distance education resources on the Internet changes almost daily, but here are some that you may want to examine:

Resource	Internet Address
American Distance Education Consortium	www.adec.edu
Chronicle of Higher Education	www.chronicle.com
Distance Education at a Glance	www.uidaho.edu/evo /distglan.html
Distance-Educator.com	www.distance-educator. com
International Center for Distance Learning	www-icdl.open.ac.uk
Web-Based Learning Resources Library	www.knowledgeability. biz/weblearning/
World Lecture Hall	www.utexas.edu/world /lecture

7.3.3   For Students About to Take or Taking On-Line Courses

Once you have decided to take a distance learning course, decide to study effectively. Studying for distance learning courses requires the same sort of discipline as studying for classroom courses, with one notable difference. For some people, class attendance is energizing. It helps stimulate their desire to study. This stimulus is, of course, absent for distance learners, but e-mail communication with other students and the instructor may serve the same purpose for some. In general, the same study habits that lead to success in regular courses also lead to success in on-line courses. In order to make the point with perhaps a little humor, we offer the following scenarios about two distance learners, Sidney and Jan.

Sidney spends twenty hours per week studying for his on-line course in animal husbandry. His friends affectionately call his room at the Queens YMCA "Pompeii," for Sidney's course materials, when they can be found at all, are likely to be located under piles of laundry, empty cereal boxes, or bags of cat litter. Sidney is a night person. His most productive hours, when he is most alert, are from 8 P.M. to 1 A.M. He reserves this prime time for playing video games and watching his favorite videos, stacks of which help to keep his floor, except for an occasional few square inches, invisible. Sidney always studies in the morning, when, bleary-eyed, he most enjoys the cacophony created by his electric fan, the television, four parakeets, three cats, and his pet armadillo. Sidney studies sporadically, and the morning hours drag on as he anxiously awaits the mail, praying each day for the overdue check from his uncle Rudolph, who has promised to fund Sidney's education if Sidney would stay at least fifty miles from Rudolph's home in Casper, Wyoming. When Sidney reads the text for his on-line course, the words all slide through his field of vision without effort and without effect, and he is rarely able to recall content five minutes after it has been perused. Interruptions in study time always take priority, especially when Sidney's friend Morris, who is determined to teach Sidney's cats to play badminton, comes to visit.

Jan is a tank commander in the Israeli army reserve. When she awakens at 5 A.M., her golden retriever, Moshe, delivers the newspaper to her bed, turns on the coffeemaker, and sits at attention, awaiting his first command of the day. Jan's most effective hours are in the morning, and three days a week she spends three morning hours concentrating intently on the materials for her on-line course in financial planning. Her Jerusalem condominium is quiet during her study time not only because Jan's only electrical appliances are her coffeemaker and microwave oven, but also because her neighbors have learned that life in the neighborhood is much more pleasant if Jan is not disturbed. As she studies, her room floods with morning light, and Jan methodically crosses off her well-planned list each successive course requirement as she accomplishes it.

Sidney and Jan may not be exactly typical students, but you get the idea. To study effectively you must be organized, set aside prime time in a quiet place, and concentrate completely on your study materials.

Morgan (1991) has identified two approaches that students take to distance learning. When following the first, less effective method, which Morgan calls the *surface approach*, students focus on the signs. This is to say that they see the trees rather than the forest. They concentrate on the text or instruction itself rather than on catching the idea or spirit of what is going on. They focus on specific elements of the task rather than on the whole task. Less effective students like to memorize data, rules, and procedures, which become crutches, substitutes for the more important task of understanding concepts. They also unreflectively associate concepts and facts, failing to understand how specific facts are related to certain concepts, and therefore confusing principles with evidence for those principles. Moreover, they consider assignments as mere tasks, or requirements imposed by the instructor, instead of as ways to learn skills or understand concepts that meaningfully relate to the goals of the course or to the realities of life.

As an alternative to this surface method, Morgan proposes a deep approach, in which the student focuses on the concepts being studied and on the instructor's arguments as opposed to the tasks or directions for assignments. The deep approach encourages students to relate new ideas to the real world, to constantly distinguish evidence (data) from argument (interpretations of data), and to organize the course material in a way that is personally meaningful.

Brundage, Keane, and Mackneson (1993) have found that successful distance learners are able to do the following:

- Assume responsibility for motivating themselves
- Maintain their own self-esteem irrespective of emotional support that may or may not be gained from the instructor, other students, family, or friends
- Understand their own strengths and limitations, and ask for help in areas of weakness
- Take the time to work hard at effectively relating to the other students
- Continually clarify for themselves and others precisely what it is that they are learning and become confident in the quality of their own observations
- Constantly relate the course content to their own personal experience

One final thought: Studies indicate that the drop-out rate for distance learners is higher than that for students in traditional courses. In part this is because distance learners tend to underestimate their other obligations and the time it will take to successfully complete their on-line course. Before you begin, be sure that you allow enough time not only to complete your course, but to do so with a reasonable measure of enjoyment. Good luck in your adventure in distance education. Armed with the information in this introduction, your chances of success are good.

DOING SOCIAL RESEARCH

Social analysis is the systematic attempt to explain social events by placing them within a series of meaningful contexts. We call this activity *social science*, and we conduct it using methods that are often quantitative in nature. These quantitative methods of research are much the same in social science as they are in any other scientific field. To understand them, we should begin with a brief look at what we mean by the terms *science* and *scientific method*.

8.1   THINKING SCIENTIFICALLY

We tend to use the word *science* too loosely, referring to things that are not strictly science. Hoover and Donovan (1995:4–5) describe three common uses of the term *science* that divert our understanding from what science really is. First, people often—and wrongly—think of science as technology. In fact, technology is a product of science. Technology results from the application of science to different tasks. For instance, the technology involved in sending people to the moon came into existence, over time, as people decided how to use discoveries they made through the application of scientific principles. Although the lunar module that landed in the Sea of Tranquillity is definitely a "piece of technology," it is not "science."

A second misconception is that science is a specific body of knowledge that discloses to us the rules by which the natural world works. To say that "science tells us" something is misleading. For example, it is not science that "tells" us smoking is dangerous to our health. It is people, who, investigating the effects of smoking tobacco on a variety of human pathologies, conclude that smoking is a very harmful practice. The body of knowledge these people produce is evidence, accumulated through scientific inquiry, of the effects of smoking. It is important not to mistake the body of knowledge for the mode of inquiry that helps researchers to produce it.

Finally, Hoover and Donovan point out that it is also misleading to think of science as an activity conducted only by a specialized group of researchers called scientists. This notion implies that some people use the scientific approach to understanding reality while others do not. In fact, all people use some form of scientific thinking to aid them in their struggle to deal with the uncertainties of life. Sometimes the thinking process is a bit crude, as when we decide what to eat by determining through trial and error what tastes good. But it is scientific thinking nonetheless.

So if science is not simply technology or a body of knowledge available only to people we call scientists, then what is it? Let us define science as a method of inquiry, a process of thinking and asking questions by which we arrive at an understanding of the world around us. Conceived of in this way, science does not exist in machines or in books or even in the natural phenomena around us, but in the mind. More specifically, science is a way of formulating questions and investigating answers—a set of rules for inquiry created to help achieve valid and reliable answers.

Historically, the scientific approach to knowledge has not done well when competing with other approaches. This is largely because, throughout the centuries, knowledge acquired through scientific investigation often threatened established values, norms, and institutions by which those in power maintained control of their world—values, norms, and institutions founded on such approaches to knowledge as myth, dogma, and superstition. Those who used science to understand and predict events were often viewed negatively by the powerful. Galileo was censured by both church and state when he used the scientific method to arrive at conclusions that challenged existing beliefs about the center of the universe. Using science to support the conclusion that the sun was in fact the center around which all things revolved, his outcome flew in the face of the Roman Catholic dogma that held the earth to be the center.

So it is safe to say that science is never practiced in a social vacuum. Today, leaders in Western countries tend to rely on science, rather than superstition or dogma, to establish credibility for what they say and do. But the scientific approach to seizing and maintaining power is very new in the history of the world.

8.2   THE SCIENTIFIC METHOD

The goal of science is to explain reality. The scientific method attempts to explain reality through the development and testing of theories, which are general explanations for the existence or cause of certain classes of phenomena. For example, two centuries before Christ, Ptolemy constructed a theory to explain the movement of the stars in the sky. His theory suggested that the sun and planets all revolve around earth. Ptolemy's theory, which described the general relationship of the planets and stars to earth, explained much of what could be observed in the sky at night. More precise observations, however, later began to cast doubt on Ptolemy's theory.

Once they are constructed, theories must be tested to see if they actually explain the phenomena that they are intended to explain. We test theories in a two-step process:

1. We create specific statements that should be true if the theory is correct.
2. We then devise tests of these statements. A statement devised to test a theory is known as a *hypothesis*. A substantial part of what social science does is to test research hypotheses.

The development of this two-step scientific method was a historical and cultural breakthrough. Accomplished slowly at the end of the Middle Ages by brilliant thinkers in different European countries, it stands as one of the watershed events that differentiate the ancient world from the modern. We will now briefly examine the elements of the scientific method.

8.2.1   Formulating and Testing Research Hypotheses

A research hypothesis is an educated guess. It is a declarative sentence stating that a specific relationship exists between two or more phenomena. Consider the following example of a research hypothesis: "When a person's anxiety rises, his or her intolerance of others increases." This hypothesis states that there is a specific relationship between two variables: (1) a person's anxiety; and (2) the person's tolerance of other people. In addition, the hypothesis states the nature of the relationship between the two variables: An increase in the first is associated with an increase in the second.

A researcher constructs a hypothesis for the sole purpose of testing whether it is "true"—that is, whether a certain relationship exists between two phenomena that the formulator of the hypothesis is investigating. Hypotheses help define the question that our research is trying to answer. Suppose that we want to know if family relationships are affected by economic conditions. Eventually, we would like to develop a theory that will help explain how different economic conditions lead to different ways in which family members relate to one another. But before we can understand general patterns of relationships and create a theory to explain these patterns, we must become much more specific in our inquiry. Hypotheses help us to select specific aspects of a problem or question and explore them one at a time.

For instance, in our example of the economy and family relationships, we might propose the following hypothesis: "When the economy is strong, the divorce rate decreases, and when the economy is weak, the divorce rate increases." We notice, however, that there will be difficulties in testing this hypothesis. For example, what are "strong" and "weak" economies? Our hypothesis will need to be more specific. We will perhaps find that a combination of selected economic indicators, such as the rate of unemployment or the amount of manufacturing production, will help us to define strong and weak in economic terms. The problem has now become more, rather than less, complicated. How will we know if family relationships are influenced by only one of these factors and not others? What if only certain combinations of these factors, and not other combinations, might have an effect upon relationships? To answer these questions, we need to start with one simple hypothesis, then test others in a careful, systematic way. Our first hypothesis might be: "When the national unemployment rate is greater than 7 percent, the divorce rate will remain above 50 percent."

Two types of hypotheses are commonly used in social science. The first may be called *causal*, the second *relational*. Causal hypotheses attempt to show that one phenomenon causes another. Relational hypotheses, on the other hand, attempt to indicate whether two phenomena are related to each other in a specific way, without demonstrating that one causes the other. Testing our hypothesis ("When the national unemployment rate is greater than 7 percent, the divorce rate will remain above 50 percent") will indicate only whether a relationship exists between unemployment and divorce, not whether unemployment causes divorce. Relations between hypotheses may be either positive or negative. A positive relation exists when an increase in one variable is associated with an increase in another. A negative relation exists when the presence of one variable coincides with the lack of another variable.

After hypotheses are constructed, we test them by observing the behavior of the variables that they contain. For example, let us phrase our hypothesis like this: "Extended periods of unemployment increase the likelihood of divorce."

8.2.2   Variables

The phenomena being observed are designated as different types of variables. The dependent variable is the phenomenon that is in some way affected by other variables. In our example, divorce is the dependent variable.

The independent variable is the phenomenon that may have some effect on the dependent variable. In our example, the time period in which a person is unemployed is the independent variable and divorce is the dependent variable.

Antecedent variables are phenomena that act on or relate to independent variables. In our example, if we hypothesized that "extended periods of unemployment occur in states with fewer high-tech industries," then the number of high-tech industries in a state would be an antecedent variable.

Intervening variables are variables other than the independent variable that affect the dependent variable directly. In our example, if we said that "divorce rates decrease when it rains," then rain would be an intervening variable.

Identifying the dependent, independent, antecedent, and intervening variables is very important in conducting research because it helps you to carefully define the relationships that you are examining.

Hypotheses are constructed to find out what relationship, if any, exists between the independent and dependent variables. To test a hypothesis, therefore, you need to measure the amount of change in the dependent variable as you observe change in the independent variable. To do this, you must complete two tasks.

The first task is to find accurate measurements of the dependent and independent variables as they vary over time or in different circumstances. For measurements to be accurate, they must be both valid and reliable. Valid measurements measure the effects they are supposed to measure instead of measuring something else. Reliable measurements are those that can be made under different conditions and still yield the same result.

The second task is to determine the effects of antecedent and intervening variables on the dependent variable so that you will know how much effect the independent variable has had. For example, if the voter turnout is greater in one community than another, and the communities have different registration time periods, you must determine how much of the difference in turnout was due to the registration periods as opposed to other factors, such as the percentage of independent voters or the occurrence of rain.

Conducting a study that is reliable and valid requires an analysis that utilizes accepted statistical methods. The instructor for your course in social science research methods will help you determine the correct methods for your analysis.

8.2.3   Problems for the Scientific Study of Society

A hypothesis can often be difficult to test. When attempting to test hypotheses in social science, we often encounter three general problems:

Data insufficiency or incongruity.   After we have stated our hypothesis, we may discover through investigation that sufficient data are not available. Sometimes the records that we need have not been kept consistently or accurately, or have been compiled according to different systems or categories. If we want to compare divorce rates in the United States and Italy, for example, we may find that the American and Italian governments have different reporting requirements and that the procedures used to validate data may be much more reliable in one country than in another.

Multiplicity and ambiguity of variables.   It is often difficult to cope with the sheer number of variables that may affect the result of our study; likewise it can be difficult to isolate the effects of one variable from those of others. If we want to find out what decreases the divorce rate, for example, we may need to try to sort out the competing effects of family histories, customs, religious beliefs, and economic factors.

Methodological uncertainty.   The third problem with the scientific study of society originates in epistemology—that is, the study of the nature of knowledge itself. Testing hypotheses, an approach fundamental to the scientific method, is an inductive process. One requirement of induction is the examination of numerous specific cases in hopes of finding general principles that help explain or predict behavior. For example, if all known cases of oak trees have acorns, one may conclude that all oak trees have acorns. But there may be a flaw in this sort of reasoning. In his book *The Logic of Scientific Discovery* (1959), Karl Popper pointed out that to show that some examples of a certain phenomenon behave in a certain manner is not to demonstrate that others will also. Even if all known examples of a phenomenon behave in a certain way, there may be examples in the future that will deviate from the pattern. Thus, the fact that all known oak trees have acorns does not mean that an oak tree without acorns will never be found.

Furthermore, said Popper, scientific observation is always selective. We must choose to observe before the actual observation takes place, and when we do observe, our observation will always take place within a particular context. This fact suggests that hypotheses are observations not of reality but merely of one context, one view of reality. Hypotheses, therefore, are not genuine observations, but only bold guesses. Since we can never say with certainty that a hypothesis is true, Popper explains that the only time we can be sure of a hypothesis is when it is disproved. Scientific progress is thus made not by verifying hypotheses but by refuting them. Because of Popper's works and those of others, this is indeed the way research often proceeds: by working not to prove hypotheses but to refute them.

A hypothesis established precisely for the purpose of being refuted is called a *null hypothesis*. Returning to a previous example, if we wanted to prove that extended registration periods increase voter turnout, we would begin by testing a null hypothesis: "Extended registration periods do not increase voter turnout." If we can find a case in which an extended registration period does increase voter turnout, we will have disproved the null hypothesis. We will not have proven that extended registration periods always increase voter turnout, but we will at least have taken the first step by showing that extended registration periods can increase voter turnout. Science thus proceeds by disproving successively specific null hypotheses.

No matter how we decide to treat hypotheses, there is still a question about how useful they are when it comes to major scientific discoveries. According to Kuhn (1970), even the refutation of null hypotheses is not a viable strategy if one wants to achieve the occasional new perspective that revolutionizes science. When Copernicus proposed his heliocentric theory of astronomy, the Ptolemaic model of the solar system was well entrenched in the scientific community. Kuhn calls established patterns of scientific inquiry *paradigms* and says that they are essential to the progress of science. A paradigm establishes the foundations of knowledge in a particular discipline until the paradigm is displaced by a new one.

Discrepancies in the Ptolemaic paradigm were met by increasingly complicated explanations devised to make observation conform to the theory. Copernicus's system was so different from Ptolemy's that it became a new scientific paradigm. At first, Copernicus's theory had little evidence from observation to support it. Kuhn argues that Copernicus did not come up with his new theory by disputing the Ptolemaic system. Instead of gradually and successively refuting hypotheses, Copernicus had a flash of intuition. A paradigm, for Kuhn, is never refuted by evidence; it can only be overturned when another one takes its place.

Social science, says Kuhn, needs a paradigm to establish its identity, its mission. Not having one, social science winds its way endlessly through a series of disagreements over methods and goals. Therefore, although the scientific method remains the normal way of adding to our common store of knowledge about society, the great breakthroughs of the future may as likely come from exceptional moments of human creativity as from the steady testing of statements within our normal range of exploration.

8.2.4   The Stages of Social Research

How do those who practice scientific inquiry go about "doing" social research? What are the steps involved in approaching a research problem scientifically? Actually, as we have stated, thinking scientifically and using science to help us make decisions are a part of our everyday life. However, if we wish to use this approach to aid in the investigation of problems that are germane to sociology, the scientific method is more structured and stepwise. Whether researchers are pursuing a problem in sociology, political science, criminal justice, psychology, or any area that relies on the scientific method, they use the following steps:

1. Define a research problem.
2. Formulate a meaningful hypothesis.
3. Conduct a literature review to determine what is known about the research problem.
4. Identify dependent, independent, and intervening variables.
5. Formulate a research design.
6. Conduct the study.
7. Analyze and interpret the results.

8.3   COMMON QUANTITATIVE RESEARCH DESIGNS

Four of the most common quantitative research designs utilized by sociologist are the following:

1. Surveys
2. Experiments
3. Scientific observation
4. Content analysis

These designs are outlined and discussed in Chapter 11.

How to Write Different Types of Sociology Papers

CHAPTER 9

SOCIAL ISSUE PAPERS

9.1 ISSUE REACTION PAPERS

The purpose of being assigned to write an issue reaction paper is to develop and sharpen your critical thinking and writing skills. The model originated from Professor Stephen Jenks, formerly of the University of Central Oklahoma. Your objective in writing this type of paper is to define an issue clearly and to formulate and clarify your position on that issue by reacting to a controversial statement. Completing this assignment requires accomplishing the following six tasks:

1. Select a suitable reaction statement.
2. Explain your selection.
3. Clearly define the issue addressed in the statement.
4. Clearly state your position on the issue.
5. Defend your position.
6. Conclude concisely.

9.1.1 Select a Suitable Reaction Statement

Your first task is to find or write a statement to which to react. Reaction statements are provocative declarations. They are controversial assertions that beg for either a negative or a positive response. Your instructor may assign a reaction statement, you may find one in a newspaper or on the Internet or hear one on television, or you may construct one yourself, depending on your instructor's directions. The following statements may elicit a polite reply but will probably not stir up people's emotions. They are, therefore, not good reaction statements:

It's cold out today.

Orange is not green.

Saturday morning is the best time to watch cartoons.

The following statements, however, have the potential to be good reaction statements, because when you hear them you will probably have a distinct opinion about them:

Abortion is murder.

Capital punishment is necessary.

Government is too big.

Welfare is bad.

Such statements are likely to provoke a reaction, either negative or positive depending on the person who is reacting to them. While they may be incendiary, they are also both ordinary and vague. If your instructor assigns you a statement to which to react, you may proceed to the next step. If you are to select your own, select or formulate one that is provocative, imaginative, and appropriate to the course for which you are writing the paper. Professor Johnson, for example, once assigned this statement in his Social Problems class:

Parents should not use corporal punishment to discipline their children.

Consider the following examples of reaction statements for other sociology classes:

Juveniles who commit heinous crimes should be certified and tried as adults.

Social service agencies should be run more like businesses.

The Supreme Court should take an active role in determining social policy.

Police officers should not carry weapons of deadly force.

Workers should be forced to retire by age sixty-five.

Where do you find good reaction statements? A helpful way is to think about subjects that interest you. When you hear something in class that sparks a reaction because you either agree or disagree with it, you know you are on the right track. Be sure to write your statement and ask your instructor for comments on it before beginning your paper. Once you have completed your selection, state it clearly at the beginning of your paper.

9.1.2   Explain Your Selection

After you have written the reaction statement, write a paragraph that explains why it is important to you. Be as specific as possible. Writing "I like it" does not tell the reader anything useful, but sentences like the following are informative: "Innocent people are being shot down by violent gangs in the inner city. We must crack down on gang violence in order to make the inner city safe for all who live there."

9.1.3   Clearly Define the Issue Addressed in the Statement

Consider the statement assigned by Professor Johnson: "Parents should not use corporal punishment to discipline their children." What is the most important issue addressed in this statement? Is it the notion that corporal punishment diminishes children's self-esteem, that spanking children will somehow cause them to feel hostile and aggressive? Or is it the possibility that parents might lose control of their children if they don't spank them? Perhaps some aspects of the statement are more important than others. As you define the issue addressed in the statement, you provide yourself with some clarification of the statement that will help you state your position.

9.1.4   Clearly State Your Position on the Issue

In response to Professor Johnson's statement, you might begin by saying: "It seems reasonable to assume that no one likes to be hit and that being hit causes feelings of resentment and hostility. Parents who say you can't discipline children without spanking them obviously are confused about the meaning of the word discipline." The reader of this response will have no doubt about where you stand on this issue.

9.1.5   Defend Your Position

You should make and support several arguments to support your stand on the issue. When evaluating your paper, your instructor will consider the extent to which you did the following:

- Identified the most important arguments needed to support your position
- Provided facts and information, when appropriate
- Introduced new or creative arguments to those traditionally made on this issue
- Presented your case accurately, coherently, logically, consistently, and clearly

9.1.6   Conclude Concisely

Your concluding paragraph should sum up your argument clearly, persuasively, and concisely. When writing this assignment, follow the format directions in Chapter 3 of this manual. Ask your instructor for directions concerning the length of the paper, but in the absence of further directions, your paper should not exceed five pages (typed, doublespaced).

The following sample issue reaction paper (starting on page 159) was written by a student in a Social Problems class at the University of Central Oklahoma. As you read it, try to identify its strengths and weaknesses.

SAMPLE ISSUE REACTION PAPER

A Positive Response to the Reaction Statement

"Electronic voting machines should not be used
to elect our government officials."

by

Mark Brennaman

for

Social Problems 2203

Section 23816

Dr. William Johnson

University of Central Oklahoma

April 8, 2005

The controversy over "hanging and dimpled chads" on Florida ballots in the presidential election of 2000 has intensified efforts to require the use of electronic voting machines in our elections. There are many different methods of voting in the United States, ranging from paper ballots to mechanical voting machines, butterfly punch cards and, in a growing number of jurisdictions, electronic voting machines. Ballots have been modernized over time, ostensibly to ensure the accuracy and speed of election night reporting of results. However, computerized methods of counting votes have caused an unacceptable degree of controversy, and should not be used to elect our officials if we are to maintain voter confidence in our government.

The primary reason computer-based voting is a bad idea is that the manufacturers of electronic voting machines refuse to reveal their source code even to election officials. Because source codes control the storage and display of data, unscrupulous officials could use them to manipulate election outcomes. To foster confidence in voting results the process needs to be as transparent as possible. Without the ability to examine the source code to ensure that an election is not rigged, there can be no confidence that the results of an election truly represent the will of the people.

Manufacturers of the voting computers claim the source code is "proprietary" and cannot be revealed to anyone outside their companies for fear that others will misappropriate the programming. Voting is "proprietary" too; it belongs exclusively to the people, not a private company. Without the ability to examine the source code there is simply no way to verify the fairness of any election outcome. Programming the voting computers outside public view can easily rig the outcome for candidates supported by the voting machine manufacturers.

Another reason why computerized voting damages voter confidence is that sometimes computers crash. What to do with a vote cast at the time a computer freezes? Will that vote not count? What if poll workers are unable to re-boot a crashed computer? Will all previous votes cast be lost in cyberspace entirely? The risk is too great that votes will not be counted in the event of a computer malfunction.

Another potential problem is that recounts, one potential way of discovering voting errors, will become a thing of the past if voting computers are used. In the past when the outcome of an election was close the apparent losing candidate could file for an official recount. In some cases errors have been caught and a new winner has been declared when paper ballots or mechanical voting machine totals were recounted. Electronic voting results will be the same every time a recount function command is entered on computers—garbage in, garbage out.

Another objection to using voting computers is that they are not currently programmed to provide a paper trail, which many believe is essential to guaranteeing the accuracy of elections. Representatives of computer voting machine manufacturers have claimed that it would be too difficult to program these computers to provide a check-and-balance paper trail. One person opposing the use of computers recently mused on a CNN talk show, "We can drive a little rover on the surface of Mars with a computer joystick on Earth, and we can't program voting computers to spit out a paper receipt?"

Defending the use of computer voting machines, one manufacturer spokesperson recently said on yet another television talk show, "The public wants electronic voting machines because they want fast results of an election." However, a search of public interest groups clambering for instant election results comes up empty. The media, not the public, is interested in fast results. What the public is interested in are true and accurate election results.

Even more alarming than the potential for error in using computer voting machines at polling places is the prospect of voting over the Internet. Hackers routinely break into so-called secure Web servers just to prove they can. Some hackers have even compromised data during their cybermeddling. Having the outcome of

SAMPLE ISSUE REACTION PAPER (*CONT.*)

a national election decided in the bedroom of a seventh-grade hacker would destroy the credibility of voting altogether. Our current premise for voting is "one man, one vote," but if the results of elections can be left to the whim of some cyberkid who hacks into these computer voting machines and alters the vote count, the new premise might well be "one gigabyte, thirty million votes."

Why does it matter that electronic voting seems to be on the fast track for national approval? Simply put, it will further erode the confidence voters have in the election process itself and erode the confidence people have in their government. Confidence was already shaken somewhat when the outcome of the 2000 presidential election was decided not at the ballot box or at the Electoral College, but at the bench of the Supreme Court.

Voter turnout has been declining for years. Participation in our democracy will likely decline even more once people begin to feel like their vote won't count. Widening the chasm between the voters and their government can be described as the *allegiant divide*. Citizens will come to believe they have no real stake in the operation of their government, and electronic voting might well lead to anarchy or, worse, the loss of freedoms that we cherish.

Therefore, electronic voting machines should not be used to elect our government officials. Instead, we should abandon the idea of using computers to register votes. We should also rid ourselves of mechanical voting machines and the butterfly punch card ballots and return to the old-fashioned paper ballot. The paper ballot should have large empty boxes in which voters can place an "X" to vote for their candidate.

Sure, it will take many more hours to tally the results, but we will have bolstered the active participation of people in the process of electing our officials. Society will benefit by having government servants elected in a fair and verifiable manner. Conversely, our society will be harmed if a devious computer programmer can select officials on our behalf.

9.2   SOCIAL ISSUE ANALYSIS PAPERS

9.2.1   Basic Concepts of Social Analysis

In 1956, sociologist C. Wright Mills published *The Power Elite,* a social and political analysis of American society. According to Mills (1956), the United States is controlled by a "power elite" composed of influential business, government, and military leaders who interact with each other socially and professionally.

> The power elite is not an aristocracy, which is to say that it is not a political ruling group based upon a nobility of hereditary origin. It has no compact basis in a small circle of great families whose members can and do consistently occupy the top positions in the several higher circles that overlap as the power elite. But such nobility is only one possible basis of common origin. That it does not exist for the American elite does not mean that members of this elite derive socially from the full range of strata composing American society. They derive in substantial proportions from the upper classes, both new and old, of local society and the metropolitan 400. The bulk of the very rich, the corporate executives, the political outsiders, the high military, derive from, at most, the upper third of the income and occupational pyramids. Their fathers were at least of the professional and business strata, and very frequently higher than that. They are native-born Americans of native parents, primarily from urban areas, and, with the exception of the politicians among them, overwhelmingly from the East. They are mainly Protestants, especially Episcopalian or Presbyterian. In general, the higher the position, the greater the proportion of men within it who have derived from and who maintain connections with the upper classes. The generally similar origins of the members of the power elite are underlined and carried further by the fact of their increasingly common educational routine.
>
> Overwhelmingly college graduates, substantial proportions have attended Ivy League colleges, although the education of the higher military, of course, differs from that of other members of the power elite. . . . The inner core of the power elite consists, first, of those who interchange commanding roles at the top of one dominant institutional order with those in another: the admiral who is also a banker and a lawyer and who heads up an important federal commission; the corporation executive whose company was one of the two or three leading war material producers who is now the Secretary of Defense; the wartime general who dons civilian clothes to sit on the political directorate and then becomes a member of the board of directors of a leading economic corporation. Although the executive who becomes a general, the general who becomes a statesman, the statesman who becomes a banker, see much more than ordinary men in their ordinary environments, still the perspectives of even such men often remain tied to their dominant locales. In their very career, however, they interchange roles within the big three and thus readily transcend the particularity of interest in any one of these institutional milieux. By their very careers and activities, they lace the three types of milieux together. They are, accordingly, the core members of the power elite. (Pp. 269–297)

The Power Elite brought to social and political analysis a new perspective on social relationships and how they define the structures of political power in society. The idea that segments of society form ruling elites has a history reaching back in history to before Plato and Aristotle. Mills, however, explained how power elites operate in society in general, and he painted a graphic and detailed portrait of the American power structure as it existed in the 1950s.

While Mills examined many social and political issues, his major objective was to explore the social and political forces that make things happen in society. As a sociology student, your attempts to analyze social issues and events will probably not be as all-encompassing or far-reaching as Mills's. However, your social issue analysis paper will have the same general goal that Mills's study had: to help readers understand social processes. Furthermore, your paper will have a more specific primary objective: to apply the techniques of sociological analysis to a specific social issue or problem.

Determining your audience.   Before writing your paper, consider your audience. For whom are you writing? When you write a social issue paper, your audience consists of the following:

- The instructor of the course, who wants you to analyze carefully and insightfully, and write well
- College students and others who study sociology, who want to improve their chances of success in their careers, or who simply want to better understand the social and political process in order to affect events or teach sociology to others
- Yourself

Keep all three audiences in mind as you write. It is sometimes difficult to determine how much background material or how much basic discussion of an important but tangential subject you should include in an analysis. What would one of your classmates need to know about your topic to understand your thesis? A clear understanding of your paper's purpose will help you to pinpoint your audience and tailor your material accordingly.

9.2.2   Writing Social Issue Analysis Papers

There are four basic steps in writing a good social issue analysis paper. These steps are recursive, meaning that although they must all be undertaken, they need not necessarily be taken consecutively, and some of them will be taken repeatedly:

1. Select a social issue to study.
2. Narrow the focus of your study.
3. Conduct your research.
4. Write the paper.

Selecting an issue to study. In most cases, your teacher will ask you to select an issue that is germane to the course. For example, in a course on the family as a social institution, you might choose to write on a topic like one of these:

The Future of "Traditional Families" in America
Problems of Two-Paycheck Families
Current Challenges for African-American Families
Special Needs of Single-Parent Families

In a course in majority–minority relations you might write on one of the following topics:

The Melting Pot vs. Multiculturalism
Assimilating Native Americans into Mainstream American Culture
Racial Discrimination in the Media
Sexual Harassment in the Workplace
Women of Color in the Feminist Movement

While it is not a requirement, personal experience or interest can sometimes help you decide which issue to write about. For example, you may want to do a paper on some issue related to your vocational aspirations. If you are planning to be a teacher, you could investigate the quality of public education in the United States or, more specifically, in your state or district. An aspiring athlete could study a particular aspect of U.S. Olympic policy or the "gloried self" problem faced by superstar athletes described by Adler and Adler (1989). A future physician may want to look at problems in medical reimbursement or the trend toward socialized medicine. Since government policy affects every vocational interest to some degree, you may find a topic by asking yourself: "What are my career goals and interests? In what way does government affect me?" Many college students, for example, are affected by government student loan policies and the issue of an income tax deduction for college tuition.

Where you have been and what you have done in your life are important, and if you are or have been personally involved with your topic, you gain more than knowledge. Your paper becomes an experiential tool; it expands your vision and increases the options available to you. By writing a good paper on some "personal" issue, you not only contribute to your success in the class and the available knowledge on the topic, but also broaden your understanding of the life you are living.

Another general approach to finding a topic is to select a current event. Newspapers, popular magazines, and television and radio reports continually present actual problems that are meaningful issues for sociology students to investigate. Issues related to drugs, gang violence, poverty, quality of education, abortion, and religious practices are to be found in the news every day. Scan the pages of your local newspaper or read the entries in the news digest of your Internet service, and you will find many topics to write about.

Narrowing the focus for your social issue paper.   With assistance from your instructor, you should be able to narrow the issue and select a specific topic that is right for you. For example, the news is filled with reports on gangs and gang behavior, which can easily translate into many meaningful topics, including the following:

> The Role Gangs Play in Replacing Family Values
> Gangs and Violence in New York City
> Gangs, Drugs, and Minority Self-Concept

Suppose that you select the family as the general issue area that you would like to study. You can narrow your topic by selecting a specific focus for your paper:

> *Definitional focus:* What is the traditional family, and how does it differ from other forms of family organization?
>
> *Geographic focus:* What is family life like in Concord, New Hampshire? Is it different from family life in Papua, New Guinea?
>
> *Historical focus:* How has the family changed over time?
>
> *Systems focus:* How does the traditional family as an American institution interact with other basic systems or institutions in society, such as churches, schools, or government agencies?
>
> *Interaction focus:* What are the roles played in the family? What social, economic, political, or environmental forces affect these roles?
>
> *Future focus:* What does the future hold for the family? What can be projected from what you have learned about the issue?

9.2.3   Contents of a Social Issue Analysis Paper

Your social issue analysis paper should contain the following elements. The format for each is described in Chapter 3 of this manual:

- Title page
- Abstract, outline, or table of contents—ask your instructor which of these to include
- Body or text, which includes source citations
- References
- Appendixes (where applicable)

The following sample social issue analysis paper (starting on page 167) was written by a student in a Social Stratification class at the University of Central Oklahoma. You may use it as a model for writing your paper.

Aspects of Social Stratification in the
Access and Use of Computers and the Internet

by

Mark Brennaman

for

Social Stratification 4443

Section 23870

Dr. William Johnson

University of Central Oklahoma

November 20, 2004

Sample Social Issue Analysis Paper (*cont.*)

Table of Contents

Abstract

Aspects of Social Stratification in the Access
and Use of Computers and the Internet

The growth of computer and Internet use has occurred unevenly among the various social identity groups. Primarily due to the high cost of computers at the beginning of our Information Age, wealthier white members of society led the way in adopting the new technology. Low-income, minority, and rural and central-city individuals were slow to acquire computers and the skills to use them, and this discrepancy has been described as the *digital divide*.

Beginning in 1995 the National Telecommunications and Information Administration (NTIA) has conducted studies tracking the growth of computer and Internet use. Since 1995 the divide has narrowed as the cost of computers has come down and connecting to the Internet has become easier. A divide still exists, however, which various government and corporate programs are attempting to address.

Emerging as a new kind of divide is the debate over the use of computers and the Internet in government elections. While this divide is not based on socioeconomic differences, many voters are expressing a lack of confidence in the accuracy of computer-based voting. There exists a robust debate over whether computers are appropriate for elections, given the ability to "hack" computers and the lack of a paper trail in this type of voting. The increasing lack of voter confidence is termed the *allegiant divide*—a growing chasm between the government and the governed.

There is a digital divide, but how wide that chasm is depends on what aspect of society one examines. Computer and Internet use is still relatively young, and this topic will continue to be the subject of study for many years to come.

SAMPLE SOCIAL ISSUE ANALYSIS PAPER (*CONT.*)

THE PROBLEM

The Digital Divide

The proliferation of computers over the past twenty years and the growth of the Internet over the past ten years have spawned a new aspect of social stratification known as the *digital divide*. Individuals who lack access to computers and the Internet are said to experience "information poverty" as they are unable to use computers to access banking, seek jobs, communicate with friends, or retrieve other information (Facer and Furlong 2001).

Many studies have examined differences in computer skills and access to the Internet between the *haves* and the *have nots,* focusing on the disparity of levels of access and use among different income and ethnic groups, gender, education levels, and geographic locations.

Socioeconomic Status

A series of studies by the National Telecommunications and Information Administration (NTIA) of the U.S. Department of Commerce have concluded that access to computers and the Internet is directly related to socioeconomic status (Clark and Gorski 2002). Those in lower economic brackets not only disproportionately lack ownership of computers and the skills to operate them but have also shouldered the brunt of job displacement as robots have been deployed on assembly lines and for other workplace uses.

Low-income students who lack computers at home are likely to attend schools that do not have computers or Internet connection (Clark and Gorski 2002). The divide between students in poorer schools and those in wealthier schools is aggravated by the fact that many of the wealthier schools offer after-hours access to computers to students even though they are more likely to have access at home. Low-income students without computer access at school are also deprived of the experience at home.

In 1997 the President's Committee of Advisors on Science and Technology (1997) set as a goal that schools should have a student-to-computer ratio of 4 or 5 to 1. A 2000 federally funded study found that the average school had reached a 5 to 1 ratio, but the poorest schools had 9 students per computer (NCES 2001). Despite efforts to increase access to computers and the Internet, there still exists a large gap in computer access between students from households with incomes under $15,000 and students from households with higher incomes (Clark and Gorski 2002).

Ethnicity

According to the NTIA (2000), Internet and computer use increased for all social identity groups between 1998 and 2000, but the increase of use by racial or ethnic groups still lagged behind when considered by gender, income, and geographic location. During this period Asian American households had the highest rate of access at 56.8%, while white households had the second highest rate of access at 46.1%. Black and Hispanic households had the lowest Internet penetration rates at 23.5% and 23.6% respectively for the same two-year period. It is interesting to note that no projections were made for American Indians, Aleuts, and Eskimos because the sampled populations were too small to generate credible results.

Gender

By 2000 the gap between male and female use of computers and the Internet became virtually indistinguishable. The NTIA (2000) found that 44.6% of men and 44.2% of women used computers and the Internet in the year 2000. Although the gender gap appears to have been closed, there are interesting differences between males and females when age is considered. The NTIA (2000) found that younger boys and girls had equal use of the Internet. Women used the Internet more than men of college age and during the prime working age. Finally, when older adults were surveyed, men were more likely to use the Internet.

Sample Social Issue Analysis Paper (*cont.*)

Low-Literate Adults

The most significant barrier to low-literate adults using the Internet is that the content on the Web is written at a 10th grade reading level, while at least half of the U.S. population reads at an 8th grade level or below (Zarcadoolas, Blanco, and Boyer 2002). This barrier is borne out in the federal *Falling through the Net* studies, which reported that adults with only an elementary school education had a 4% Internet use, compared to a 74.5% Internet use for adults with at least a bachelor's or higher degree (NTIA 2000).

Even as the gap in access to the Internet is narrowing for most demographic groups, low-literate adults still face navigation barriers once they do go on-line. Working to make Internet navigation easier for people with physical and visual disabilities, the World Wide Web Consortium (W3C) has designed clearer links and graphics that also help those with lower levels of education (Zarcadoolas et al. 2000).

Geographical Location

Two geographic areas have traditionally been underserved with respect to telephone and computer access. The first *Falling through the Net* report by NTIA (1995) discovered that the "most disadvantaged in terms of absolute computer and modem penetration are the most enthusiastic users of on-line services that facilitate economic uplift and empowerment" (p. 3).

Rural areas and inner-city areas lag behind the rest of the country, but the gap is closing somewhat (NTIA 2000). The national telecommunication policy of universal service was once centered strictly on telephone access, but now the debate has reconfigured itself to determine whether the policy should include Internet service (Gillett 2000). One barrier to Internet use that people in rural areas have experienced is an inability to connect with a service provider as a local call.

Prior to changes in telecommunication laws in 1996, people in rural areas had to make long distance calls to connect to the Internet. New laws taking effect in

1996 created "expanded area service," or flat-rate calling zones, which allowed people in rural areas to connect their modems to service providers in a more populated area (Nicholas 2003).

The federal *Falling through the Net* report of 2000 indicates that rural areas made significant increases in penetration of Internet use but that central-city penetration fell behind other parts of the country (NTIA 2000). The lack of telephone subscribership in inner-city areas explains why those in a lower socioeconomic status are also underrepresented in terms of use of Internet services.

AN OPPOSING VIEW OF THE DIGITAL DIVIDE

Not everyone is convinced that the so-called digital divide is real, or if it does exist, that it matters. Michael Powell, the current chairman of the Federal Communications Commission, believes the notion of a digital divide is an "ill-advised version of the 'Mercedes divide' in the United States" (Strover 2003:275). Powell's view is that some people can afford luxury cars and others cannot, but those without a Mercedes are not necessarily at a disadvantage. Others who believe a divide once existed have come to believe that the gap in the use of technology has narrowed for some groups, such as those identified by ethnicity and income, and has been eliminated between men and women (Servon 2002).

Servon (2002) suggests there are *four myths about the digital divide* that need to be debunked in order for the nation to formulate appropriate information technology policies: The first is that providing access to computers and the Internet will eliminate the digital divide. She states that the phenomenon of the digital divide has been narrowly defined as a problem of access and that even though people have access to the technology not much else changes. She points out that those who use computers for low-order tasks such as word processing still do not benefit in our information age to the same extent as those who use

SAMPLE SOCIAL ISSUE ANALYSIS PAPER (*CONT.*)

computers for higher-order tasks such as data analysis and design. The second myth is that technology can solve social problems. Servon (2002) states that . . .

> although the potential of [Internet technology] to create opportunities for disadvantaged groups must be pursued aggressively, there must also be a pragmatic assessment about what it can and cannot do. Technology alone will not level deep-seated historical inequalities. (P. 225)

The third is that on-line communication diminishes the need for personal contact. She believes that both virtual and face-to-face interactions are mutually reinforcing. Increasing computer skills help people form new relationships that can help them attain resources to move out of poverty. The final myth is that information technology levels spatial inequalities. Servon (2002) points out that even though the Internet allows people to access information from around the world, the technology is still rooted in geography. The telecommunication infrastructure's penetration is much greater in wealthier areas than in rural or poor urban areas; the same areas that can be classified as poor areas also "suffer from information poverty" (p. 226).

There have been many programs, both public and private, to increase the availability of computers in schools, libraries, and community centers. With the burgeoning availability of technology, the public debate has shifted from the digital divide to digital opportunities. Physical access to computers and the Internet may have improved for everyone, but there still appears to be a divide in the skills people have in the use of technology at home and in the workplace (Strover 2003).

THE SECOND-LEVEL DIGITAL DIVIDE

Over the past five years the availability of computers in schools has grown considerably. Nationally, public schools had nearly one computer for every four students, and almost all classrooms are connected to the Internet (Samuelson 2002). It appears that access to computers and the Internet is growing for all classes of people, but there still exists a disparity of skills in using the technology.

With a steady increase in the number of people having access to the Internet, some scholars have moved beyond measuring the difference between those who are connected and those who are not. Studies are beginning to measure inequalities in the level of skills people have when using computers and the Internet (Hargittai 2002). Moving to the study of skills as opposed to mere access to information technology serves to better demonstrate how the technology is used. It is one thing to have physical access to computers, but without the skills to use the technology, effectively a digital divide still exists.

In a study of the second-level digital divide, Hargittai (2002) found that young people could navigate the Internet better than older people, and that those with more education were more adept at using computers. Her study showed that online skills between males and females are nearly equal. She concluded that public policies to increase access to the Internet need to have a parallel policy of increasing training, and stated that "... like education in general, it is not enough to give people a book, we also have to teach them how to read in order to make it useful" (p. 14).

EFFORTS TO CLOSE THE GAP

Despite the Internet barriers experienced by the poor, the less educated, those in rural and inner cities, and minorities, there are many programs active in the United States to close the digital divide. Most notable among various programs are the Bill and Melinda Gates Foundation, which has linked more than 7,000 libraries in the United States and Canada (Sargent 2004). Another effort to narrow the information gap is the creation of community technology centers. The first such center was opened in 1983 in New York City Harlem by Antonio Stone to provide personal computer training for low-income people. There are now more than 4,000 technology centers in the United States to boost computer and Internet access to those who otherwise would still be part of the divide (Sargent 2004).

In a March 2002 speech to the trustees of the Greenwich Library in Greenwich, Connecticut, William Harrison (2002), the CEO of J. P. Morgan Chase & Company, discussed closing the digital divide as part of a response to the third Information Revolution. He pointed out the first Information Revolution was over 5,000 years old—the invention of the written language. He went on to say that the second Information Revolution began with the invention of Gutenberg's printing press. The third Information Revolution, Harrison said, was the creation of the Internet.

Harrison's (2002) company created a program to close the digital divide known as Our Neighborhood Digital Education Community, or ON_DEC. The project put a computer with Internet access in the homes of 1,300 students and all 300 faculty and staff (including janitors) of Ditmas Intermediate School in Brooklyn, a school serving a poor neighborhood. The results were positive. In addition to fostering a new sense of being connected among students and teachers, the project contributed to many positive changes in the school. Prior to the installation of the computers, the school experienced a 20% rate of students transferring to other schools. By the next year, after ON_DEC was launched, only 15% of students transferred to other schools, and after the first full year of the project that number dropped to about 12%. Disciplinary problems dropped by 58% during the same period. Harrison (2002) noted that ". . . maybe all this isn't so amazing, after all. When people see a real opportunity to improve their own lives, they will seize it with both hands" (p. 25).

A NEW KIND OF DIVIDE: USING COMPUTERS IN ELECTIONS

The controversy of the presidential election of 2000 has given rise to a new kind of divide with respect to computers and information technology. As a result of counting errors blamed on punch card ballots with their "hanging and dimpled chads," there has been considerable debate over whether computers and even Internet voting ought to replace all other methods of electing government officials.

Proponents of using computers for voting give three basic arguments for electronic voting: (1) it will increase participation; (2) it will enhance administrative efficiency; and (3) it is the logical next step in voting technology. Given that voter turnout has been declining since 1960, they argue that the enthusiasm younger people have for computers and the Internet is likely to increase voter participation, especially if voting is allowed over the Internet so people will not have to go to a traditional polling place to cast their votes. They also say that using computers can reduce the cost of elections, since computers can tally vote totals in seconds rather than hours, as happens when totals taken from mechanical voting machines must be transcribed by hand, and they claim that computer voting will eliminate counting errors and make it easier for voters to make their selections. And they argue that our election system already uses electronic technology in creating voter rolls and ballot counting (in the case of scanning machines). They say that the possibility of election fraud is not sufficient enough to abandon the idea of electronic voting given that fraud has always been present, even when paper ballots have been used. And they point out that every new method of voting encounters resistance ((Gibson 2001–2002).

Opponents of electronic voting say that the digital divide promotes discrimination against the poor and minorities. Gibson (2001–2002) points out that even though government reports claim that the divide is closing, there is still a significant gap among the poor and those in inner cities. Opponents of electronic voting also point to the security of the computers themselves. A component of computer voting is the use of "smart cards" that identify individual voters. The smart cards must be inserted into a computer to allow voting, but opponents fear that these cards have the ability to be programmed to allow voters to cast more than one vote (Hulme 2004). Perhaps the most vehement argument against using computers for voting is that the computers do not provide a paper trail that can be used in the event of a recount (Hulme 2004). Recounts will be a practice of the past since the vote totals will be exactly the same every time a total function is entered on the computer. Colorado recently decided not to use computers for voting until the issue has been further debated on the national level. Upon debating legislation regarding computer use, the Colorado legislature decided that, absent a paper trail, the state will wait for a federal law providing standards that address security issues (Brown 2004).

At present voters lack confidence in voting computers and doubt that election results will be the true will of the people. This chasm might well give rise to voters feeling more and more distant from their government, a chasm that can be described as the *allegiant divide.*

CONCLUSIONS

From a conflict or institutional perspective (Rothman 2005), the digital divide appears to extend the gap between the *haves* and the *have nots.* Attempts to ameliorate this gap have met with mixed reviews. Although the distance between male and female computer and Internet use has all but vanished, the gap between those in the lower and upper socioeconomic strata may be widening. Those embracing the order perspective (Rothman 2005) might conclude that this is simply a manifestation of one major function of social stratification—finding and training the most talented individuals to fill those positions ranked as most important by society. However, from a conflict perspective this widening gap is another reality of the oppression experienced by the poor and others in lower socioeconomic strata.

Continuous studies will have to determine where the most significant divides are in terms of universal use of computers and the Internet. Where the divide appears to be closing, further study needs to be done in terms of the skills that each demographic group brings to the task of computing, information retrieval, and communication. The development of computer voting also deserves extensive study as the debate over accuracy and voter confidence continues. In the final of their seven-part series on the digital divide, Clark and Gorski (2003) conclude that . . .

> . . . it is crucial that both multicultural education and digital divide researchers . . . recognize that efforts to altogether eliminate the digital divide must be understood as but one part of a larger effort to eradicate the persistence and proliferation of inequity in every aspect of education and society. (P. 32)

REFERENCES

Brown, Fred. 2004. "We're Still Fretting About Voting." *The Denver Post,* April 11. Retrieved April 11, 2004 (http://www.denverpost.com/Stories/0,1413,36~ 145~2072026,00.html).

Clark, Christine and Paul Gorski. 2002. "Multicultural Education and the Digital Divide: Focus on Socioeconomic Class Background." *Multicultural Perspectives* 4(3):25–36.

———. 2003. "Turning the Tide of the Digital Divide: Multicultural Education and the Politics of Surfing." *Multicultural Perspectives* 5(1):29–32.

Facer, Keri and Ruth Furlong. 2001. "Beyond the Myth of the 'Cyberkid': Young People at the Margins of the Information Revolution." *Journal of Youth Studies* 4(4):451–469.

Gibson, Rachel. 2001–2002. "Elections On-Line: Assessing Internet Voting in Light of the Arizona Democratic Primary." *Political Science Quarterly* 11(4):561–583.

Gillett, Sharon. 2000. "Universal Service: Defining the Policy Goal in the Age of the Internet." *The Information Society* 16:147–149.

Hargittai, Eszter. 2002. "Second-Level Digital Divide: Differences in People's On-Line Skills." *First Monday* 7(4):1–20. Retrieved March 12, 2004 (http://www.first monday.org-/issues/issue7_4/hargittai/).

Harrison, William. 2002. "Closing the Digital Divide." *Executive Speeches,* August/September, pp. 23–25.

Hulme, George. 2004. "E-Voting Systems Face Security Questions." *Information Week,* February 9, p. 28.

National Center for Education Statistics (NCES). 2001. *Stats in Brief: Internet Access in U.S. Public Schools and Classrooms: 1994–2000.* Washington, D.C., cited in Christine Clark and Paul Gorski. 2002. "Multicultural Education and the Digital Divide: Focus on Socioeconomic Class Background." *Multicultural Perspectives* 4(3):25–36.

National Telecommunications and Information Administration. 1995. *Falling through the Net: A Survey of the 'Have Nots' in Rural and Urban America.* Washington, D.C. Retrieved April 9, 2004 (http://www.ntia.doc.gov/ntiahome/fallingthru.html).

———. 2000. *Falling through the Net: Toward Digital Inclusion.* Washington, D.C.. Retrieved April 10, 2004 (http://www.ntia.doc.gov/ntiahome/fttn00/Falling.htm#33).

Nicholas, Kyle. 2003. "Geo-Policy Barriers and Rural Internet Access: The Regulatory Role in Constructing the Digital Divide." *The Information Society* 19:287–295.

President's Committee of Advisors on Science and Technology. 1997. *Report to the President on the Use of Technology to Strengthen K–12 Education in the United States.* Washington, D.C., cited in Christine Clark and Paul Gorski. 2002. "Multicultural Education and the Digital Divide: Focus on Socioeconomic Class Background." *Multicultural Perspectives* 4(3):25–36.

Rothman, Robert A. 2005. *Inequality and Stratification: Race, Class, and Gender.* 5th ed. Upper Saddle River, NJ: Pearson Prentice Hall.

Samuelson, Robert. 2002. "Debunking the Digital Divide." *Newsweek,* March 25, p. 37.

Sargent, Mark. 2004. "Community Technology Centers: A National Movement to Close the Digital Divide." *The Digital Divide Network.* Retrieved April 10, 2004 (http://www.digitaldividenetwork.org/content/stories/index.cfm?key=245).

Strover, Sharon. 2003. "Remapping the Digital Divide." *The Information Society* 19:275–277.

Servon, Lisa. 2002. "Four Myths about the Digital Divide." *Planning Theory & Practice* 3(2):222–227.

Zarcadoolas, Christina, Mercedes Blanco and John F. Boyer. 2002. "Unweaving the Web: An Explanatory Study of Low-Literate Adult's Navigation Skills on the World Wide Web." *Journal of Health Communication* 7:309–324.

CRITICAL EVALUATION
OF SOCIOLOGICAL LITERATURE

10.1   BOOK REVIEWS

10.1.1   *The Objective of a Book Review*

Successful book reviewers answer two questions for their readers: What is the book trying to do? How well is it doing it? People who read a book review want to know if a particular book is worth reading, for their own particular purposes, before buying or beginning to read it. These potential book readers want to know what a book is about, and the book's strengths and weaknesses, and they want to gain this information as easily and quickly as possible.

Your goal in writing a book review, therefore, is to help people decide efficiently whether to buy or read a book. Your immediate objectives may be to please your instructor and get a good grade, but these objectives are most likely to be met if you focus on a book review's audience: people who want help in selecting books to read. In the process of writing a review according to the guidelines given in this chapter, you will also learn about the following:

- The book you are reviewing and its content
- Professional standards for book reviews in sociology
- The essential steps to reviewing books that apply in any academic discipline

This final objective, learning to review a book properly, has more applications than you may at first imagine. First, it helps you to focus quickly on the essential elements of a book, to draw from a book its informational value for yourself and others. Some of the most successful professional and business people speed-read many books. They read these books less for enjoyment than to assimilate knowledge quickly. These readers then apply this knowledge to substantial advantage in their professions. It is normally not wise to speed-read a book you are reviewing, because you are unlikely to gain from such a fast reading enough information to evaluate the book's qualities fairly. However, writing book reviews helps you to become proficient in quickly locating the book's most valuable information and paring away material that is of secondary importance. The ability to make such discriminations is of fundamental importance to academic and professional success.

In addition, writing book reviews for publication allows you to participate in the discussions of the broader intellectual and professional community of which you are a part. People in law, medicine, teaching, engineering, administration, and other fields are frequently asked to write reviews of books to help others in their profession assess the value of newly released publications.

10.1.2   Elements of a Book Review

Book reviews in the social sciences contain the same essential elements of all book reviews. Since social science is nonfiction, book reviews within the disciplines focus less on writing style and more on content and method than reviews of works of fiction. Your book review should generally contain four basic elements, though not always in this order:

1. Enticement
2. Examination
3. Elucidation
4. Evaluation

Enticement.   The first sentence should entice people to read your review. Social studies do not have to be dull. Start your review with a sentence that both sums up the objective of the book, and catches the reader's eye. Be sure, however, that your opening statement is an accurate portrayal of the book as well as an enticement to the reader.

Examination.   Your book review should encourage the reader to join you in examining the book. Tell the reader what the book is about. When you review a book, write about what is actually in the book, not what you think is probably there or what ought to be there. Do not tell how you would have written the book, but tell instead how the author wrote it. Describe the book in clear, objective terms. Include enough about the content to identify for the reader the major points that the author is trying to make.

Elucidation.   Elucidate, or clarify, the book's value and contribution to sociology by defining (1) what the author is attempting to do; and (2) how the author's work fits within current similar efforts in the discipline of sociology or scholarly inquiry in general. The elucidation portion of book reviews often provides additional information about the author. How would your understanding of a book be changed, for example, if you knew that its author is a leader in the feminist movement? Include in your book review information about the author that helps the reader understand how this book fits within the broader concerns of social science.

Evaluation.   After your reader understands what the book is attempting to do, she will want to know the extent to which the book has succeeded. To effectively evaluate a book, you should establish evaluation criteria and then compare the book's content to those criteria. You do not need to define your criteria specifically in your review, but they should be evident to the reader. The criteria will vary according to the book you are reviewing, and you may discuss them in any order that is helpful to the reader. Consider including the following among the criteria that you establish for your book review:

- How important is the subject matter to the study of culture and society?
- How complete and thorough is the author's coverage of his subject?
- How carefully is the author's analysis constructed?
- What are the strengths and limitations of the author's methodology?
- What is the quality of the writing in the book? Is the writing clear, precise, and interesting?
- How does this book compare with other books written on the same subject?
- What contribution does this book make to sociology?
- Who will enjoy or benefit from this book?

When giving your evaluation according to these criteria, be specific. If you write, "This is a good book; I liked it very much," you have told the reader nothing of interest or value. But if you say, for example, "Smith's book provides descriptions of most of the major sociological theories, but it fails to describe the full extent of Weber's concept of bureaucracy," then you have given your reader some concrete information.

10.1.3   Reflective and Analytical Book Reviews

Two types of book reviews are normally assigned by instructors in the humanities and social sciences: the reflective and the analytical. Ask your instructor which type of book review she wants you to write. The purpose of a reflective book review is for the student reviewer to exercise creative analytical judgment without being influenced by the reviews of others. Reflective book reviews contain all the elements covered in this chapter—enticement, examination, elucidation, and evaluation—but they do not include the views of others who have also read the book.

Analytical book reviews contain all the information provided by reflective book reviews but add an analysis of the comments of other reviewers. The purpose is to review not only the book itself but also its reception in the professional community. To write an analytical book review, insert a review analysis section immediately after your summary of the book. To prepare this review analysis section, use the *Book Review Digest* and *Book Review Index* in the library to locate other reviews of the book that have been published in journals and other periodicals. As you read these reviews, use the following four steps:

1. List the criticisms (strengths and weaknesses) of the book found in these reviews.
2. Develop a concise summary of these criticisms, indicate the overall positive or negative tone of the reviews, and discuss some of the most frequent comments.
3. Evaluate the criticisms of the book found in these reviews. Are they basically accurate in their assessment of the book?
4. Write a review analysis of two pages or less that states and evaluates Steps 2 and 3, and place it in your book review immediately after your summary of the book.

10.1.4   Format and Length of a Book Review

The directions for writing papers provided in Part I of this manual apply to book reviews as well. Unless your instructor gives you other specifications, a reflective book review should be three to five pages in length, and an analytical book review should be from five to seven pages. In either case, a brief, specific, concise book review is almost always preferred over one of greater length.

10.2   ARTICLE CRITIQUES

An article critique evaluates an article published in an academic journal. A good critique tells the reader what point the article is trying to make and how convincingly it makes this point. Writing an article critique achieves three purposes. First, it provides you with an understanding of the information contained in a scholarly article and a familiarity with other information written on the same topic. Second, it provides an opportunity to apply and develop your critical thinking skills as you attempt to critically evaluate the work of a sociologist. Third, it helps you to improve your own writing skills as you attempt to describe the selected article's strengths and weaknesses so that your readers can clearly understand them.

10.2.1   Choosing an Article

The first step in writing an article critique is to select an appropriate article. Unless your instructor specifies otherwise, select an article from a scholarly journal (e.g., *American Journal of Sociology, American Sociological Review, Sociological Quarterly, Social Forces,* or *Free Inquiry in Creative Sociology*) and not a popular or journalistic publication (e.g., *Time, Newsweek,* or the *National Review*). Chapter 6 of this manual contains a substantial list of academic journals that pertain to sociology. Your instructor may also accept appropriate articles from academic journals in other disciplines, such as history, political science, or criminal justice, many of which are also contained in this list.

Three other considerations should guide your choice of an article. First, browse article titles until you find a topic that interests you. Writing a critique will be much more satisfying if you have an interest in the topic. Hundreds of interesting journal articles are published every year. The following articles, for example, appeared in a 1998 issue (Vol. 26, No. 1) of *Free Inquiry in Creative Sociology:*

"Social Bonding and Juvenile Male Violence: An Empirical Investigation"

"Understanding Adolescent Work in Social and Behavioral Contexts"

"Examining Courtship, Dating, and Forced Sexual Intercourse: A Preliminary Model"

"Positive Deviance: A Classificatory Model"

"Disabilities and the Workplace: Employment Opportunities Perceptions of College Students"

The second consideration in selecting an article is your current level of knowledge. Many sociology studies, for example, employ sophisticated statistical techniques. You may be better prepared to evaluate them if you have studied statistics.

The third consideration is to select a current article, one written within the twelve months prior to making your selection. Much of the material in sociology is quickly superseded by new studies. Selecting a recent study will help ensure that you will be engaged in an up-to-date discussion of your topic.

10.2.2   Writing the Critique

Once you have selected and carefully read your article, you may begin to write your critique, which should cover the following four areas:

1. Thesis
2. Methods
3. Evidence
4. Evaluation

Thesis.   Your first task is to find and clearly state the thesis of the article. The thesis is the main point the article is trying to make. In a 1998 article in *Free Inquiry in Creative Sociology,* Professors Cynthia Y. A. Jacob-Chien of the University of Northern Iowa and Richard L. Dukes of the University of Colorado at Colorado Springs examine "Understanding Adolescent Work in Social and Behavioral Contexts." In this article Jacob-Chien and Dukes (1998) state their thesis in the introduction:

Traditional explanations of crime and delinquency imply that adolescent work is a useful control mechanism. . . . [Some] theories appear to overlook the notion that the workplace can be an environment that displays significant sources of deviant activities. We expect that . . . *work intensity will have a negative effect on well-being and academics and a facilitating effect on delinquent and substance use behavior.* (P. 23) (Italics ours)

Sometimes the thesis is more difficult to ascertain. Do you have to hunt for the thesis of the article? Comment about the clarity of the author's thesis presentation, and state the author's thesis in your own paper. Before proceeding with the remaining elements of your paper, consider the importance of the topic. Has the author of the article written something that is important for sociology students or professionals to read?

Methods.   What methods did the author use to investigate the topic? In other words, how did the author go about supporting the thesis? In your critique, carefully answer the following two questions. First, were appropriate methods used? In other words, did the author's approach to supporting the thesis make sense? Second, did the author employ the selected methods correctly? Did you discover any errors in the way he conducted his research?

Evidence.   In your critique, answer the following questions: What evidence did the author present in support of the thesis? What are the strengths of the evidence presented by the author? What are the weaknesses of the evidence presented? On balance, how well did the author support the thesis?

Evaluation.   In this section, summarize your evaluation of the article. Tell your readers several things. Who will benefit from reading this article? What will the benefit be? How important and extensive is that benefit? What is your evaluation of the article? What suggestions do you have for repeating this study or one like it? Your evaluation might begin like this:

> Jacob-Chien and Dukes's article titled "Understanding Adolescent Work in Social and Behavioral Contexts" is an excellent presentation on measuring the effect of intensive work on a variety of social and behavior aspects of adolescence. They examine the weaknesses of several theoretical explanations that see adolescent work as a "useful control mechanism," while concluding that the current structure of work for teens "has become an unwholesome process in the personal growth of adolescents."

When writing this assignment, follow the directions for formats described in Chapter 3 of this manual. Ask your instructor for directions concerning the length of the paper, but in the absence of further directions, your paper should not exceed five pages (typed, double-spaced).

The sample article critique that follows (starting on page 187) was written by a student in Professor Johnson's Social Psychology class at the University of Central Oklahoma. As you read it, ask yourself how well this student followed the previously described guidelines.

SAMPLE ARTICLE CRITIQUE

Critique

of

Johnson, J. D., N. E. Noel and J. Sutter-Hernandez. 2000. "Alcohol and Male
Acceptance of Sexual Aggression: The Role of Perceptual Ambiguity."

Journal of Applied Social Psychology 30(6):1186–1200.

by

Nancy K. Hamilton

for

Social Psychology 2303

Section 105

Professor William A. Johnson, Jr., Ph.D.

University of Central Oklahoma

October 10, 2000

THESIS

Studies have established that alcohol use disrupts cognitive functions, and the fact that alcohol intoxication is a factor in a significant proportion of "date rape" incidents has also been well established by prior research. This study attempts to document the relationship between the level of alcohol consumption and male acceptance of sexual aggression.

The researchers examined how the interpretation of subtle versus explicit behavioral cues, as related to perceived sexual intent, is impacted by blood alcohol level. In this study, it was expected that the effects of alcohol consumption would be moderated by the behavior of the female (i.e., that when the female appeared receptive to the sexual advances, intoxicated male subjects would consider sexual aggression to be more acceptable than would sober subjects). If the thesis were correct, sexual aggression would be unacceptable even to intoxicated subjects, provided the female's behavior indicated a clear and consistent message of disinterest.

METHODS

Researchers recruited 118 volunteers through posters and class announcements at a medium-sized Southeastern state university. The study participants included university staff and students, students' friends, and students' relatives. The study excluded those volunteers with self-reported alcohol/drug problems, alcohol-related arrests (other than one charge of DUI), and those with significant medical or psychiatric problems. Study participants were tested for blood alcohol level (BAL) at the beginning of the session, and only those with an initial BAL of 0.00 percent were included in the study results. To minimize the probability of "demand bias," participants were told the experiment was intended to measure the effect of alcohol on visual acuity and social perceptions.

Subjects were given one of four beverages on the basis of random selection. Those in the control group got ice water, and knew they were part of the control group. The placebo group got tonic water with 0.08-ml alcohol/kg body weight. The low-dose group got 0.33-ml alcohol/kg body weight, and the moderate-dose group got 0.75-ml alcohol/kg body weight. Drinks were served in such a way that participants other than those in the control group did not know what dosage they had received. Subjects were given 20 minutes to consume the beverage and then spent 25 minutes completing a visual-acuity task. Then the subjects were asked to participate in two social perception experiments, one of which was the videotaped interaction of a male/female couple at the beginning of a "blind date." Subjects were shown two interactions, one in which the female was enthusiastic about the upcoming date, touched the male's arm, and laughed extensively, and one in which the female maintained a rigid posture, frequently checked her watch, and reminded the male of her need to end the date at the prescribed time. Both sequences ended as the couple left for the movies. Participants were then asked three questions: Should the man try to have sex with the woman, even if it means using force? Would you try to have sex with the woman, even if it meant using force? How responsible would the female be if the male forced her to have sex? Responses to the third question were rated on a 9-point scale ranging from 1 (not responsible at all) to 9 (totally responsible).

The authors of this study were diligent in structuring the experiment in a way that minimized unintended influences: (1) Care was taken to ensure that participants were not influenced by their own or the researchers' expectations; (2) there were clear distinctions between the behaviors exhibited by the females in the two scenarios; and (3) variations in the experimental treatments (alcohol dosage) were consistent across experimental groups.

EVIDENCE

Researchers found a strong positive correlation between increased alcohol consumption, acceptance of sexual aggression, and attribution of responsibility to the female. As expected, study participants consistently rejected sexual aggression

SAMPLE ARTICLE CRITIQUE (*CONT.*)

toward the female in the unreceptive scenario, but accepted sexual aggression toward the female in the receptive scenario, and were more accepting of that aggression as they become more intoxicated. Responsibility for the aggression was assigned to the female in the receptive scenario and to the male in the unreceptive scenario. These findings supported the thesis that unambiguous behavioral cues would be recognized and accepted even when the males were intoxicated, but that in a state of intoxication the males would attend to the most obvious behavioral cues and be more inclined to disregard other inhibitory cues (such as legal and moral sanctions against sexual aggression).

Participants' responses to the three questions indicated that BAL and the acceptance of sexual aggression increased in tandem, as did the attribution of female responsibility for the aggression, and those responses support the thesis of the experiment.

EVALUATION

This study is valuable to anyone who has occasion to be in social situations where alcohol consumption occurs. We know that males are influenced by the effects of alcohol in their interpretation of female behavior that appears to be sexually receptive. Consequently, women need a clear understanding of how their actions may be perceived and interpreted by male companions who are under the influence of alcohol. In the end, when a woman says "no," that should always mean "no." However, it is important to understand that this message can be obscured in a haze of intoxication from alcohol.

In continuing the pursuit of this and related research, it would be instructive to see if these findings apply across broader economic and educational lines, and to study how female intoxication impacts the perception of sexual aggression and the attribution of responsibility for that aggression.

10.3   LITERATURE REVIEWS

Your goal in writing a research paper is to provide your readers an opportunity to increase their understanding of the subject you are addressing. They will want the most current and precise information available. Whether you are writing a traditional library research paper, conducting an experiment or survey, doing an observational study, or preparing an analysis of a policy enforced by a social service agency, you must know what has already been learned in order to give your readers comprehensive and up-to-date information or to add something new to what is already known about the subject. For example, if your topic is how marital satisfaction is influenced by sex, you will need to survey the professional journals to discover what is already known about this subject. When you seek this information, you will be conducting a literature review, a thoughtful collection and analysis of available information on the topic you have selected for study. It tells you, before you begin your experiments or analyses, what is already known in this area.

Why do you need to conduct a literature review? It would be embarrassing to spend a lot of time and effort preparing a study, only to find that the information you are seeking has already been discovered by someone else. Also, a properly conducted literature review will tell you many things about a particular subject. It will tell you the extent of current knowledge, sources of data for your research, examples of what is not known about the subject (which generates ideas for formulating hypotheses), methods that have been used for research, and clear definitions of concepts relevant to your own research.

Let us consider an example. Suppose you are enrolled in a political sociology class and have been assigned to research the question: "How are voter attitudes affected by negative advertising?" First, you will need to establish a clear definition of "negative advertising," then find a way to measure attitudes of voters, and finally use or develop a method of discerning how attitudes are affected by advertising. Using research techniques explained in this and other chapters of this manual, you should begin your research by looking for studies that address your research question or similar questions at the library, on the Internet, and through other resources. You will discover that many studies have been written on voters' attitudes and the effects of advertising. As you read these studies, certain patterns will appear. Some research methods will appear to have produced better results than others. Some studies will be quoted in others many times—some confirming and others refuting what previous studies have done. You will constantly be making choices as you examine these studies, reading very carefully ones that are highly relevant to your purposes, and skimming those of only marginal interest. As you read, constantly ask yourself the following questions:

- How much is known about this subject?
- What is the best available information, and why is it better than other information?
- What research methods have been used successfully in relevant studies?
- What are the possible sources of data for further investigation of this topic?

- What important information is still unknown, in spite of previous research?
- Of the methods that have been used for research, which are the most effective for making new discoveries? Are new methods needed?
- How can the concepts being researched be more precisely defined?

You will find that this process, like the research process as a whole, is recursive: Insights related to one of the above questions will spark new investigations into others; these investigations will then bring up a new set of questions, and so on.

Literature reviews can be either a complete product or part of a larger, more comprehensive creation. For example, your instructor may request that you include a literature review as a section of the paper you are writing. Your written literature review may be from one to several pages in length. It should tell the reader the following:

- The best available information on the selected topic from previously compiled or published studies, articles, or other documents
- What these studies conclude about the topic
- The apparent methodological strengths and weaknesses of these studies
- What remains to be discovered about the topic
- What appear to be, according to these studies, the most effective methods for developing new information on the topic

Your literature review should consist of a written narrative that answers, not necessarily consecutively, the above questions. The success of your own research project depends in large part on the extent to which you have carefully and thoughtfully answered these questions.

The following example is extracted from a student research paper submitted in Professor Johnson's Sociological Research and Statistics class. This review is designed to assess the available information on marital satisfaction as it relates to several potentially influential variables: age, sex, number of children, number of years married, and extramarital affairs. It is a portion of a research paper like the review described in the Survey-Based Quantitative Research Papers section in Chapter 11. While some reviews are meant to be extensive in their survey of the topic and to stand alone, this model presents the information as succinctly as possible in one section of a research paper. Some instructors refer to this shorter, more concise presentation as "article format."

This sample literature review also models the ASA citation system described in Chapter 4 and the headings/subheadings format described in Chapter 3. When writing this assignment you should follow the guidelines outlined in these two chapters. Ask your instructor for directions concerning the length of the paper. Depending on the type of review you are writing, the length can vary greatly. If your review is an assignment that stands alone, your instructor may wish you to include a title page like the one with the following sample review (starting on page 193).

SAMPLE LITERATURE REVIEW

Marital Satisfaction:

A Review of the Literature

by

LaKrista Evans

for

Sociology of the Family 3303

Section 5635

Professor Maria Juarez

Colorado State University

November 15, 2001

SAMPLE LITERATURE REVIEW (*CONT.*)

REVIEW OF LITERATURE

Age

While early research found little or no association between age and marital sat-isfaction, more current research has concluded otherwise (Stephenson 1988; Trimble 1978; Tucker and O'Grady 1991). Tucker and O'Grady (1991) suggest that the younger the individual (especially under twenty years of age), the lower the marital satisfaction and the higher the likelihood of divorce. Stephenson (1988) reports that women's marital satisfaction may decline as they age, but that men's satisfaction increases. This may be the result of society's tendency to view female aging as negative, while aging men are often considered to have be-come more sophisticated.

In addition, Trimble (1978) believes that individuals going through the so-called midlife crisis often experience a loss of intimacy that results in marital dissatisfaction. According to Trimble (1978:107), around the age of forty "men and women may experience a kind of alienation from each other. This in turn pro-duces a crisis in the marriage that sometimes ends in divorce."

Sex

Some studies disclose little difference between the sexes in rates of marital hap-piness (Rowers 1991; Gorman 1992), while others reveal that women have high-er dissatisfaction rates than men (Dion and Dion 1993; Stephenson 1988). This may be due to the increasing independence of women as they enter into the workforce, become financially secure, and establish a larger pool of eligibles. In addition, different expectations about communication often create a strong bar-rier to a successful marriage. For example, women tend to discuss feelings and their relationships, while men would prefer to avoid these issues (Satran 1995). Satran (1995:92) observes that "the happiest couples speak each other's lan-guage." Whatever the reasons may be, women seem to be more dissatisfied with the actual degree of intimacy (Dion and Dion 1993). In addition, men tend to perceive their marriage as having more psychological and physical benefits than women do (Campbell 1989; Dion and Dion 1993; Fowers 1991).

Number of Children

The large majority of professional literature agrees that the transition to parenthood affects marital satisfaction (Abbey et al. 1994; Campbell 1989; Hunt 1995; Kephart and Jedlicka 1991; Levy-Skiff 1994; Lewis 1989; Stephenson 1988; Turner and Helms 1994). Although some research concludes otherwise, most believe children cause a decrease in marital happiness (Lewis 1989; Turner and Helms 1994). Usually this unhappiness is greater among women, probably due to the added responsibilities. This unhappiness increases if the husband does little to help out with the added responsibilities (Abbey, Andrews, and Halman 1994; Hunt 1995; Levy-Skiff 1994).

While Stephenson (1988) points out that no consistent findings have determined whether the actual number of children affects marital satisfaction, one might assume that as the number of children increases, added responsibilities, especially for the wife, increase as well. This in turn would create a deficiency in intimate relations, which could then lead to a decrease in marital satisfaction.

Number of Years Married

There are fewer studies concerned with length of marriage and its association with overall marital satisfaction. Of those assessing the impact of this variable, most agree that marital satisfaction tends to decline with time (Brinkerhoff and White 1991; Glenn 1993; Stephenson 1988). This could be a direct result of a lack of intimacy as the marriage progresses; it has consistently been found that the frequency of sexual intercourse declines steadily after the first year of marriage (Brinkerhoff and White 1991). In contrast to the above conclusion, Glenn (1993)

SAMPLE LITERATURE REVIEW (CONT.)

found that while women's satisfaction decreases with the length of marriage, men's satisfaction actually increases.

Extramarital Affairs

Kinsey and many other researchers agree that approximately 50 percent of males and 25 percent of females have engaged in extramarital sexual behavior at least once (Libby and Whitehurst 1977; Turner and Helms 1994). Whipple and White (1995) claim that more recent surveys indicate about 60 percent of men and 50 percent of women have been involved in this behavior.

Many researchers believe that extramarital affairs are highly associated with low marital satisfaction (Kinder and Cowan 1989; Libby and Whitehurst 1977; Pittman 1993; Turner and Helms 1994). But Pittman (1993) has observed some marriages as being stable and happy before the affair, with the rate of dissatisfaction in the marriage occurring after the affair begins. "The decision that they were not in love with their marriage partner was an effort to explain and justify their behavior" (Pittman 1993:36). However, most researchers agree that, in the majority of cases, a low degree of marital satisfaction precedes an extramarital affair.

10.4   ANNOTATED BIBLIOGRAPHIES

10.4.1   What Is an Annotated Bibliography?

A bibliography is, simply, a listing of written items—essays, reviews, books—that share one or more important characteristics: They were all written by the same author, perhaps, or they all deal with the work of a particular author or else focus on a particular field of study. The sort of annotated bibliography we will be dealing with in this chapter is a listing and brief description of articles, books, or other sources on a given topic. Depending on the uses for which it is intended, the annotated bibliography may be organized in various ways. For example, if the purpose of the bibliography is to chart the growth and development of critical interest in its topic, then the listed items may appear in chronological order according to the dates when they were first published. Most frequently, however, the items listed in an annotated bibliography are simply organized alphabetically, each one placed either by the last name of its author or, if no author's name is available, by the first important word in its title.

There are usually two components to each item in an annotated bibliography:

1. The bibliographical citation, using one of the standard citation systems, such as the MLA system or the ASA system described in Chapter 4
2. The annotation, a brief description or summary (usually 100 to 250 words) of the contents of the source

Sometimes the annotation attempts to be strictly objective in nature, meaning that it only describes the contents and purpose of the source without offering an opinion as to its quality. Scholars in some disciplines refer to this type of objective annotation as an *abstract*. Another type of annotation offers a brief assessment or appraisal of the source in addition to a description. We'll call this type an *evaluative annotation*.

Annotated bibliographies are usually limited to a specific theme, area, topic, or discipline. Taken together, the annotations provide a lucid and balanced account or synopsis of the state of research on its subject.

10.4.2   Why Write an Annotated Bibliography?

The purpose for writing an annotated bibliography can differ with the audience and the assignment. It might be a project in a course you are taking or a requirement for research in the organization or agency for which you work. (Your supervisor or colleagues may wish to know more about a particular topic.) Depending on the assignment, the annotated bibliography may serve a number of purposes, such as the following:

- To review the literature on a particular subject
- To illustrate the quality of your research

- To give your research historical perspective
- To illustrate the types of sources available in a given area
- To describe other items relating to a topic of interest to the reader
- To explore a particular subject for further research

10.4.3   Who Uses Annotated Bibliographies?

One of the great benefits of an annotated bibliography is that it saves time for those who consult it. Since extensive and scholarly annotated bibliographies provide a comprehensive overview of material published on a topic, they can give both researchers and practitioners a swift impression of the types of research already conducted on that topic, as well as a notion of the types of research left to do. An annotated bibliography can make researchers aware of articles or books they should read to advance their own research. Practitioners can scrutinize annotated bibliographies rapidly in order to see what new research their colleagues have conducted or what new practices have been developed in their fields and whether it would be worth their time to locate and read the entire article or book annotated.

But there is another important use for annotated bibliographies written by students. There are few ways of developing the descriptive and analytical skills needed in most scholarly disciplines more effectively than by compiling and writing an annotated bibliography. By summarizing and evaluating articles on a particular topic you are both learning valuable information about that topic and gaining confidence in assimilating and connecting facts the way scholars do. You are learning mastery of the material and the mental processes that comprise your discipline.

10.4.4   What Is the Content of an Annotated Bibliography?

The specific structure and approach to writing an annotated bibliography may vary with the professional community for which you are writing it. For example, in some situations an annotated bibliography may have an introductory paragraph or two in order to define its audience, purpose, rationale, and topic. In other situations, it may not. Here are a list and description of the most commonly found elements of an annotated bibliography:

Introduction.   In addition to defining your audience and expressing your purpose, your introduction should also describe the scope of your bibliography (the specific areas or types of works upon which you are focusing) and explain the reasons why you have limited your exploration to these parameters. It is also important to let your reader know clearly what kind of annotations you are providing, whether objective or evaluative. If you say your annotations are objective, then you are telling your reader that every opinion or theory expressed in each annotation belongs to the source and its author. If, however, the annotation is evaluative, then at least some of the material in it expresses *your* opinion about the quality of the source, an opinion that the writer might not share. You must not let your reader think that every opinion or theory expressed in the annotation belongs to the source when, in fact, that is not the case.

Citations.   Like a regular (unannotated) bibliography or a works cited page at the end of a research paper, an annotated bibliography provides a full bibliographic entry for each source it lists. Make sure you follow a bibliographical format approved by your instructor or by the publication for which you are writing. Chapter 4 of this manual gives guidelines for the ASA system of bibliography.

Annotations.   For most annotated bibliographies, the annotations should be one or two paragraphs that together range from about 100 to 250 words. To some extent the conventions of the professional community in which you are writing will dictate the contents of your annotations, as well as your specific purpose and audience. If you are writing your annotated bibliography for a course, your instructor will provide guidelines. It can be helpful to your reader for you to establish a consistent form for your annotations, perhaps beginning each time with a clear statement of the source's thesis, then a brief description of the argument used to prove or justify that thesis, followed, if required, by your evaluation of the work's value and achievement.

To quote or not to quote?   How much of your annotation should be direct quoting as opposed to your own wording? This is an important question to address, and one whose answer depends to a large extent on the uses you project for your bibliography. Importing the thesis sentence directly from the source, for example, may help you to be accurate about the source's purpose—but it may also establish a tone or a level of complex reasoning that the rest of a brief annotation cannot sustain. You do not want to give the impression that you are merely pasting together passages from the source without having thoroughly understood them yourself. Remember: While the style and tone of the source belong to the source's author, the style and tone of the annotation belong to you. You want your annotation, though it is small, to have the coherence and confidence of a well-made paragraph.

Depending on your project or assignment, your annotations may provide one or more of the following:

Summation.   As stated above, while *some* annotations offer evaluative comments, *most* annotations summarize the source. Here is a tip about summarizing: Although it is logical, when summarizing, to ask yourself what the source is about, it is rarely a good gambit to begin a brief annotation with the phrase, "This source is about. . . ." Why not? Because a sentence beginning with these words cannot help but end with a generalization about the source's subject that will be vaguer than a simple restatement of the source's thesis.

Here are introductory sentences from two objective annotations of the same source. Which sentence more effectively sets up the rest of the annotation?

Rafelson's article is about racial profiling and how it is misused in school counseling programs.

Rafelson argues that racial profiling should be prohibited in school counseling programs because it results in preferential treatment for certain minorities at the expense of others.

Sentence one establishes the *topic* of the source, but sentence two establishes the *thesis,* which is a more comprehensive and necessary task.

After relating the thesis of the source, you might describe such elements as methodology, results, and conclusions. The required length of the annotations will determine how detailed your summary should be.

Evaluation.   Your assignment may require you to include a brief critique or appraisal in each annotation. If you are writing evaluative annotations, ask yourself the following questions: What is the overall goal of this source? Does the source achieve its goal? Do you find the contents of the source useful in relation to your own research? How does the source compare with other sources in your bibliography? Is the information reliable? How biased is it?

Reflection.   If you are compiling this annotated bibliography in order to facilitate your own research project, you will probably want to examine the perspective taken in each source to ascertain how it fits into your research on the topic. The perspective could be a political one (liberal or conservative), a subject-matter perspective (sociological, psychological, medical, and so on), or some other perspective. It might help to point out similarities or contradictions between sources. For example, you might say, "Like Munson, Eversol approaches racial profiling from a sociological perspective. However, while Munson focuses on how law enforcement has used racial profiling to increase the probability of arrests, Eversol analyzes the practice of businesses profiling blacks to apprehend shoplifters." You might then want to reflect on how this source has changed how you think about your topic and how it fits into your research project.

The following sample short-version annotated bibliography (on page 201) is fictitious. It describes articles that might be written on racial profiling. The annotations in this example are like abstracts, since they are summative and contain no evaluative component.

Pages 202–203 show longer, abstract-type annotations for the same sample articles.

Annotated Bibliography
Racial Profiling

Jones, William B. 2003. "Targeting Blacks in Shoplifting Surveillance: Unjust and Inaccurate." *Social Issues* 26(2):37–45.

Jones argues that while racial profiling of shoplifters by major department stores is an unjust practice, the process also fails to target those most likely to shoplift. No data exists that supports the probability that blacks are more likely to shoplift than other racial groups. Targeting blacks in surveillance procedures only increases the opportunity to catch those blacks that shoplift and improves the chances of success for whites that shoplift.

Monroe, Victor G. 2003. "Using Racial Profiling to Impede the Trafficking of Illicit Drugs." *Drug Enforcement Bulletin,* August 14, pp. 42–45.

Using racial profiling to impede drug trafficking, contends Monroe, is not a good way to decrease the flow of illicit drugs in the United States. Race should never be a factor in probable cause, and the harm done from this practice far outweighs any perceived benefit. He supports applying legal sanctions to those practicing racial profiling to catch drug traffickers.

Arnold, Eugene H. 2003. "Terrorism and Racial Profiling." *Journal of International Terrorism* 17(3):510–518.

Arnold believes that the use of racial profiling to help control terrorist activities is both justified and necessary. Applying a random intervention policy wastes precious time investigating those with little potential for terrorism, while allowing those most likely to put others in harm's way—Middle Eastern, Muslim males between fifteen and twenty-nine years of age—to avoid careful examination.

Annotated Bibliography

Racial Profiling

Jones, William B. 2003. "Targeting Blacks in Shoplifting Surveillance: Unjust and Inaccurate." *Social Issues* 26(2):37–45.

Jones argues that while racial profiling of shoplifters by major department stores is an unjust practice, the process also fails to target those most likely to shoplift. No data exists that supports the probability that blacks are more likely to shoplift than other racial groups. Targeting blacks in surveillance procedures only increases the opportunity to catch those blacks that shoplift and improves the chances of success for whites that shoplift. Jones takes issue with Elsner and Squires, whose study, published in the June 2002 *Journal of Crime and Criminology,* supports racial profiling on the basis of its cost-effectiveness. While Jones concedes that targeting a single race reduces the cost to businesses by allowing them to streamline their security operations, he argues that this cost-effectiveness is offset by the increase in white shoplifting. Instead of using racial profiling, Jones recommends that businesses invest in more extensive human-relations training for security personnel.

Monroe, Victor G. 2003. "Using Racial Profiling to Impede the Trafficking of Illicit Drugs." *Drug Enforcement Bulletin,* August 14, pp. 42–45.

Using racial profiling to impede drug trafficking, contends Monroe, is not a good way to decrease the flow of illicit drugs in the United States. Race should never be a factor in probable cause, and the harm done from this practice far outweighs any perceived benefit. Monroe supports this argument by discussing recent, disastrous attempts of government agencies in six different countries to base a drug interdiction policy on data regarding race. While two of the six

---

SAMPLE 2: ANNOTATED BIBLIOGRAPHY (*CONT.*)

---

countries, the Netherlands and Luxembourg, reported a slight drop in the importation of marijuana and cocaine during their interdiction campaigns, all six of the countries eventually abandoned racial profiling for two reasons: The legal tangle it caused in the courts and the negative effect such profiling had on race relations within each country. Monroe provides information charting the effects of racially based drug policing programs on morale and social and economic development among minority populations in the United States. A former state attorney-general, Monroe concludes with an argument supporting the application of legal sanctions against those practicing racial profiling to catch drug traffickers.

Arnold, Eugene H. 2003. "Terrorism and Racial Profiling." *Journal of International Terrorism* 17(3):510–518.

Arnold believes that the use of racial profiling to help control terrorist activities is both justified and necessary. Applying a random intervention policy wastes precious time by focusing on those with little potential for terrorism, while allowing those most likely to put others in harm's way—Middle Eastern, Muslim males between fifteen and twenty-nine years of age—to avoid careful examination. Arnold constructs a three-part defense of his position, establishing first the legal argument for racially geared antiterrorist policies, then the economic argument, and, finally, what he calls the moral argument. Borrowing heavily on scripture from both the Old Testament and the Koran in the last third of the article, Arnold defines a religious imperative for racial profiling that, he admits, will not be to everyone's taste but that may provide direction and control for a problem that threatens to spiral out of control.

QUANTITATIVE RESEARCH PAPERS

As explained in Chapter 8, sociologists, like other scientists, rely on the scientific method in their attempt to understand and explain social phenomena. This often requires the quantification of data in order to apply more objective procedures. Some of the common research designs for quantitative data are described following.

11.1 QUANTITATIVE RESEARCH DESIGNS

Since sociologists investigate a wide variety of issues and problems, their quantitative research can take many forms. Four of the most common quantitative research designs are the following:

1. Surveys
2. Experiments
3. Direct observation
4. Content analysis

You will find detailed instructions for conducting a survey in the next section of this chapter (Survey-Based Quantitative Research Papers). Therefore, we will not discuss surveys in this brief introduction to quantitative research.

The processes of conducting experiments, performing scientific observation, and making content analysis studies require extensive additional knowledge and are normally only undertaken by students in upper-division courses or at the graduate level. However, it is important for all sociology students to have some basic knowledge of these procedures. Therefore, we provide a brief introduction to experiments, direct observation, and content analysis here.

11.1.1 Experiments

Experimentation is the fundamental method of acquiring knowledge in the physical sciences. As a research method it has one primary and substantial benefit: Experimentation allows the researcher to control the variables, making it easier than it might otherwise be to determine the effect of the independent variable upon the dependent variable. Experiments are more difficult to conduct in the social sciences than in the physical sciences because the research subjects are human beings and because the number of variables is normally large. In spite of these difficulties, however, social scientists are now successfully conducting more experiments than they have in the past.

Experiments in the social sciences are set up according to several different basic designs. The first is the simple post-test measurement. For example, a lecture on the social consequences of using marijuana may be followed by a test of the knowledge of the participants who heard the lecture. The test-retest method is more accurate. A researcher using this method might measure the effects of a lecture upon the attitudes of the people in an audience by first having the members of the audience complete a survey, then listen to the lecture, and finally complete the survey again. The researcher could then measure the differences in opinion registered before and after the survey. Without the first survey, the researcher cannot be sure of the level of knowledge or the respondents' attitudes before the test was given, and the effects of the lecture or speech, then, are less certain.

The alternative-form type of experiment uses two different measures of the same concept. In a research project concerning the effects of peer pressure on adolescents, for example, the analyst could measure subjects' propensity to conform in one test and then their desire for acceptance in another test. The split-halves device is similar to the alternative-form measurement, except that two measures of the concept under study are applied at the same time.

All experimental designs confront the following problems:

- *Control of variables:* Can the environment be controlled to rule out other factors?
- *Time passage:* People get tired, or for some other reason take a different attitude.
- *Varying acts of measurement:* Different pollsters may record the responses differently.
- *Statistical regression:* Someone who is on the high end of a test score range may register a high score only temporarily.
- *Experimental mortality:* Subjects drop out.
- *Instrument decay:* The instrument may not be used as carefully the second time.
- *Selection error:* Control and experimental groups may not be equivalent.

Researchers have developed a number of complex methodologies to overcome these problems. Multigroup designs, for example, test multiple independent variables against the same dependent variable. Factorial designs may test the effects of several independent variables in different combinations. A simple 2×2

factorial design, for example, might test combinations of four possible results from two different actions a researcher might take to test the social acceptability of her actions. Let's suppose that the researcher made an identical presentation of information on the health hazards of smoking to four different groups of people and later had the groups complete a questionnaire that would indicate their acceptance of her presentation. Normally the researcher would wear a traditional business suit when addressing a group, but since the experiment's goal is to study how socially acceptable her appearance is to her audiences, she decides to alter her customary dress in each group setting, using a straw hat and a pink leotard. The chart below illustrates the four possible variations in her appearance:

	Wear Pink Leotard	Do Not Wear Pink Leotard
WEAR A STRAW HAT	(1) Both hat and leotard	(2) Hat but no leotard
DO NOT WEAR A STRAW HAT	(3) Leotard but not hat	(4) Neither hat nor leotard

A factorial design based upon the choices set forth in the above chart would test the results of presentation participant acceptance according to each of the four situations.

Researchers conduct dozens of different types of experimental designs, using different combinations of strategies. The above factorial design is intended to be used as part of a field experiment—an experiment conducted within a natural setting, which in our example above would be four regular high school health classes.

In the following example the groups who participate in the experiment have not been left in their natural setting or randomly assigned, but rather have been preselected by the researcher. Some researchers claim that this type of interference with subjects creates a quasi-experimental design and raises questions about the impact of the experimental treatment on the outcome measurement.

Let us suppose that we will design an experiment to test this research hypothesis: "Students who are anxious because they believe their instructor will have access to their evaluations of the instructor's effectiveness before the assignment of the students' final grades will give the instructor a higher evaluation than if they had no such anxiety."

For our experiment, the teacher will use two course sections of his Introduction to Sociology class, the sections being similar in size and student make-up. Section 1, the control group, will be given the teacher evaluation form in the usual manner. The teacher will leave the room while a monitor—a student in the class—dispenses the forms, reads the instructions, gathers the forms after they have been completed, seals them in an envelope, and then leaves the room, supposedly to take them where they will be kept from the teacher until final grades have been assigned to transcripts. As part of the instruction, the teacher emphasizes the fact that he does not have access to the results until final grades have been recorded.

Section 2, the experimental group, will follow the same procedure with one exception. The monitor, again a student in the class, will first disclose information she has been given about teachers being allowed to look at the evaluations prior to the final grades being assigned. She will state that this is something she has heard from several reliable sources, but that she is unwilling to disclose those sources. Everything else in the evaluation process will be carefully controlled to emulate the procedure used with the control group. The evaluations are then tallied to determine if the experimental group's perception that the teacher has access to their evaluations before the final grades are assigned caused them to give their teacher significantly higher evaluations than the control group did.

Experiments in sociology like the one above encounter certain difficulties. See if you can answer the following questions:

- Is this an experiment or a quasi-experiment? Why?
- What is the dependent variable of the experiment?
- What is the independent variable?
- What are the important antecedent and intervening variables?
- What else would need to be done to control the antecedent and intervening variables?
- What ethical issues might preclude running an experiment of this kind?

11.1.2 Direct Observation

A number of techniques are used for data collection. Direct observation of social phenomena is conducted by trained observers who carefully record selected behaviors. Observation may be structured, which means that a definite list of phenomena is compiled and studied. Or observation may be unstructured, in which case observation attempts to take in every action in a certain setting that may possibly be significant. In either case, successful observation for purposes of social science research always follows clear guidelines and standard procedures.

Direct scientific observation is difficult to conduct for several reasons. First, researchers usually consider observation data to be qualitative and therefore subjective in nature. Although much of the data can be quantified, qualitative considerations are hard to avoid. Another problem is that social events can be difficult, time-consuming, and expensive to observe, and an entire event, such as an election, may require several observers whose activities are highly coordinated and regulated.

11.1.3 Content Analysis

Content analysis is a method of analyzing written documents that allows researchers to transform nonquantitative data into quantitative data by counting and categorizing certain variables within the data. Content analysts look for certain types of words or references in the texts, and then categorize or count them. A content analyst of news articles on women, for example, might count the number of times the authors of the articles portray women in a positive manner.

Content analysts of "events data" focus on a particular event or a series of events over time. A number of content analysts have examined the major wars of this century and have attempted to identify factors that are common in situations of war. Compilations of events data, such as the World Handbook of Political and Social Indicators (Russett 1977), provide a listing of the important political events (e.g., elections, coups, wars) for most countries of the world. These listings help to compare trends in selected types of events from one country to another. Press reports, statistics, televised and radio reports, personal records, newspapers, and magazines provide inexhaustible mines of data for content analysts. Government documents are an especially rich source of material for political scientists. Different types of government documents include presidential papers; the Code of Federal Regulations; the Congressional Record; federal, state, and local election returns; historical records; judicial decisions; and legal records. The data analyzed in content analysis are most often the words contained in books, journals, magazines, newspapers, films, and radio or television broadcasts. But content analysis may also be conducted on photographs, cartoons, or music.

An example of content analysis design is found in the research of Levin, Arluke, and Mody-Desbareau (1986), who coded 311 celebrity and noncelebrity profiles that appeared in the four most widely circulated gossip magazines—*National Enquirer, Star, Globe,* and *National Examiner*—from February through July of 1983. The researchers concluded that while the profiles of noncelebrities mostly emphasized extraordinary acts of heroism, strength, or charity, celebrities were usually featured for some mundane or minor event, such as a shopping spree or quarrel with a spouse or lover. The researchers found a hidden message in the articles they reviewed: The ordinary, "little" person in the world should be content with his collective place in life (Levin and Fox 1997).

11.2 SURVEY-BASED QUANTITATIVE RESEARCH PAPERS

11.2.1 *Scope and Purpose of a Sociological Survey Paper*

A survey is simply a device for identifying and counting events, actions, perceptions, attitudes, or beliefs. Sociological surveys are the barometers of society. They describe a society's quality of life and the characteristics of its culture. They tell us who we are. There is little doubt that the skillful use of surveys dramatically increases the accuracy of our perceptions of ourselves.

As a student of sociology, you will find that writing your own sociological survey paper will serve two purposes. First, in learning how to construct, conduct, and interpret a sociological survey, you will add to your understanding of society and of one of the most basic processes of sociological research. By writing this paper you will gain a skill—if only at the introductory level—that you may actually use in your professional life. Public and private organizations often conduct surveys on attitudes and preferences in order to make their services more effective and desirable. Second, you will learn how to evaluate critically published surveys. Knowing the strengths and weaknesses of the surveying process will help you to obtain some of the fundamental knowledge necessary to appraise the validity of surveys you read about in books, journals, magazines, and newspapers.

This chapter explains how to construct and conduct a simple sociological survey and how to apply to your survey results some elementary data analysis and evaluation techniques. Your instructor may want to add supplemental tasks, such as other statistical procedures, and your class text in sociology methods will explain much more about the process of sociological research. The following set of directions, however, will provide a general framework that will help you to create and interpret a sociological survey.

11.2.2   Steps for Writing a Sociological Survey Paper

1. Focus on a specific topic.   The first step in writing a sociological survey paper is to select a topic that is focused on one specific issue. While nationally conducted surveys sometimes cover a broad variety of topics, confining your inquiry to one narrowly focused issue will allow you to gain an appreciation for even a single topic's complexity and for the difficulties inherent in clearly identifying opinions. Precision is vital to the success of a sociological survey. Topics for sociological papers are nearly as numerous as the titles of articles in a daily newspaper. Sociological surveys are conducted on topics pertaining to local, state, national, or international politics. You will usually increase the interest of the audience of your paper if you select an issue that is being widely discussed in the news. Many issues of health and safety are publicized on a regular basis. General topic headings found almost daily in the news include the following:

- Drugs
- Crime
- Education
- Abortion
- Family life

2. Formulate a research question and hypothesis.   After you have selected a topic, your task is to determine what you would like to investigate about that topic. One student who was interested in family relationships, for example, wanted to try to identify the factors that contribute to and detract from marital satisfaction. The first thing you need to understand when conducting survey research is that you must phrase your questions carefully. If you simply ask, "What do you think makes for a happy marriage?" you will probably receive obvious replies from a substantial majority of your respondents, replies that may not have much to do with actual marital satisfaction. To find out what really makes for a good marriage, you will need to design more specific questions. The following sections of this chapter will help you to do this.

However, to create these specific questions, you will first need to formulate a research question and a research hypothesis. A research question asks exactly what the researcher wants to know. Here are some examples of research questions posed by national surveys:

What factors contribute to family stability?

What social conditions contribute to violence?

What are the social issues about which Americans are most concerned?

Research questions for papers for sociology classes, however, should be more specific and confined to a narrowly defined topic. Consider the following:

What is the relationship, if any, between ethnicity and philanthropy?

To what extent do the people surveyed believe that their own personal actions, such as working hard toward a goal, will actually make a difference in their lives?

What is the relationship, if any, between sexual orientation and choice of vocation?

It is important to note that while you are formulating a hypothesis or hypotheses from your research question, hypotheses can only be accepted or rejected through the application of decision-making statistics. These techniques require special skills that you may or may not have acquired. Since the statistical techniques outlined below are only descriptive, their application can only suggest direction and trends. Therefore, it would be inappropriate to make a decision about the correctness of your hypothesis in the absence of decision-making statistics.

3. Select your sample.   Researchers usually conduct sociological surveys to find out how large groups of people—such as Americans in general, African Americans, women, or welfare recipients—behave in certain situations. It is normally unnecessary and too costly to obtain data on every member of the group under consideration, so most surveys question a small but representative percentage of the total group that is being studied. The individual units studied in a sociological survey are usually called *elements*. An element might be a group—such as an ethnic group, social organization, or church denomination—but it is most often an individual. The population is the total number of elements covered by the research question. If, as in our sample survey research design, the research question is "Are left-handed fifth-grade boys more likely than right-handed fifth-grade boys to identify with sports heroes?" then the population is all fifth-grade boys in the United States. The sampling frame consists of all fifth-grade boys who attend the school in which your survey will take place. The sample is the part of the population that is selected to respond to the survey. A representative sample includes numbers of elements in the same proportions as they occur in the general population. In other words, if 81 percent of the population of fifth-grade boys in the United States are right-handed and 19 percent are left-handed, then 81 percent of a representative sample of fifth-grade boys will also be right-handed and 19 percent will be left-handed. Conversely, nonrepresentative samples do not include numbers of elements in the same proportions as they occur in the general population.

How large must a sample be to accurately represent the population? This question is difficult to answer, but two general principles apply. The first is that a large sample is more likely, simply by chance, to be more representative of a population than a small sample. The second is that the goal of a representative sample is to include representatives of all of the strata that are included in the whole population.

Let us consider the case of a student who has designed a research survey to determine the degree of marital satisfaction experienced by students at her college. The target population for the survey is the married students enrolled at the college. The next question becomes: How can our student researcher get a representative sample—meaning one in which the percentages of student marital satisfaction are the same as the percentages in the much larger target population? Generalizing from a sample to a population contains some error. The objective is to draw the most representative sample—one with the lowest error—from the population. A random sample has the lowest chance of error because every element in it has an equal opportunity of being selected. However, circumstances often do not allow the researcher to use this sampling technique.

Sometimes the researcher is able to control error from certain variables by stratifying the sample, or subdividing it into different layers based on prior knowledge of how these variables are distributed in the population. If, for example, before sampling a university population, we know that 58 percent of the student body is female, 13 percent are minorities, the average age is twenty-eight, and 54

SAMPLE SURVEY RESEARCH DESIGN

Research question: Are left-handed fifth-grade boys more likely than right-handed fifth-grade boys to identify with sports heroes?

Research hypothesis: Left-handed fifth-grade boys are more likely than right-handed fifth-grade boys to identify with sports heroes.

Elements: Individual fifth-grade boys

Population: American fifth-grade boys

Sampling frame: Fifth-grade boys at Hoover Elementary School

Sample: 84 students in Mr. Wimbly's and Mrs. Baker's classes, out of the total population of 420 fifth-grade boys at Hoover Elementary School

percent of the students attend all or part of their program at night, we can strati-
fy the sample according to these variables before making random selections. Again,
obtaining a stratified sample, like a purely random sample, is very difficult—if not
impossible—when the population in question is college students.

Faced with such problems, the most reasonable and economical question
becomes: Can the survey be completed in select classes that represent the student body? For example, would sampling classes that are diversified by age, sex,
ethnic background, major field, and so on, lower the error enough to allow the
researcher to feel comfortable generalizing to the target population as a whole?
Our answer depends to some extent on the degree to which the makeup of the
classes parallels the stratification of the university. While this is often the best
sampling procedure available in such a complex environment as a university, the
problem with the method lies in our inability to gauge the amount of error. When
we read about a plus or minus 3 or 4 percent error in samples that have been
taken for opinion polls and other scientific endeavors, it is important to understand that the researchers have applied controlled procedures to judge the error
involved in generalizing to the population being sampled. So while we may have
given careful thought to selecting classes that are stratified much like the student
body of the university, the absence of random selection prevents us from accurately measuring the error involved in generalizing to the population.

As you begin to work on your own sociological survey, you will find it most
convenient to select as your sample the class in which you are writing your paper.
The disadvantage of this sample selection is that your class may not be representative of your college or university. Even if this is the case, however, using
the class will enable you to learn the procedures for conducting a survey, which
is the primary objective of this exercise.

RESEARCH WITH HUMAN SUBJECTS.   Sociological surveys often ask people for personal information. The people whose responses are sought are then known as
human subjects of the research. Most colleges and universities have policies
concerning research with human subjects. Sometimes administrative offices,
known as *institutional review boards,* are established to review proposals for research to ensure that the rights of human subjects are protected. It may be necessary for you to obtain permission from your institutional review board or
college to conduct your survey. Be sure to comply with all policies of your college or university with respect to research with human subjects.

4. Construct the survey questionnaire.   Your research question is your primary guide for constructing survey questions. As you begin to write your questions, ask yourself what it is that you really want to know about the topic. Suppose
that your research question is: "What are the views of sociology students regarding the role of the government in regulating abortions?" If you ask as one of
your survey questions, "Are you for abortion?" you may get a "no" answer from
70 percent of the respondents. If you then ask, "Are you for making abortion illegal?" you may get the answer "no" from 81 percent of your respondents. These
answers seem to contradict each other. By asking additional questions, you may

determine that, although a majority of the respondents finds abortion is regrettable, only a minority wants to make it illegal.

But even this may not be enough information to get a clear picture of people's opinions. The portion of the population that wants to make abortion illegal may be greater or smaller according to the strength of the legal penalty to be applied for having an abortion. In addition, some of the students who want no legal penalty for having an abortion may want strict medical requirements imposed on abortion clinics, while others may not. You will need to design additional specific questions to accurately determine respondents' views on these issues.

You must consider carefully the number of questions to include in your questionnaire. The first general rule, as mentioned, is to ask a sufficient number of questions to find out precisely what it is you want to know. A second principle, however, conflicts with this first rule. This second principle—which may not be a problem in your sociology class—is that people generally do not like to fill out surveys. Short surveys with a small number of questions are more likely to be answered completely than long questionnaires. The questionnaire for your paper in survey research methods should normally contain between ten and twenty-five questions.

Surveys consist of two types of questions—closed and open. Closed questions restrict the response of the respondent to a specific set of answers, normally two to six. Multiple-choice examination questions are typical closed questions. Open questions do not restrict respondents to preselected answers, but allow them to answer in any manner they choose. Therefore, open questions call for a more active and thoughtful response than do closed questions. The increased time and effort may be a disadvantage, though, because in general the more time and effort a survey demands, the fewer responses it is likely to get. However, open questions have the advantage of providing an opportunity for unusual views to be expressed. For example, you might get the following response to the question "What should be done about gun control?": "All firearms should be restricted to law enforcement agencies in populated areas. Special privately owned depositories should be established for hunters to be able to store rifles in hunting areas, where they can be used for target practice or outdoors during hunting season."

Open questions are preferable to closed questions when you want to expand a range of possible answers to find out how much diversity there is among opinions on an issue. For practice working with open questions, you should include at least one in your survey questionnaire. Perhaps the greatest difficulty with open questions is quantifying the results. The researcher must examine each answer and then group responses according to their content. For example, it might be possible to differentiate responses that are clearly in favor of, clearly opposed to, and ambivalent toward gun control. Open questions are of particular value to researchers who are doing continuing research; the responses they obtain help them to create better questions for the next survey they conduct.

In addition to the regular open and closed questions on your survey questionnaire, you will want to add what are often called *identifiers*—questions that ask for personal information about the respondents. If you ask questions about gun control, for example, you may want to know if men respond differently from women, if Caucasians respond differently from African Americans, or if young people respond differently from older people. Identifier questions, sometimes referred to as *demographic variables,* concern such things as the respondent's gender, age, political party, religion, income level, or other items that may be relevant to the particular survey topic. For an example of a questionnaire containing both closed and identifier questions, see page 78.

5. Collect data.   After you have written the survey questionnaire, you need to conduct the survey. You will need to distribute it to the class or other group of respondents. Be sure to provide on the survey form clear directions for completing it. If the students are to fill out the survey in class, read the directions out loud to the class and ask if there are any questions before the students begin.

6. Tabulate data.   If your sample is only the size of a small sociology class, you will be able to tabulate the answers directly from the survey form. If you have a larger sample, however, you may want to use data collection forms such as those available from the Scantron Corporation (on-line at scantron.com). You may already be using Scantron forms when you take multiple-choice tests in some of your classes now. On Scantron forms—which are separate from your survey form—respondents use a number 2 pencil to mark multiple-choice answers. The advantage of Scantron forms is that they are processed through computers that tabulate the results and sometimes provide statistical measurements. If you use Scantron sheets, you will need access to computers that process the results, and you may need someone to program the computer to provide the specific statistical measurements that you need.

7. Analyze data.   After you have collected and tabulated the completed questionnaires, you will need to analyze the data that they provide. There are many statistical procedures especially designed to describe data and to imply the correctness of hypotheses. Several useful types of statistics are easily processed with the aid of common computer programs. Ask your instructor for advice about which statistical methods to use and which software package to choose. Each software package will provide its own directions for entering data and determining results. The following example describes one way to collect, tabulate, and analyze data.

AN EXAMPLE.   Using the marital satisfaction questionnaire on page 78, suppose we survey a sample of 200 married students at Coweta State College. Taken together, the first ten items on this questionnaire are an example of a summative scale—because they are all measuring some component of the same variable (marital satisfaction), they can be added to yield a score that represents this variable. Notice that respondents are asked to rate each of the ten items on a scale that ranges from 1 (least degree) to 5 (greatest degree). After adding the ratings for the ten items, the marital satisfaction scale yields a score that ranges from 10 (very unsatisfied) to 50 (very satisfied). Each individual in the sample receives a score on this scale that represents his or her level of marital satisfaction.

These scores allow us to associate each of the identifier variables on the questionnaire (sex, number of children, and so on) with marital satisfaction. For example, if we choose to describe how sex relates to marital satisfaction, we can compare the level of male marital satisfaction to that of female marital satisfaction. In order to do so, we must find some number that lies between the extremes of marital satisfaction (10 to 50) to represent each of the categories (male and female). Since we are dealing with scores, we can use the mean (arithmetic average) to represent each category. We can calculate the mean by simply adding all the male scores and dividing that sum by the number of males in the sample (42 + 37 + 48 + 41 + 37 + ... / 94 = 42.35) Then we do the same for the females. This gives us a mean value for males (42.35) and a mean value for females (38.47). We now have a way to describe the difference between males and females in their level of marital satisfaction.

You've heard the saying that "a picture is worth a thousand words." That's also true with data analysis. If we describe our analysis with charts, graphs, or figures, the reader is more likely to see and understand what we are trying to communicate. The following figure is one way to visualize our results.

Marital Satisfaction Scale

Charts and graphs are helpful in visualizing how sex and marital satisfaction are related. While there are several types of charts or graphs (e.g., bar, pie, line) that visually describe data, the bar chart is a popular choice for a problem like ours. The bar chart that follows presents the same analysis as the preceding figure, but the visual presentation is more appealing to some people.

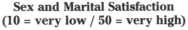

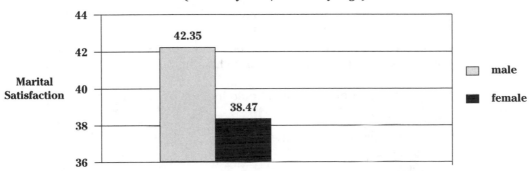

This chart was created in Microsoft Word by clicking on *insert,* then opening the *picture* option and clicking on *chart.* There are many options in the chart selection. The preceding chart is a simple bar chart with a legend and labels for the axes, along with values on the y (vertical) axis. Both of these charts allow the reader to visualize the difference between males and females as it is depicted on the marital satisfaction scale.

While we have done a good job of *describing* the association between sex and marital satisfaction, it's important to understand that we cannot make an inference or decision about this association without the application of inferential or probability statistics. Both visual presentations clearly indicate that males scored higher than females in marital satisfaction, but without the application of probability to this difference, we cannot determine if it is really due to the sex of the respondents or to chance.

Our example shows that charts and figures are helpful tools in describing data. The remaining identifier variables on this questionnaire can be described in the same manner.

11.2.3   The Elements of a Sociological Survey Paper

A sociological survey paper is composed of five essential parts:

1. Title page
2. Abstract
3. Text
4. References
5. Appendixes

1. Title page.   The title page should follow the directions given in Chapter 3. The title of a sociological survey paper should provide the reader with two types of information: the subject matter of the survey and the population being surveyed. Examples of titles for papers based on in-class surveys are "University of South Carolina Student Opinions on Welfare Reform," "Middlebury College Student Attitudes About Sexual Harassment," and "The 2000 Presidential Election: Ohio University Student Opinions on a Recount in Florida."

2. Abstract.   Abstracts for a sociological survey paper should follow the directions given in Chapter 3. In approximately 150–200 words, the abstract should summarize the subject, methodology, and results of the survey. An abstract for the example used in this chapter might be like the one in Chapter 3 on page 66.

3. Text.   The text of the paper should include five sections:

1. Introduction
2. Literature review
3. Methodology
4. Results
5. Discussion

SAMPLE INTRODUCTION

University students often have problems discovering financial aid programs, and, once such programs are identified, accessing channels to apply for funds. The purpose of this paper is to define Howard University student attitudes toward federal student aid programs. In particular, this study seeks to understand how students view the criteria for aid eligibility and the efficiency of application procedures. Further, the survey is expected to indicate the amount of knowledge students have about the federal student aid process. The primary reason for conducting this study is that the results will provide a basis for identifying problems in the aid application and disbursement process, and facilitate discussion among administrative officers and students about solutions to problems that are identified.

INTRODUCTION.   The introduction should explain the purpose of your paper, define the research question and hypothesis, and describe the circumstances under which the research was undertaken. Your purpose statement will normally be a paragraph in which you explain your reasons for conducting your research. You may want to write something like the sample introduction that follows. Next, the introduction should state the research question and the research hypotheses. The research question might be, "Is student knowledge of federal student aid related to student attitudes about the effectiveness of the aid programs?" A hypothesis might be, "Student ratings of the effectiveness of federal student aid programs is positively correlated with student knowledge of the programs."

LITERATURE REVIEW.   As stated in Chapter 10, the goal in writing a research paper is to provide your readers an opportunity to increase their understanding of the subject you are addressing. The purpose of a literature review is to demonstrate that the person conducting the study is familiar with the professional literature that is relevant to the survey and to summarize the content of that literature for the reader. The subject matter of the survey may be gender discrimination in secondary education programs. In this case, the purpose of the literature review would be to briefly inform your readers about (1) the history, content, and social implications of gender differences in secondary educational programs; and (2) the current status of discriminatory practices. In providing this information you should cite appropriate documents, such as previous studies on the subject. Chapter 10 gives detailed instructions for completing this section of your paper and an example of a literature review from a survey paper appears on pages 193–196.

METHODOLOGY.   The methodology—sometimes labeled *design*—section of your paper describes how you designed and conducted your study. It should also briefly describe the format and content of the questionnaire: How many questions were asked? What kinds of questions (open, closed, and so on) were asked, and why were these formats selected? The methodology section should also briefly address the statistical procedures used in data analysis: What statistical methods are used? Why were they selected? What information are these procedures intended to provide? Finally, the methodology section should explain how the sample was drawn and what population is being sampled.

RESULTS.   The results—sometimes labeled *findings*—section of your paper should present the findings of your study. Here you report the results of your statistical calculations. Raw data should not be included. The descriptive statistics you create from the data should be presented in tables and/or charts. Interpret the results as they relate to your hypothesis. Remember, hypotheses can only be accepted or rejected through the application of decision-making statistics. Allow your descriptive statistics to assist you in determining the accuracy of the hypothesis, but avoid statements that bring finality to your conclusion.

DISCUSSION.   In your discussion—sometimes labeled *conclusions*—section, draw out the implications of your findings: What is the meaning of the results of your study? How do the results of your study relate to those you described in your review of literature section? What conclusions can you draw? What questions remain unanswered? At the end of this section, provide the reader with suggestions for further research that are derived from your research findings.

4. References.   Your references and source citations in the text should be completed according to the guidelines in Chapter 4. If your instructor is using the article format referred to in Chapter 4, you should double-space after the last line of the discussion section of your survey paper and type "REFERENCES" in all caps. Double-space again and begin listing your references. Some instructors prefer a separate page for the references. In this case, insert a page break and type "REFERENCES" at the top of the page, double-space, and list your sources. Remember that, as stated in Chapter 4, only those sources cited in the paper can be included in the reference section, and all reference listings must be cited somewhere in the paper.

5. Appendixes.   See Chapter 3 for further guidelines on including appendixes at the end of the paper. The only thing that must be included in an appendix for a sociological survey paper is a copy of the questionnaire used in the study like the example on page 78. Other material that might be appropriate for inclusion in a survey paper appendix includes the following:

- Tables or charts of survey data not sufficiently important to be included in the text but helpful for reference
- Summaries of survey data from national or regional surveys on the same subject, if such surveys are available and discussed in your text

QUALITATIVE RESEARCH PAPERS

There are differences in doing social research from qualitative and quantitative perspectives that go beyond the use of numbers. We discuss some of these differences below, and describe in some detail the qualitative approach, especially as it relates to utilizing case studies.

12.1   WHAT IS QUALITATIVE RESEARCH?

Any research that produces results and is not quantitative can be classified as qualitative research. Qualitative research generally seeks to describe and/or analyze individuals, groups, organizations, agencies, communities, or some pattern of social interaction. Some of the methods used by qualitative researchers include observation, participant observation, open-ended surveys, unstructured interviews, and life histories. Basically, any method that allows the researcher to see the world from the perspective of those being studied could be called a qualitative design.

Qualitative research is usually as follows:

- *Empathetic:* The researcher attempts to understand why those being studied think, feel, and act the way they do.
- *Longitudinal:* The analysis generally takes place over time, with change an important part of the description and/or analysis; there is an emphasis on process.
- *Descriptive:* People, places, and settings are usually described in detail, with rich text replacing the numbers used in quantitative research.
- *Unstructured:* Unlike hypothesis-testing research, the "strategy is . . . open, so that in some cases the investigator may not have decided in advance precisely what is to be investigated" (Bouma and Atkinson 1995:207). This open, unstructured approach to research allows unexpected topics or events to be investigated, and makes for theory-building rather than theory-testing.

12.2   COMPARING QUANTITATIVE AND QUALITATIVE RESEARCH

While we tend to dichotomize the quantitative and qualitative approaches to social research into those using and not using statistics, respectively, this limits our understanding of some basic differences that go beyond the numbers comparison. The following table utilizes certain descriptive words to compare these approaches to social research:

Quantitative Research	Qualitative Research
Structured	Open
Logical	Intuitive
Measured	Subjective
Directional	Exploratory

The next table, which summarizes Bryman's (1994) description of certain aspects of research as they relate to both qualitative and quantitative research, also highlights the differences:

Aspect of Research	Quantitative	Qualitative
Relationship between researcher and subject	Distant	Close
Research strategy	Structured	Unstructured
Nature of data	Hard, reliable	Rich, deep
Relationship between theory and research	Confirmatory	Emergent

12.3   CASE STUDIES AS QUALITATIVE RESEARCH

One of the most common forms of qualitative research is the case study, although in some instances this approach can also be quantitative. We will take the remainder of this chapter to describe and outline this approach to qualitative research, followed by an example of a qualitative case study.

12.3.1   Definition and Purpose

A case study is an in-depth investigation of a social unit such as a person, gang, business, political party, or church undertaken to identify the factors that influence the manner in which the unit functions. Some examples of case studies are as follows:

An evaluation of the industrial efficiency of a Western Electric plant

A study of ritual and magic in the culture of the Trobriand Islanders

A study of the social service agency behavior of forest rangers

A description of the role of secretary in the corporation

Case studies have long been used in law schools, where students learn how the law develops by reading actual court case decisions. Business schools began to develop social service agency case studies to help students understand actual management situations. Courses in social organization, public administration, and social institutions adopt the case study method as a primary teaching tool less often than business or law schools, but case studies have become a common feature of many courses in these areas.

Psychologists have used the case histories of mental patients for many years to support or negate a particular theory. Sociologists use the case study approach to describe and draw conclusions about a wide variety of subjects, such as labor unions, police departments, medical schools, gangs, public and private bureaucracies, religious groups, cities, and social class (Philliber, Schwab, and Sloss 1980:64). The success of this type of research depends heavily on the open-mindedness, sensitivity, insights, and integrative abilities of the investigator.

Case studies fulfill many educational objectives in the social sciences. As a student in a sociology course, you may write a case study in order to improve your ability to do the following:

- Carefully and objectively analyze information
- Solve problems effectively
- Present your ideas in clear written form, directed to a specific audience

In addition, writing a case study allows you to discover some of the problems you will face if you become involved in an actual social situation that parallels your case study. For example, writing a case study like the example included at the end of this chapter can help you to understand the following:

- Some of the potentials and problems of society in general
- The operation of a particular cultural, ethnic, political, economic, or religious group
- The development of a particular problem, such as crime, alcoholism, or violence within a group
- The interrelationships—within a particular setting—of people, structures, rules, politics, relationship styles, and many other factors

12.3.2   Using Case Studies in Research

Isaac and Michael (1981:48) suggest that case studies offer several advantages to the investigator. For one thing, they provide useful background information for researchers planning a major investigation in the social sciences. Case studies often suggest fruitful hypotheses for further study, and they provide specific examples by which to test general theories. Philliber et al. (1980:64) believe that through intensively investigating only one case, the researcher can gain more depth and detail than might be possible by briefly examining many cases. Also, the depth of focus in the study of a single case allows investigators to recognize certain aspects of the object being studied that would otherwise go unobserved. For example, Becker et al. (1961) noticed that medical students tend to develop a slang that Becker and his associates refer to as "native language." Only after observing the behavior of the students for several weeks were the researchers able to determine that the slang word *crocks* referred to those patients who were of no help to the students professionally because they did not have an observable disease. The medical students felt the "crocks" were robbing them of their important time.

Bouma and Atkinson (1995:110–114) call attention to the exploratory nature of some case studies. Researchers, for example, may be interested in what is happening within a juvenile detention center. Before beginning the project, they may not know enough about what they will find in order to formulate testable hypotheses. The researchers' purpose in doing a case study may be to gather as much information as possible in order to help in the formulation of relevant hypotheses. Or the researchers may intend simply to observe and describe all that is happening within the case being studied.

12.3.3   Limitations of the Case Study Method

Before writing a case study you should be aware of the limitations of the methods you will be using in order to avoid drawing conclusions that are not justified by the knowledge you acquire. First, case studies are relatively subjective exercises. When you write a case study, you select the facts and arrange them into patterns from which you may draw conclusions. The quality of the case study will depend largely upon the quality of the facts you select and the way in which you interpret those facts.

A second potential liability to the case study method is that every case study, no matter how well written, is in some sense an oversimplification of the events that are described and the environment within which those events take place. To simplify an event or series of events makes it easier to understand but at the same time distorts its effect and importance. It can always be argued that the results of any case study are peculiar to that one case and, therefore, offer little as a rationale for a general explanation or prediction (Philliber et al. 1980:65). A third caution about case studies pertains strictly to their use as a learning tool in the classroom: Remember that any interpretations you come up with for a case study in your class, no matter how astute or sincere, are essentially parts of an academic exercise and therefore may not be applicable in an actual situation.

12.3.4   Types of Case Studies Written in Sociology

Sociology case studies usually take one of two basic forms. The first might be called a *didactic* case study, because it is written for use in a classroom. It describes a situation or a problem in a certain setting but performs no analysis and draws no conclusions. Instead, a didactic case study normally lists questions for the students to consider and then answer, either individually or in class discussion. This sort of case study allows the teacher to evaluate student analysis skills and, if the case is discussed in class, to give students an opportunity to compare ideas with other students.

The second form, an *analytical* case study, provides not only a description but an analysis of the case as well. This is the form of case study most often assigned in a sociology class, and the example at the end of this chapter parallels this type of qualitative research.

Sociologists conduct case studies for a variety of specific purposes. An *ethnographic* case study, for example, is an in-depth examination of people, an organization, or a group over time. Its major purpose is to lead the researchers to a better understanding of human behavior through observations of the interweaving of people, events, conditions, and means in natural settings or subcultures.

Ethnographic case studies examine behavior in a community or, in the case of some technologically primitive societies, an entire society. The term *ethnography* means "a portrait of a people," and the ethnographic approach was historically an anthropological tool for describing societies whose cultural evolution was very primitive when compared to the "civilized" world (Hunter and Whitten 1976:147). Anthropologists would sometimes live within the society under scrutiny for several months or even years, interviewing and observing the people being studied.

The in-the-field nature of ethnographies has caused them to sometimes be referred to as *field studies,* and some social researchers classify studies of subcultural groups as small as gangs as ethnographies.

12.4   A QUALITATIVE CASE STUDY PAPER

The subjective nature of case studies means that they are often written in the first person. The example included below is a student's qualitative research project in Professor David Ford's Sociology of Religion class at the University of Central Oklahoma. Students in this class were assigned a case study of some religious group in the community with which they were not familiar. They were given this assignment as an introduction to qualitative research. Since most students had not been exposed to this type of research or the theoretical tools necessary for in-depth analysis, Professor Ford's requirements were more descriptive than analytical. Students were required to perform the following in their case studies:

- Conduct at least one interview with clergy of this religious group
- Conduct at least one interview with a layperson of this religious group
- Attend a minimum of two meetings of this religious group; these meetings could be two formal services or one formal service and one more informal service, such as a Bible study or prayer meeting
- Use interviews, participant observation, and information from official publications of this religious group to write this case study
- Write an in-depth description of this religious group

Students were then required to address the following areas in writing their papers:

- A general description of the religion represented (introduction)
- The belief structure of this religious group
- The physical settings of the religious meetings
- A description of the worship or other services or meetings attended
- Observations about the roles of men and women in this religious group
- Observations about the roles of clergy and laypeople in this religious group
- Personal observations and feelings—What did you learn? (conclusions)

The following paper (starting on page 225) is an example submitted by one of the students who was given Professor Ford's assignment.

SAMPLE ANALYTICAL CASE STUDY PAPER

"The Refreshing: A Twenty-First-Century Experience":

An Analytical Case Study of a

Nondenominational Evangelical Church

by

Michelle Thompson

for

Sociology of Religion 3573

Section 5237

Dr. David Ford

University of Central Oklahoma

November 7, 2000

INTRODUCTION

Coming from a varied religious background made the search for a new religious group more difficult. Friends had mentioned a charismatic church, the Refreshing, located in southwest Oklahoma City. This nondenominational evangelical church has beliefs that are founded in Christian fundamentalism. The Refreshing is in a covenant relationship with and accountable to the Christian Center in Lawton, Oklahoma, and the Bahamas Faith Ministries International in Nassau, Bahamas. In order to familiarize myself with this church I attended two services, gathered some general information, and interviewed a clergy member and a layperson. They provided insight into the group's religious doctrine and belief structure that would have taken multiple visits, if not months of observation, to obtain. The Refreshing church has a well-defined set of goals in the form of vision and mission statements.

THE BELIEF STRUCTURE

Vision

In their vision statement, the Refreshing church is described as an evangelistic and disciple ministry focusing on responding to the environmental needs of the twenty-first century. Responding to this ever-changing environment requires a keen consciousness and obedience to biblical principles to make a significant impact on society. The church consists of a body of believers who provide a house full of God-kind-of-faith. God's Holy Spirit commits them to remaining fresh in their obedience to God according to his word. The church strives to remain fresh and sharp in its continued development of skills by renewing members' minds. One method to accomplish this is by proselytizing—compelling others to come into the kingdom of God and reach their destiny through Christ. The church provides the community with development training and life survival skills for the purpose of producing twenty-first century, destiny-filled leaders. This vision requires activity by all clergy members to make it a reality.

Mission

Their mission is to provide a place where all people (regardless of race, class, or socioeconomic background) can experience a "refreshing" of mind, body, and spirit as well as love, hope, and purpose. They believe that members will receive a fresh start through godly principles and move effectively into their destiny.

Doctrine

According to the Refreshing doctrine, the Chief Cornerstone, Jesus Christ, governs the Refreshing. The pastors (willing vessels) of the Refreshing strive to maintain a strong commitment to both biblical principles and experiences. They have a sense of responsibility to aggressively teach God's word and welcome His Spirit. Great value is placed on the full range of gifts described in the scriptures; thus members are encouraged to exercise within the guidelines provided by the New Testament. The Refreshing is characterized by team preaching and pastoral care provided through a team of elders and appointed leaders, based upon scripture. Over the past few decades, the ministerial leaders have been created through various forms of education, training, and equipping (some formal and some informal). They have been "chosen" and put in place for this generation and generations to come.

According to doctrine, the church's beliefs are truths to be affirmed, boundaries to be observed, and principles to be practiced by all that represent the Refreshing. Scriptures are the inspired Words of God, without error. The writings comprise the complete revelations of God's will for salvation of men and the final authority for an all-Christian faith and life.

Beliefs

They believe in the Trinity, one God, creator of all things, infinitely perfect and eternally existing in three persons: the Father, the Son, and the Holy Spirit. God the Father is an infinite personal Spirit, perfect in holiness, wisdom, power, and

SAMPLE ANALYTICAL CASE STUDY PAPER (*CONT.*)

love. A concrete belief of this religion is that God actively and mercifully intervenes in the affairs of men, that He hears and answers prayer, and that He saves from sin and death all that come to Him through His Son Jesus Christ. The Son, Jesus Christ, is God and man. He was conceived by the Holy Spirit and born of the Virgin Mary. He lived a sinless life and died on the cross as a sacrifice for human sins. He rose bodily from the dead and ascended into heaven. Jesus Christ is now the High Priest and advocate at the right hand of the Father. The Holy Spirit is fully God, equal with the Father and the Son. The Holy Spirit convinces nonbelievers of their need for Christ and gives new birth to believers. The Holy Spirit indwells, sanctifies, leads, teaches, and empowers believers for godly living and service. All biblical gifts of the Spirit continue to be distributed by the Spirit today, as these gifts are divine provisions central to spiritual growth and effective ministry. These gifts are to be eagerly desired, faithfully developed, and lovingly exercised according to biblical guidelines.

The creation of man was in God's own image. However, man is a sinner by nature and action, and is, therefore, spiritually dead. Those who repent sin and trust in Jesus Christ as Savior are spiritually born again to new life by the Holy Spirit. Salvation is a free gift of God and is received by man through faith in Jesus Christ apart from any human merit, works, or rituals. The shed blood of Jesus Christ and His resurrection provided forgiveness of sins.

The Second Coming of Christ is their future hope, and has vital bearing on the personal life and service of the believers. Following this coming is the resurrection from the dead of the believers to everlasting joy with the Lord and of the unbelievers to judgment and everlasting conscious punishment. Christ will also, at this time, bring about the ultimate defeat of Satan. The kingdom of God will be completely fulfilled in the heavens and the new earth, in which He will be worshipped forever.

SAMPLE ANALYTICAL CASE STUDY PAPER (*CONT.*)

Ordinances

The Refreshing ordinances are similar to other Christian churches—believer's baptism and the Lord's Supper. Baptism is a testimony to the death of sin and resurrection of new life in Christ. The Lord's Supper symbolizes the death of the Lord Jesus Christ and salvation through faith in Him. All believers should participate in the ordinances.

Responsibilities

The Christian responsibility is found in the great commandments: "Love the Lord your God with all your heart, soul, and mind. Love your neighbor as yourself." Glorifying God, enjoying Him, and fulfilling His great commission to go and make disciples of all nations fulfills these commands. These pursuits require personal commitments to live by the truth of God's word and to depend on the power of His Spirit. Both the Word and the Spirit call people to a life of Christ-like character, wholehearted worship, generous giving, unselfish service, and compassionate outreach to the lost. These beliefs are fundamental and unchanging.

THE SETTING

Two years ago the church began holding meetings in an urban shopping center. This sanctuary was located next door to a bar. The congregation was soon forced to look for a new location, as the bar patrons complained that the group's profession of faith disrupted their consumption of alcohol. They were fortunate to utilize a community center until finding their current location.

The church is now located at the corner of Southwest Fifty-Ninth and Walker, behind the Homeland grocery store. It sounds like this would be easy to locate, but finding the church proved very difficult. The church is actually located on a small side street. After driving in circles for fifteen minutes, I asked a police officer for directions, but he was not sure of the street or the church location. Once I located the street, it appeared that I was lost again; all that I saw was an empty field ahead of me as the road began to curve. Suddenly a large sign appeared that stated: "The Refreshing: A Twenty-First-Century Experience."

Continuing to follow the road, I noticed a large metal building in the distance. I pulled into the parking lot and began looking for directions, but nothing was visible. The exterior of the building was a dull, yellow-colored wavy metal, with a small awning projecting off the front of the building. There were only two other cars in the parking lot. Upon entering the building, I found myself in a large foyer with dark wood paneling on the walls and gray commercial grade carpet on the floor. This area had very few furnishings—two love seats and a bulletin board, which displayed upcoming events for the church. To the right was a set of unlit stairs, and on the left, doors were open to a large room full of metal chairs. This appeared to be the location of the worship service.

Upon entering the room a table with literature caught my eye. I gathered fliers on the church and familiarized myself with the surroundings. The room was unusual in its design. The walls were red brick for about the first ten feet, and then changed to a tan-colored sheet-rock material that spanned to the twenty-five-foot ceiling. Gold exterior lights were mounted around the room on the brick part of the wall, every ten feet. The lights were the only items on the walls; there were no religious symbols. The upper section of the northern wall contained one five-by-twenty-foot tinted window and another opening the same size, as the window had been removed, which allowed sight of a projection machine.

A computer and some high-tech audio equipment (equalizers and synthesizers) were located on a folding table directly beneath these windows. Eight three-by-five-foot speakers, stacked two on top of each other, were placed in the southeast corner of the room. They were placed on either side of a semicircle-shaped stage. There were three steps up to the stage, which was covered with microphones on stands, drums, and an electric keyboard. The seating for this room was set up in the same format as church pews, but consisted of one hundred beige metal chairs. On the west wall was a small bookshelf that contained many Bibles. Completing my observation of the sanctuary, I was greeted by members of the congregation and invited to sit with a woman during the worship service.

THE WORSHIP SERVICE

The worship service began with music, which was very edifying, charismatic, and loud. It continued for approximately ten minutes without interruption. During the singing, members of the congregation were standing in front of their chairs, with their arms raised in the air, singing and swaying or dancing to the beat of the music. Those that were not singing were verbally praising God.

Following the music a layperson approached the front of the room, and explained that the pastor was ill and that he would be preaching. As he began his sermon, the projection machine came to life. As he spoke of scriptures they were displayed onto the painted portion of the wall above the bricks with the help of a power-point presentation. His sermon was brief, but he spoke of praying or becoming prey. The congregation responded to questions posed and repeated the teachings as instructed. When the sermon ended, we began what is called intercession. This is best described as members individually praying and singing while moving about through the sanctuary.

The woman sitting with me said that "God had directed me to this church for a reason," and asked if she could pray with me. As she asked God to come into my life, she was holding my hands. As the prayer continued she moved her hands to the sides of my face and then placed one hand on my forehead and the other on my heart. During the prayer she spoke in both English and in tongues (glossolalia). Soon another member of the congregation walked up behind me and placed his hands on my shoulders while speaking in tongues. After praying, the woman asked me to accompany her to the altar (stage), which I agreed to do. We walked to the front of the sanctuary, kneeled at the steps, and began praying again.

When the intercession was over, the layperson minister asked for tithing. A small basket was placed at the center of the altar (stage), and members came forward to give money to the church. We prayed a closing prayer followed by announcements from the members of the congregation concerning upcoming events. As I was leaving, many members hugged me and expressed their happiness about my attendance. Since I had arrived before most of the members, they apologized that I was not hugged by all of the members of the welcoming committee upon my arrival.

My second meeting was very similar in structure to the first. However, it lasted three hours rather than one hour, like the first meeting. The pastor was in attendance for this service, which he commenced by singing and playing the electric keyboard for over thirty minutes. As he finished singing, the man who gave the sermon during my first meeting approached him to wipe the sweat from his head and face. During his sermon, the power-point presentation was again present. Again, the congregation repeated specific verses loudly, accentuating specific words as he commanded. He interpreted the scriptures for the congregation, even rephrasing them in modern-day slang. His sermon was very energetic, motivational, and directed. He spoke of those who live in the supernatural as opposed to those who live in the natural. He instructed the congregation that they should live in the supernatural as God instructed them and avoid individuals that only lived in the natural. Those "lost souls" would only drag down the members of the congregation.

We did not have an intercession during this worship service or collect the tithe. The pastor reminded members of the upcoming revival; it was described as "three nights of anointed preaching, teaching, miracles, and praise." He showed how to anoint individuals at the revival without them knowing, in an effort to invite the Holy Spirit into their life. Another announcement was a reminder of the forum to "identify, define, discuss, and provide solutions" to those who are involved with twenty-first-century youth, education systems, the juvenile justice system, mental health providers, and the members of the legal system. The service ended with a prayer. As I was leaving, a member approached and asked how I found out about the church, what I thought of the service, and invited me back.

SEX ROLES AND LAY MINISTRY

I was not surprised by their position on the roles of men and women within the church. Unlike most fundamentalist religious groups, this church pays no attention to gender. The senior pastors of the church are a man and his wife. Both men and women fill the elected elder positions. If a member feels "moved" to speak to the congregation, all that the pastor asks is that the "individual be knowledgeable of scripture." The church expresses a realization for a greater freedom in the worship service. The layperson that I interviewed stated that the pastor feels that the message does not change but that the method of delivery must change with the times.

CONCLUSIONS

I was very impressed with the energy and commitment of these people. While this church is relatively new—it was created just two short years ago—it has gathered over 250 into its fold. The clergy member explained that their members are "burned out" from traditional church settings and seeking a "refreshing" experience. The clergy and elders strive to provide an inspirational setting where members can experience the "birthing" of God's Spirit.

The focus of the church is not on the exterior, which was the reason for the lack of religious symbols, but is directed toward assisting the members' spirits to connect with God. They believe that one way to accomplish this is by involving members with every aspect of the church, from preaching to prophesying and even having direct input on the direction the church will take

The innovative ideas that are used in this church make the worship service exciting and energizing, while providing what they believe are the fundamental teachings of God. The Refreshing congregation has a goal they believe is determined by God, and they will let nothing stand in the way of accomplishing this goal. I believe they have found their niche in the religious realm.

GLOSSARY

achieved status A social position within a stratification system that a person assumes voluntarily and that reflects a significant measure of personal ability and choice—for example, educational attainment.

ageism Prejudice and discrimination against the elderly.

age-sex pyramid A graphic representation of the age and sex of a population.

alienation The experience of powerlessness in social life in which the individual feels disassociated from the surrounding society.

animism The belief that natural objects—such as winds, clouds, rocks and the like—are conscious forms of life that affect humanity.

anomie A state of normlessness in which social control of individual behavior has become ineffective and society provides little moral guidance to individuals.

ascribed status A social position a person inherits at birth or assumes involuntarily later in life on the basis of characteristics over which he or she has no control.

assimilation The process by which minorities gradually take on the values of the dominant culture.

authoritarianism A political system that denies popular participation in government, or a personality syndrome that finds comfort in such structure.

authoritarian personality A personality pattern believed by social psychologists to be associated with a psychological need to be prejudiced.

authority Power people perceive to be legitimate rather than coercive.

autosystem A system or institution whose major purpose is the perpetuation of itself.

beliefs Specific statements that people hold to be true; a community-held set of convictions related to a supernatural order.

blue-collar occupation Lower prestige work that involves mostly manual labor, including production, maintenance, and service work.

bureaucracy Formal organization designed to perform tasks efficiently by explicit procedural rules.

bureaucratic inertia   The tendency of bureaucratic organizations to perpetuate themselves. Bureaucracies become autosystems that exist to maintain their existence.

bureaucratic ritualism   A preoccupation with rules and regulations to the point of obstructing organizational goals. Associated individuals are said to have "trained incapacity" or bureaucratic personality.

capitalism   An economic system in which natural resources and the means of producing goods and services are in private hands and are used to create more wealth for its owners.

capitalist   One who owns a factory or other productive enterprise and embraces the economic system of capitalism.

case studies   Observational studies of a given social unit, such as an individual, organization, neighborhood, community, or culture. Ethnographic or field research often describes a single unit or case.

caste system   Social stratification based on ascription.

cause and effect   A relationship between two variables in which change in one (the independent variable) causes change in another (the dependent variable).

charisma   Extraordinary personal qualities that can turn members of an audience into followers without the necessity of formal authority.

church   A formal religious organization well integrated into the larger society; a shared place of moral and ethical concerns.

cohabitation   The sharing of a household by an unmarried couple committed to a long-term relationship.

cohort   A category of people with a common characteristic, usually their age—for example, all persons born during the Great Depression (1929–1939).

colonialism   The process by which some nations enrich themselves through political and economic control of other nations.

concept   An abstract idea that represents some aspect of the world, such as descriptive properties or relations, inevitably in a somewhat simplified form.

constant   A characteristic of a sample or population that does not take on different values and is the same from one element to the next. For example, if a sample contained all males, gender would be a constant because it does not vary.

corporation   An organization with a legal existence, including rights and liabilities, apart from those of its members.

correlation   The measured strength of an association between two or more variables.

correlation coefficient   A number whose magnitude shows how strongly two or more variables are correlated, or related to one another. Values range from +1.00 to –1.00, with strength of association increasing as the value approaches either extreme.

counterculture   Cultural patterns that strongly oppose conventional culture. The individual member will usually experience alienation from the values and expectations of the dominant culture.

credentialism   Evaluating people on the basis of their credentials, especially educational degrees.

crime   The violation of a norm formally enacted into criminal law.

crimes against property (property crimes)   Crimes involving theft of property belonging to others.

crimes against the person (violent crimes)   Crimes against people that involve violence or the threat of violence.

criminal justice system   The lawful response to alleged crimes using police, courts, and state-sanctioned punishment.

criminal recidivism   A tendency by people previously convicted of crimes to commit subsequent offenses.

crude birth rate   The number of live births in a given year for every 1,000 people in a population.

crude death rate   The number of deaths in a given year for every 1,000 people in a population.

cult   A religious organization that is substantially outside the cultural traditions of a society.

cultural lag   The observation that some cultural elements (material culture and technology) change more quickly than others (values and norms), with potentially disruptive consequences.

cultural relativism   The practice of evaluating any culture by its own standards.

cultural transmission   The formal and informal learning process by which culture is passed from one generation to the next.

cultural universals   Traits found in every culture.

culture   The beliefs, values, behavior, and material objects shared by a particular people.

culture shock   The individual disorientation accompanying sudden exposure to an unfamiliar way of life.

democracy   Rule by the people.

democratic socialism   An economic and political system that combines significant government control of the economy with free elections.

demography   The scientific study of human population.

denomination   A religious group, not linked to the state, that claims doctrinal autonomy.

dependent samples   Two random samples whose elements are not mutually exclusive. An example would be when the same subjects are measured on some variable before (pre-) and after (post-) experimental manipulation, and the two samples were not independently selected.

dependent variable   The variable that is being affected or influenced by another variable. In a causal analysis, the dependent variable is caused by the independent variable; it is the effect.

descent   The system by which members of a society trace kinship over generations.

descriptive statistics   Statistics (numbers) used only to describe the data—in other words, percentages, charts, graphs, and so on; no hypotheses are tested.

deterrence   The attempt to discourage criminality through fear of punishment.

deviance   The recognized violation of cultural norms.

discrimination   Treating groups of people unfavorably based on categorical, rather than individual, grounds.

distribution   A listing of all the values or outcomes for a particular variable. It often takes the form of a frequency distribution or a percentile distribution.

division of labor   Specialized economic activity separating work into distinct parts.

dramaturgical analysis   The investigation of social interaction in terms of theatrical performance.

dyad   A social group with two members involving the presentation of selves.

ecology   The study of the interaction of living organisms and their natural environment; the spatial distribution of people and activities and the resulting interdependence, as in a community.

economy   The social institution that organizes a society's production, distribution, and consumption of goods and services.

ecosystem   A physical environment composed of the interaction of all living plants and animals in it.

education   The social institution through which society provides its members with important knowledge, including facts, skills, and values.

ego   Freud's designation of a person's conscious attempts to balance the pleasure-seeking drives of the human organism and the demands of society.

element   A single member of a population.

empirical distribution   A list of the different values for a variable and the number of times each value appears in the sample. It is also referred to as a *frequency distribution*.

endogamy   Marriage between people of the same social category.

ethnocentrism   The practice of judging another culture or group by the standards of one's own culture; usually involves taking the position that one's own culture or group is best.

ethnomethodology   The study of the way people make sense of their everyday surroundings. Sometimes referred to as ethnography, it is widely utilized in case studies.

euthanasia (mercy killing)   Assisting in the death of a person suffering from an incurable illness.

exogamy   Marriage between people of different social categories.

experiment   A research method that investigates cause-and-effect relationships under very controlled conditions.

extended family (consanguine family)   A social unit including parents, children, and other kin.

faith   Belief anchored in conviction rather than scientific evidence.

family   A set of persons who are related to each other by blood, marriage, or adoption, and who usually live together.

feminism   A social movement that advocates social equality for men and women, in opposition to patriarchy and sexism.

feminization of poverty   The trend by which women represent an increasing proportion of the poor.

fertility   The incidence of childbearing in a society's population.

folkways   Patterns of behavior common in and typical of a group.

formal organization   A large-scale, special-purpose group that is organized to achieve specific goals.

frequency distribution   A distribution of the values of a variable and the number of times each value occurs in the data; sometimes called an *empirical distribution*.

functional illiteracy   Reading, writing, and problem-solving skills that are judged to be inadequate for everyday living.

Gemeinschaft   A type of social organization (community) in which people are bound together by kinship and tradition.

gender   The significance a society attaches to the biological categories of female and male, sometimes labeled *feminine* and *masculine*.

gender roles   Attitudes and activities that a society links to each sex; often referred to as *sex roles*.

gender stratification   The differential ranking of males and females in societies where sex determines access to scarce resources.

genocide   The systematic killing of an entire race or people.

gerontocracy   A form of social organization in which the elderly have the most wealth, power, and privileges.

gerontology   The study of aging and the elderly.

Gesellschaft   A type of social organization in which relationships are contractual, impersonal, voluntary, and limited.

global economy   Economic activity across national borders.

global perspective   A view of the larger world and one's society's place in it.

government   A formal organization that directs the political life of a nation.

greenhouse effect   A rise in the earth's average temperature (global warming) due to an increasing concentration of carbon dioxide in the atmosphere.

groupthink   Group conformity that limits individual understanding of an issue.

hate crime   A crime motivated by racial, ethical, or other bias.

hermaphrodite   A human being with a combination of female and male internal and external genitalia.

high culture   Cultural patterns that distinguish a society's elite.

holistic medicine   An approach to health care that emphasizes prevention of illness and takes account of a person's entire physical and social environment.

homogamy   Marriage between people with the same social characteristics.

horticulture   The practice of raising crops.

hunting and gathering   A stage of cultural evolution in which simple tools were used to hunt animals and gather vegetation.

id   Freud's designation of the human being's basic drives.

ideology   Cultural beliefs that justify particular social arrangements.

incest taboo   A norm forbidding sexual relations or marriage between closely related family members.

income   Wages or salary from work and earnings from investments.

independent variable   In a causal analysis, the cause of the dependent variable (the effect).

industry   The production of goods using sophisticated fuels and machinery.

infant mortality rate   The number of children per 1,000 live births who die during their first year of life.

inferential statistics   The type of statistics used to make inferences from sample data to populations through hypothesis testing. Probability is used to make a decision about the association between two or more variables; a null hypothesis is accepted or rejected based on the probability of an event occurring by chance.

in-group   An esteemed social group commanding a member's loyalty.

institutional discrimination   Discrimination against an individual or group that is supported by the values and organizations of a society.

intergenerational social mobility   The social standing of children in relation to their parents.

intragenerational social mobility   A change in social position occurring during a person's lifetime.

kinship   A social bond, based on blood, marriage, or adoption, that joins people into families.

labeling theory   The assertion that deviance and conformity result not so much from what people do as from the response of others to those actions.

language   A system of symbols that allows people to communicate with one another.

latent functions   The unrecognized and unintended effect of social action.

level of measurement   The mathematical properties of a variable. Different levels of measurement (data) include nominal (numbers are used to label mutually exclusive categories); ordinal (numbers are used to rank a variable on some criterion); interval (the distance between values is both known and constant—a unit of measurement that allows one to add, subtract, divide, and multiply without accumulating error); and ratio (has all the properties of interval data as well as a fixed meaningful zero point).

level of significance   The probability level (usually .05) used to determine the acceptance of a hypothesis or rejection of the null hypothesis. Sometimes referred to as *rejection level* or *alpha level.*

life expectancy   The average expectation of life at a given age, or the average number of years of life remaining for persons of a particular age.

looking-glass self   Cooley's term referring to a conception of self derived from the responses of others: We see ourselves as we think others see us.

macro-level orientation   A concern with large-scale patterns that characterize society as a whole.

manifest functions   The recognized and intended consequences of social action.

marriage   A legally sanctioned relationship, involving economic cooperation as well as normative sexual activity and childbearing, that people expect to be enduring.

mass media   Impersonal communications directed to a vast audience by means of a technological medium.

mass society   A society in which industry and bureaucracy erode traditional social ties.

master status   A social position with exceptional importance for identity, often shaping a person's entire life.

matriarchy   A form of family organization in which power and authority are vested in the hands of the females.

mean   A measure of central tendency. The mean is the arithmetic average of a group of interval level numbers (scores). Because it takes into account every score, it is affected by extremely low and extremely high scores.

mean deviation   A measure of dispersion for continuous data. In a distribution of scores, the mean deviation is the average absolute difference of each score from the mean of the scores. It measures, then, the average distance of each score from the mean. It is calculated by summing the absolute value of the difference between each score and the mean, and then dividing by the total number of scores.

measurement   The process of determining the value of a variable in a specific case.

measure of association   A statistic that indicates the strength of the relationship between two or more variables. The appropriate measure of association depends on the level of measurement of the variables involved.

measure of central tendency   Descriptive statistics that represent the most typical or representative score in a distribution of scores. The appropriate measure of central tendency depends on both the level of measurement and the dispersion of the data.

measure of dispersion   Descriptive statistics that reflect the amount of variability in a distribution of scores. These measures reveal how different the scores are from one another. The appropriate measure of dispersion depends on both the level of measurement and whether there are extreme scores in the data. When the magnitude of the measure of dispersion is large, it means that the scores are very different from one another and that there is a substantial amount of variability in the data.

mechanical solidarity   Social bonds based on collective conformity to tradition.

median   The score that is the exact middle score in a distribution of ranked scores. It is, therefore, the score at the 50th percentile. In a rank-ordered distribution of scores, the position of the median can be found using the formula $(n + 1)/2$, where n is the number of scores.

medicalization of deviance   The transformation of moral and legal issues into medical matters.

medicine   The social institution that focuses on combating disease and improving health.

meritocracy   Social stratification based on personal merit.

micro-level orientation   A concern with small-scale patterns of social interaction in specific settings.

midpoint of a class interval   In a grouped frequency distribution, the midpoint is exactly midway between the lower and upper class limits and is determined by adding the upper and lower limits (stated or true limits) and dividing by 2. The midpoint of the class interval 100–200 would be $(100 + 200)/2 = 150$.

migration   The movement of people into and out of a specified territory.

military-industrial complex   A close association among the government, the military, and defense industries.

minority   A category of people, distinguished by physical or cultural traits, that is socially disadvantaged.

miscegenation   The biological process of interbreeding among racial groups.

mode   A measure of central tendency. The mode is the most frequently occurring score in a distribution of scores or the most frequently occurring interval in a grouped frequency distribution.

modernity   Social patterns linked to industrialization.

modernization   The process of social change in a society or a social institution initiated by industrialization.

modernization theory   A model of economic development that explains global inequality in terms of technological and cultural differences among societies.

monarchy   A type of political system that transfers power from generation to generation within a single family.

monogamy   Marriage involving two partners.

monopoly   Control of a market by a single producer.

mores   Norms that are widely observed and have compelling moral significance.

mortality   The incidence of death in a society's population.

multiculturalism   An educational program recognizing the cultural diversity of a population and promoting the equality of all cultural traditions.

multinational corporation   A large business that operates in many countries.

natural environment   The earth's surface and atmosphere, including various living organisms as well as the air, water, soil, and other resources necessary to sustain life.

negative correlation   A correlation or association between two variables wherein the scores co-vary in opposite directions. High scores on one variable are related to low scores on the second variable, and low scores on one variable are related to high scores on the other.

neocolonialism   The economic and/or political policies by which a nation indirectly maintains its influence over other areas.

nonverbal communication   Communication using body movements, gestures, and facial expressions rather than speech.

norms   Rules by which a society guides the behavior of its members.

nuclear family (conjugal family)   A social unit containing one, or—more commonly—two adults and any children.

null hypothesis   The hypothesis of no difference or no association that is the object of a hypothesis test. The null hypothesis is tested against the alternative or research hypothesis, and it is the one that is rejected or not rejected in favor of the alternative.

oligarchy   The rule of the many by the few.

oligopoly   Domination of a market by a few producers.

organic solidarity   Social bonds based on specialization and interdependence.

outgroup   Social group toward which one feels competition or opposition.

participant observation   A research technique in which investigators systematically observe people while joining in their routine activities.

pastoralism   The domestication of animals.

patriarchy   A form of family organization in which power and authority are vested in the hands of the males.

peer group   A group whose members have interests, social position, and age in common.

percent   A descriptive statistic obtained by dividing the frequency of a subset of events by the total number of events and dividing by 100. For example, if there are 50 property crimes out of a total of 75 crimes, the percent of property crimes is 50/75, or 66.7 percent, of the total.

personality   An individual's pattern of thoughts, motives, and self-conceptions.

personal space   The surrounding area over which a person makes a claim to privacy.

perspective   A particular theoretical model or school of thought.

pluralism   A state in which people of all races and ethnicities are distinct but have social parity.

pluralist model   An analysis of politics that views power as dispersed among many competing interest groups.

political revolution   The overthrow of one political system in order to establish another.

politics   The actual act of distributing power and making decisions.

polity   The social institution that distributes power and makes decisions.

polygamy   Plural marriage, or marriage that involves more than one spouse simultaneously.

popular culture   Cultural patterns widespread among a society's people, usually limited to the arts and entertainment.

population   The entire collection or universe of objects, events, or people that a researcher is actually interested in and from which a sample is drawn. The population is often referred to as the *universe of cases*.

positive correlation   A correlation or association between two variables wherein the attributes co-vary in the same direction. For example, as religiosity increases, faith in people increases, and vice versa.

positivism   A path to understanding based on science, not on philosophic presuppositions or metaphysics.

postindustrial economy   A productive system based on service work and high technology.

postmodernity   Social patterns typical of a postindustrial society.

power   The ability to achieve desired ends despite opposition.

power-elite model   An analysis of social life that views power as concentrated among the rich.

prejudice   A rigid and problematic generalization about a category of people.

prescribe   To set down as a rule or direction to be followed.

presentation of self   Goffman's term for the ways in which individuals, in various settings, try to create specific impressions in the minds of others.

primary group   A small social group in which relationships are close, personal, and enduring.

prioritize   The condition of ranking items in the order of their importance.

profane   That which people define as an ordinary element of everyday life.

profession   A prestigious, white-collar occupation that requires extensive formal education.

proletariat   People who sell their productive labor; Marxian term for the "masses."

public opinion   The attitudes of people throughout a society about one or more controversial issues.

puppet government   A government in one country that is under complete control of a government of another country.

qualitative variable   A variable whose values differ in quality and kind rather than quantity. With a qualitative variable, one value is different from another, but numerical expressions such as "more than" or "less than" are meaningless. An example of a qualitative variable would be gender. Males are different from females, but we cannot say that males have "more gender" than females.

quantitative variable   A variable whose values differ in quantity. With a quantitative variable, you can make distinctions based on numerical properties, such as "more than" or "less than." An example of a quantitative variable would be the number of prior arrests a convicted offender has. A person with one prior arrest has fewer than a person with three prior arrests.

race   A category composed of men and women who share biologically transmitted traits that members of a society deem socially significant.

racism   The belief that one racial category is innately superior or inferior to another.

random selection   A way of ensuring that the sample selected is representative of the population from which it was drawn. In random selection, each element of the population has a known, nonzero, independent, and equal chance of being selected.

range   A measure of dispersion. With continuous data, the range is the difference between the highest score and the lowest score. With rank-ordered categorical data, the range is defined as the difference between the midpoints of the highest and lowest class intervals.

ratio-level variable   A continuous, quantitative variable in which the distance between values is both known and equal. Unlike an interval-level variable, a ratio-level variable has an absolute or true zero point, which implies the complete absence of the characteristic. An example of a ratio-level variable would be a robbery victimization rate per 100,000 for persons between the ages of twenty and forty.

rationality   Deliberate calculation of efficient means to accomplish any particular task.

rationalization   Weber's term for the change from tradition to rationality as the dominant mode of human thought.

recycling   Reuse of resources that we would otherwise discard as waste.

reference group   A social group that becomes a point of reference for making evaluations and decisions.

refugees   Persons who flee their native country seeking safety from persecution.

rehabilitation   Reforming the offender to forgo further offenses.

relative deprivation   A perceived disadvantage relative to some standard of comparison.

relative poverty   The deprivation of some people in relation to others.

reliability   The quality of consistency in measurement attained through repetition.

religion   A social institution involving beliefs and practices that distinguish the sacred from the profane.

religiosity   The importance of religion in social life.

religious fundamentalism   A conservative religious doctrine that opposes intellectuals and worldly accommodation in favor of the restoration of traditional religious systems.

replicate   To reproduce, model, or simulate. In science, studies are replicated to increase or decrease confidence in their findings.

research method   A strategy for systematically carrying out research. Sometimes referred to as the *design* of a study.

resocialization   Formal or informal socialization intended to radically alter an individual's personality.

retrospective labeling   The interpretation of someone's past consistent with present deviance.

robotics   The field of research and development of robots.

role   Normative patterns of behavior for those holding a particular status.

role conflict   Incompatibility among roles corresponding to two or more statuses.

role model   Someone who sets the example.

role set   A number of roles attached to a single status.

role strain   Incompatibility among roles corresponding to a single status.

routinization of charisma   Weber's term for the development of charismatic authority into some combination of traditional and bureaucratic authority.

sacred   That which people define as extraordinary, inspiring a sense of awe and reverence.

sample   A subset of objects, events, or people selected from a population. A sample is selected to estimate values or characteristics (parameters) of the population or to test hypotheses about the population.

satellite country   A country that is controlled by another, more powerful country.

scapegoat   A person or category of people, typically with little power, whom others unfairly blame for their own troubles.

schooling   Formal instruction under the direction of specially trained teachers.

science   A logical system that derives knowledge from direct, systematic observation.

secondary group   A large and impersonal social group based on some special interest or activity, usually of limited duration.

sect   A type of religious organization that stands apart from the larger society.

secularization   The historical decline in the influence of religion.

segregation   The physical and social separation of categories of people.

self   Mead's term for the dimension of personality composed of an individual's self-awareness and self-image.

sex   The biological distinction between females and males.

sexism   The belief that one sex is innately superior to the other.

sex ratio   The number of males for every hundred females in a given population.

sexual harassment   Comments, gestures, or physical contact of a sexual nature that are deliberate, repeated, and unwelcome.

sexual orientation   The manner in which people experience sexual arousal and achieve sexual pleasure.

sick role   Patterns of behavior defined as appropriate for those who are ill.

significance level   The probability of rejecting a null hypothesis when in reality it is true.

simple random sample   A type of probability sample in which each element of the population has a known and equal probability of being included in the sample.

social change   Any significant alteration in the structure of society.

social character   Personality characteristics common to members of a society.

social-conflict paradigm   A framework for building theory based on the assumption that society is a complex system characterized by inequality and conflict that generate social change.

social construction of reality   The process by which individuals creatively build reality through social interaction.

social control   The process by which society regulates the thoughts and behaviors of individuals.

social dysfunction   The undesirable consequences of any social pattern for the operation of society.

social epidemiology   The study of how and why health and disease are distributed throughout a society's population.

social function   The consequences of any social pattern for the operation of society as a whole or in part.

social group   Two or more people who identify and interact with one another.

social institution   An organized sphere of social life such as education or the family.

social interaction   The process by which people act and react in relation to others.

socialism   An economic system in which the government owns the means of production.

socialized medicine   A medical care system in which the government owns most medical facilities and employs most physicians.

social mobility   Capability of change of position in a stratification system.

social movement   An organized effort to encourage or oppose some dimension of change.

social stratification   A system by which a society ranks categories of people in a hierarchy.

social structure   Any relatively stable pattern of social behavior.

society   A social grouping within a limited territory guided by the culture.

sociobiology   A theoretical paradigm that explains cultural patterns in terms of biological forces.

socioeconomic status (SES)   A composite social ranking based on various dimensions of inequality or inequity.

sociology   A social science concerned with the systematic study of society.

standard deviation   The square root of the variance; a commonly used measure that indicates the degree of deviation or dispersion from the mean of all the scores in the distribution. Sometimes referred to as the standard error of the mean.

status   A general designation of social standing as measured by income or wealth.

status consistency   The degree of consistency in a person's social standing across various dimensions of inequality.

status set   All the statuses a person holds at a particular time.

stereotype   An exaggerated belief associated with a category; a prejudiced description of a category of people.

stigma   A powerfully negative label that radically changes a person's self-concept and social identity.

structural-functional paradigm   A framework for building theory based on the assumption that society is a complex system whose parts work together to promote stability.

structural social mobility   Capability of shift in the social position of large numbers of people due less to individual efforts than to changes in society itself.

subculture   Cultural patterns that distinguish some group of a society's population.

suburbs   Urban areas beyond the political boundaries of a city but usually containing more than half the population of such areas.

superego   Freud's designation of the presence of culture within the individual in the form of internalized values and norms.

survey   A research method in which subjects selected (sampled) from a larger population respond to a series of statements or questions in a questionnaire or interview.

sustainable ecosystem   The human use of the natural environment to meet the needs of the present generation without threatening the prospects of future generations.

symbol   Anything that stands for or represents something else—for example, symbolic words, phrases, and images associated with a social movement.

symbolic-interaction perspective   A framework for building theory based on the view that society is the product of the everyday interactions of individuals and how they define the situations they are in.

technology The body of knowledge applied to the practical tasks of living.

terrorism Violence or the threat of violence by an individual or a group as a political strategy.

tertiary sector The part of the economy involving services rather than goods.

theoretical paradigm A set of fundamental assumptions that guides thinking and research; a perspective from which reality is defined.

total institution A setting in which individuals are isolated from the rest of society and manipulated by an administrative staff.

totalitarianism A highly centralized political system that extensively regulates people's lives.

totem An object collectively defined as sacred or as emblematic of a clan.

tracking The division of a school's students into different educational programs based on their achievement level.

tradition-directedness Rigid conformity to time-honored ways of living.

tradition sentiments Beliefs about the world that are passed from generation to generation.

transsexual A person who feels he or she is one sex though biologically the other.

triad A social group with three members.

urban ecology Study of the link between the physical and social dimensions of cities.

urbanization The concentration of humanity into cities.

validity The quality of measurement gained by measuring exactly what one intends to measure; pertains to the accuracy of the measurement instrument.

values Culturally defined standards of desirability, goodness, and beauty that serve as broad guidelines for social life.

variable A concept whose value changes from case to case.

variance A way of measuring the deviation of the scores from the mean; the amount of error involved in using the mean to represent all other scores in the distribution.

victimless crime Violation of law in which there is assumed to be no readily apparent victim—for example, prostitution or gambling.

wealth An individual's or family's total financial assets.

white-collar crime Crimes committed by people of high social position in the course of their occupations.

white-collar occupation Higher prestige work that involves mostly mental activity.

REFERENCES

Abel, E. L. 1984. *A Dictionary of Drug Abuse Terms and Terminology.* Westport, CT: Greenwood.

Abstracts in Social Gerontology. Annual. Newbury Park, CA: Sage.

Aby, Stephan, James Nalen and Lori Fielding. 2005. *Sociology: A Guide to Reference and Information Sources.* 3d ed. Littleton, CO: Libraries Unlimited.

Aday, R. H. 1988. *Crime and the Elderly: An Annotated Bibliography.* New York: Greenwood.

Adler, Patricia and Peter Adler. 1989. "Socialization and the 'Gloried Self.'" *Social Psychology Quarterly* 52:299–310.

Aldous, Joan. 1967. *International Bibliography of Research in Marriage and the Family, 1900–1964.* St. Paul, MN: Family Social Science, University of Minnesota.

American Journal of Sociology. Annual. Chicago, IL: University of Chicago Press.

American Sociological Association. 1997. *American Sociological Association Style Guide.* 2d ed. Washington, D.C.: American Sociological Association.

American Sociological Review. Annual. Washington, D.C.: American Sociological Association.

American Statistics Index. Annual. Washington, D.C.: Congressional Information Service.

Annual Review of Sociology. Annual. Palo Alto, CA: Annual Reviews.

Bear, John and Mariah Bear. 2001. *Bear's Guide to Computer Degrees by Distance Learning.* New York: Ten Speed Press.

Becker, Howard S., Blanche Geer, Everett C. Hughes and Anselm L. Strauss. 1961. *Boys in White: Student Culture in Medical School.* Chicago, IL: University of Chicago Press.

Bibliographic Index. Annual. New York: H. W. Wilson.

Borgatta, E. F. and M. L. Borgatta, eds. 1992. *Encyclopedia of Sociology.* 4 vols. New York: Macmillan.

Bouma, Gary D. and G. B. J. Atkinson. 1995. *A Handbook of Social Science Research: A Comprehensive and Practical Guide for Students.* 2d ed. New York: Oxford University Press.

Brundage, D., R. Keane and R. Mackneson. 1993. "Application of Learning Theory to the Instruction of Adults." Pp. 131–144 in *The Craft of Teaching Adults,* edited by Thelma Barer-Stein and James A. Draper. Toronto, ON: Culture Concepts.

Bryman, A. 1994. *Quantity and Quality in Social Research.* London, UK: Unwin Hymian.

Carr, Sarah. 2000. "On-Line Psychology Instruction Is Effective but Not Satisfying, Study Finds." *The Chronicle of Higher Education,* March 10, pp. 8–12.

Charon, Joel M. 1996. *The Meaning of Sociology.* 5th ed. Upper Saddle River, NJ: Prentice Hall.

Chicago Manual of Style. 2003. 15th ed. Chicago, IL: University of Chicago Press.

Child Development Abstracts and Bibliography. Annual. Chicago, IL: University of Chicago Press.

Clark, Robin E., Judith F. Clark, Christine A. Adamec and Richard J. Gelles, eds. 2001. *The Encyclopedia of Child Abuse.* 3d ed. New York: Facts on File, Inc.

Cockerham, William C. and Ferris J. Ritchey. 1997. *Dictionary of Medical Sociology.* New York: Greenwood.

Commager, Henry S., ed. 1963. *Documents of American History.* 7th ed. New York: Appleton-Century-Crofts.

Contemporary Sociology: A Journal of Reviews. Annual. Washington, D.C.: American Sociological Association.

Cooley, Charles H. [1902] 1964. *Human Nature and the Social Order.* New York: Schocken Books.

Criminal Justice Abstracts. Annual. Hackensack, NJ: National Council on Crime and Delinquency.

Cumulative Subject Index to the Monthly Catalog of United States Government Publications, 1900–1971. 1973. Washington, D.C.: Carrollton Press.

Demographic Yearbook. Annual. New York: United Nations/Statistical Office.

De Young, Mary. 1987. *Child Molestation: An Annotated Bibliography.* Jefferson, NC: McFarland.

DiCanio, M. 1993. *The Encyclopedia of Violence: Origins, Attitudes, Consequences.* New York: Facts on File.

Durkheim, Emile. [1897] 1951. *La Suicide.* Translated by J. A. Spaulding and G. Simpson. New York: Free Press.

Engeldinger, E. A. 1986. *Spouse Abuse: An Annotated Bibliography of Violence between Mates.* Metuchen, NJ: Scarecrow.

Fargin, Paul, ed. 2002. *New York Public Library Desk Reference.* 4th ed. New York: Stonesong Press.

Farley, John E. 2000. *Majority-Minority Relations.* 4th ed. Englewood Cliffs, NJ: Prentice Hall.

Freud, Sigmund. 1930. *Civilization and Its Discontents.* New York: Cape and Smith.

———. [1913] 1952. *Totem and Taboo.* Translated by James Strachey. New York: W. W. Norton.

Gallup, George and George Gallup, Jr. 1999. *The Gallup Poll Cumulative Index: Public Opinion, 1935–1997.* New York: Scholarly Resources, Inc.

Ghorayshi, P. 1990. *The Sociology of Work: A Critical Annotated Bibliography.* New York: Garland.

Gould, J. and W. L. Kolb. 1964. *A Dictionary of the Social Sciences.* New York: Free Press.

Government Finance Statistics Yearbook. Annual. Washington, D.C.: International Monetary Fund.

Gutierrez, Lynda, Andrea Yurasits, Angela Hurdle, and Michelle Franklin, eds. 1999. *Demographics USA: County Addition.* New York: Trade Dimensions.

Hara, Noriko and Rob King. 1999. "Students' Frustrations with a Web-Based Distance Education Course." *First Monday: Peer Reviewed Journal on the Internet* 4(12):7–10.

Harris, D. K. 1988. *Dictionary of Gerontology.* New York: Greenwood.

Hartwell, Patrick. 1985. "Grammar, Grammars, and the Teaching of Grammar." *College English* 47:111.

Hess, Beth B., Elizabeth W. Markson and Peter J. Stein. 1988. *Sociology.* 3d ed. New York: Macmillan.

Hoover, Kenneth and Todd Donovan. 1995. *The Elements of Social Science Thinking.* 6th ed. New York: St. Martin's Press.

Horton, C. P. and J. C. Smith, eds. 1990. *Statistical Record of Black America.* Detroit, MI: Gale.

Howard, Angela M. and Frances M. Kavenik, eds. 2000. *Handbook of American Women's History.* New York: Sage.

Hunter, David E. and Phillip Whitten, eds. 1976. *Encyclopedia of Anthropology.* New York: Harper & Row.

International Bibliography of Sociology. Annual. London, UK: Tavistock.

International Encyclopedia of the Social Sciences. 1968. 17 vols. New York: Macmillan.

Inventory of Marriage and Family Literature. 1994. Vol. 19. St. Paul, MN: National Council on Family Relations.

Isaac, Stephen and William B. Michael. 1981. *Handbook in Research and Evaluation.* 2d ed. San Diego, CA: EdITS Publishers.

Jacob-Chien, Cynthia Y. A. and Richard L. Dukes. 1998. "Understanding Adolescent Work in Social and Behavioral Contexts." *Free Inquiry in Creative Sociology* 26(1):55–62.

Johnson, Allan G. 2000. *The Blackwell Dictionary of Sociology: A User's Guide to Sociological Language.* 2d ed. New York: Blackwell Publishers.

Kaiser Index to Black Resources: 1948–1986. 1992. Brooklyn, NY: Carlson.

Kaplan, Jeffery. 2000. *Encyclopedia of White Power: A Sourcebook on the Radical Racist Right.* New York: AltaMira Press.

Katz, Bill, Linda S. Katz, William A. Katz and Berry G. Richards, eds. 2000. *Magazines for Libraries.* 3d ed. New York: Bowker.

Kinlock, G. C. 1987. *Social Stratification: An Annotated Bibliography.* New York: Garland.

Kramer, Candice. 2001. *Success in Distance Learning.* New York: Delmar.

Kuhn, Thomas. 1970. *The Structure of Scientific Revolutions.* 2d ed. Chicago, IL: University of Chicago Press.

Lerner, Richard, M. and Jacqueline Lerner, eds. 2001. *Adolescence in America: An Encyclopedia.* New York: ABC-CLIO, Inc.

Levin, Jack, Arnold Arluke and Amita Mody-Desbareau. 1986. "The Gossip Tabloid as an Agent of Social Control." Presented at the annual meeting of the American Sociological Association.

Levin, Jack and James Alan Fox. 1997. *Elementary Statistics in Social Research.* 7th ed. New York: Addison Wesley Longman.

Lockwood, Fred and Anne Gooley. 2001. *Innovations in Open and Distance Learning: Successful Development of On-Line and Web-Based Learning.* New York: Stylus.

Lunsford, Andrea and Robert Conners. 1992. *The St. Martin's Handbook.* 2d. ed. New York: St. Martin's.

Maddox, George. L., ed. 2001. *The Encyclopedia of Aging: A Comprehensive Resource in Gerontology and Geriatrics.* New York: Springer.

Malinowski, B. 1948. *Magic, Science, and Religion.* Glencoe, IL: Free Press.

Marshall, Gordon. 1998. *A Dictionary of Sociology.* New York: Oxford University Press.

Mead, George H. [1934] 1962. *Mind, Self, and Society.* Edited by C. W. Morris. Chicago, IL: University of Chicago Press.

Mills, C. Wright. 1956. *The Power Elite.* New York: Oxford University Press.

———. 1959. *The Sociological Imagination.* New York: Oxford University Press.

Mills, J. 1992. *Womanwords: A Dictionary of Words about Women.* New York: Free Press.

Miner, Horace. 1956. "Body Ritual among the Nacirema." *American Anthropologist* 58(June):503–507.

Morgan, A. 1991. *Research into Student Learning in Distance Education.* Victoria, Australia: University of South Australia Press.

Morgan, Gordon D. 1981. *Introductory Sociology: Lectures, Readings, and Exercises.* Saratoga, CA: Century Twenty-One Publishing.

Newman, R. 1981. *Black Index: Afro-Americana in Selected Periodicals, 1907–1949.* New York: Garland.

NewsBank. Annual. Greenwich, CT: Urban Affairs Library.

New York Times Index. Annual. New York: New York Times.

Nordquest, J. 1988. *The Homeless in America: A Bibliography.* Santa Cruz, CA: Reference and Research Services.

———. 1988. *Substance Abuse I: Drug Abuse: A Bibliography.* Santa Cruz, CA: Reference and Research Services.

———. 1990. *Substance Abuse II: Alcohol Abuse: A Bibliography.* Santa Cruz, CA: Reference and Research Services.

———. 1991. *The Elderly in America: A Bibliography.* Santa Cruz, CA: Reference and Research Services.

Payton, Melissa. 2004. *The Prentice Hall Guide to Evaluating On-Line Resources* (with *Research Navigator*™): *Sociology 2004.* Upper Saddle River, NJ: Pearson/Prentice Hall.

Pearce, Catherine O., ed. 1958. *A Scientist of Two Worlds: Louis Agassiz.* Philadelphia, PA: Lippincott.

Philliber, Susan G., Mary R. Schwab and G. Sam Sloss. 1980. *Social Research.* Itasca, IL: F. E. Peacock.

Picciano, Anthony G. 2001. *Distance Learning: Making Connections across Virtual Space and Time.* Upper Saddle River, NJ: Prentice Hall.

Popper, Karl. 1959. *The Logic of Scientific Discovery.* New York: Basic Books.

Population Index. Annual. Princeton, NJ: Office of Population Research, Princeton University, and Population Association of America.

Richter, A. 1993. *Dictionary of Sexual Slang.* New York: Wiley.

Rothenberg. R. 1997. *Race, Class, Gender: A Dictionary.* New York: St Martin's Press.

Russell, Bruce M. 1977. *World Handbook of Political and Social Indicators.* New York: Greenwood.

Sage Family Studies Abstracts. Annual. Beverly Hills, CA: Sage.

Sage Race Relations Abstracts. Annual. Beverly Hills, CA: Sage.

Sanders-May, Susan. 1996. *Family Violence: Index of New Information and Bibliography.* Washington, D.C.: Abbe Publications Association.

Selth, Jefferson P. 1985. *Alternative Lifestyles: A Guide to Research Collections on Intentional Communities, Nudism, and Sexual Freedom.* Westport, CT: Greenwood.

Social Forces. Annual. Chapel Hill, NC: University of North Carolina Press.

Social Sciences Citation Index. Annual. Philadelphia, PA: Institute for Scientific Information.

Social Sciences Index. Annual. New York: H. W. Wilson.

Society. Annual. New Brunswick, NJ: Rutgers University Press.

Sociological Abstracts. Annual. New York: Sociological Abstracts.

Stanley, Harold W. and Richard G. Niemi, eds. 2000. *Vital Statistics on American Politics, 1999–2000.* Washington, D.C.: Congressional Quarterly.

Statistical Reference Index Annual Abstracts. Annual. Bethesda, MD: Congressional Information Service.

Statistical Yearbook. Annual. New York: United Nations/Statistical Office.

Statistical Yearbook. Annual. Paris, France: UNESCO.

Stinnett, Nick and John DeFrain. 1985. *Secrets of Strong Families.* Boston, MA: Little, Brown and Company.

Tierney, H., ed. 1989–1991. *Women's Studies Encyclopedia: Views from the Inside.* 3 vols. New York: Greenwood.

U.S. Bureau of the Census. Annual. *Bureau of the Census Catalog.* Washington, D.C.: Government Printing Office.

———. Annual. *County and City Data Book.* Washington, D.C.: Government Printing Office.

———. 1971. *Historical Statistics of the United States: Colonial Times to 1970.* 2 vols. Washington, D.C.: Government Printing Office.

———. 2000. *Population Division, Population Projections Branch.* April 9, 2001 (http://www.census.gov/population/projections/state/stpjpop.txt).

U.S. Department of Education. 1998. "Fall Enrollment Surveys." *Integrated Postsecondary Education Data System (IPEDS).* Washington, D.C.: National Center for Education Statistics.

U.S. Federal Bureau of Investigation. Annual. *Uniform Crime Reports for the United States.* Washington, D.C.: Government Printing Office.

U.S. Library of Congress. Annual. *Subject Catalog: A Cumulative List of Works Represented by Library of Congress Printed Cards.* Washington, D.C.: Library of Congress.

U.S. Superintendent of Documents. Annual. *Monthly Catalog of United States Government Publications.* Washington, D.C.: Government Printing Office.

Vital Statistics of the United States. Annual. 2 vols. Hyattville, MD: U.S. Department of Health and Human Services.

Weber, Max. 1930. *The Protestant Ethic and the Spirit of Capitalism.* London, UK: Unwin University Books.

———. 1969. "Some Consequences of Bureaucratization." Pp. 454–455 in *Sociological Theory,* edited by L. A. Coser and B. Rosenberg. London, UK: Macmillan.

Women's Studies Abstracts. Annual. New York: Rush.

Women's Studies Index, 1999. 2000. Detroit: Gale Group. Boston, MA: G. K. Hall Citation Indexes.

Young, Jeffrey R. 2000. "Distance and Classroom Education Seen as Equally Effective." *Chronicle of Higher Education,* February 18, pp. 6–10.

INDEX